THE PATRIOTS

THE PATRIOTS

by

JUNE DRUMMOND

LONDON
VICTOR GOLLANCZ LTD
1979

© June Drummond 1979

ISBN 0 575 02573 5

The characters in this story are imaginary. The
events described are set a little in the future.

Printed in Great Britain by
The Bowering Press Ltd,
Plymouth and London

EYE-WITNESS

Name :   unknown
Occupation :   unknown
Race :   unknown

I

SINCE 7 MARCH, they've stationed a guard in the entrance to Bayside Buildings, where the Department of the Interior has its offices. This guard is armed with a revolver and a walkie-talkie. He does not wear combat uniform—that might alarm the passersby—but the summer uniform of the South African police.

He stands in the glassed-in lobby, facing the Bay, that old blue dowager whose bosom is over-laden with the spoils of trade, industry and tourism. To some, his vigil may symbolize law and order, to others a fatuous attempt to close the stable door. To people of my persuasion, his presence suggests that the Ramsay file is not yet closed.

As you know, I witnessed some of the events of 7 March. I saw, heard, and have remembered. When the time comes, I may speak . . . or I may not. Probably not. I am a person whose middle name is confidentiality. Party politics don't interest me, except in so far as they are good or bad for business.

I was well placed as a witness. There is a low wall not far from the Customs House and I was sitting there, enjoying the sun. There was quite a breeze riffling the palms along the Esplanade. The morning rush-hour was past. Over towards the Island, a dredger was lifting its buckets, clang-clang-clang. The sound made me drowsy.

Officially, I was to visit the Department of the Interior to obtain a cholera shot, prior to attending a conference in India. I have always disliked jabs, so I went on sitting on my wall for almost an hour, watching the world go by.

Quite a number of people went into the building during that period. Some strollers, some sailors, some civil servants.

Soon after nine-thirty a truck stopped in the loading bay near the main entrance to Bayside Buildings, and unloaded first a team of men in white overalls, and then a lot of equipment, stuff that looked like fumigation gear. There were gas cylinders, trolleys, oilskin bundles. The overalls had "City Cleansing Department" in red letters across the back.

At twenty-five minutes to ten, two cars joined the truck. Their windows were plastered with election stickers. "Vote Burman." I recognized the big heavy man climbing out of the first car as Colley Burman, the Conservative candidate. Four other people joined him, two men and two women. They stood together talking on the sidewalk for a while, then went into the building.

I reflected that Burman looked grosser, merrier, and more stupid than the cartoonists had managed to convey. Men of that kind often make dangerous opponents.

In due time, the Ramsay party arrived, but instead of leaving their cars in the parking zone, they found space further along the road and walked back, so I was able to observe them better.

Ramsay was the one who drew my attention. The newspapers had been using words like impressive, articulate, dynamic. I had no way of judging if they were accurate, but I could see enormous vigour in his carriage and step. He had a quick, eager way of turning his head.

There was a woman on his left, a blonde, thin and elegant, and on his right a very tall man with dark hair. This man was carrying a briefcase. As he moved through the swing-doors, he nearly got the case jammed. The others waited for him, laughing, then followed him inside.

I had no intention of attending the Nomination Court, though members of the public are entitled to do so. They are most boring affairs, as a rule.

The court is usually convened in the office of the Returning Officer, or in some other dreary Government building. The proceedings last exactly one hour, from 10 am to 11. The court cannot rise before the hour is up, in case some last-minute candidate may materialize.

During that hour, certain things happen. The nomination papers of each candidate are handed in. They can be prepared beforehand, and handed in complete, or they can be prepared and signed in the court.

Each candidate or his agent also pays his deposit, which these days is several hundred rand. It can happen that other election officials—agents and so on—are sworn in at the same time, with the usual paraphernalia of forms, stamps, and production of identity documents.

The Returning Officer makes certain obligatory remarks about the time and place of various electoral events, and he reads parts of the Act aloud, in English and Afrikaans.

The audience in the room is invariably small : candidates, their agents, a few party stalwarts. Each candidate has to be proposed and seconded by someone who lives in the contested constituency, and these people often attend. Then you'll find pressmen, a bored photographer, a secretary and clerk of the electoral office, and of course the Returning Officer presides over all. These twenty or so people manage to preserve a polite affability towards one another.

It is hardly a colourful scene. Like the weighing-in of jockeys, it is legally part of the race, but the general public takes no notice of it.

I went on sitting in the sun. The dredger stopped work and everything seemed very quiet.

A police car swung round from the Esplanade, jerked into the parking bay. The man inside sat still for a moment, apparently listening to a radio message, then started to clamber out. His back was to me.

I heard the Post Office clock strike ten, and checked my watch against it. About three minutes after the last stroke had sounded, came the gunfire, a sharp, shattering noise, high in the air.

I looked up. The sharp noise continued, and up on the fourth floor an entire window, several feet wide, fragmented, flew out in a glittering star, and dropped. In the space where the glass had been, a man pivoted round, slumped forward onto the ledge and then slid backwards out of sight.

I could hear thin cries and screams up there, like gannets. At street level, the traffic flowed undisturbed. Across the road from me, the cop stared first at the glass on the sidewalk, then at the empty window frame. He leaned into his car and straightened with a service revolver in his fist.

Almost at the same moment a man in white overalls came plunging out through the swing-doors, moving so fast he almost lost his balance. I could see him clearly, the way his mouth was pulled back as if he was grinning. He was swinging a light machine-pistol in one hand. I started to roll behind my wall, and as I did so, the policeman fired. Three shots, I thought, tied together by the echo. The man—the runaway—seemed to leap sideways stiff-legged, like a cat. His body slammed into the bonnet of the car, slid off and bounced into the roadway. His gun landed in the gutter.

The cop went straight after the gun. He wrapped the flap of his jacket round the butt, picked it up, opened the back door of the car and slid the gun under the rear seat. Only then did he lean over and reach for the radio telephone; a sequence I thought interesting.

Meanwhile, hell was breaking loose along the street.

Those drivers who had seen or heard the cop shoot the gunman, accelerated past, but others coming after saw only a blood-covered body in the roadway. Some of these stopped their cars and ran over to have a look. In a very short time there was a jam building up in all three of the approach roads.

Pedestrians began streaming towards the parking bay. Then, realizing the victim had been shot, the more cautious among them panicked, and started trying to shove their way out again. Fists swung at the edge of the crowd.

The prowl cars arrived, and a Hippo truck spilled out riot police. These spread out, pushing the onlookers back, sealing off a section of roadway.

The cop who'd done the shooting—I noticed he was an officer—was talking to a man in plain clothes. After a while, the two of them climbed into the cop's car and drove it round into Sender Street, which leads to the underground parking reserved for Department officials.

All this time, the cadaver of the gunman lay out on the road. Some of the police stayed with it, but more of them moved into the Buildings. Two ambulances came up from the south, presumably from Addington Hospital.

I judged it wise to leave. I had no wish to be subpoenaed as a witness. Nobody appeared to have noticed me. I have undistinguished features, a fact I have often found useful.

I allowed myself to be herded with the rest of the crowd to the shelter of the side streets. I collected my car and drove quietly home, keeping the radio on in case there should be a spot message. But there was none.

10

MAURICE FABER

South African citizen, aged 37 years.
Metallurgist.
Campaign-manager to Mark Ramsay in
the Parkhaven by-election.
Married and separated.
Classified White.

II

THE FIRST WARNING came from Charlie Cameron, of the *Gazette*; brilliant slob, old-style drunken news-hound, liar and friend.

It was a fortnight before Nomination Day. That was set down for Monday 7 March, Polling Day for Wednesday 20 April. In the third week of February, at about a quarter past eight in the evening, one of the incoming 'phones in our election office started to ring, and I answered it. It was Cameron. He said something had come up that he didn't like to discuss on the 'phone, would I go in and see him right away?

That was an unusual request. But the whole campaign had taken a weird tilt, and Cameron was someone we couldn't offend. I said, "How about Dick?", meaning Dick Tuttle who's our PRO and Vice Chairman of the Party in this region. Cameron said, "No, Morry, I want you and you alone". I told him I'd be over in about twenty minutes.

It took me ten to get clear of the office. The canvassers were beginning to come in from the Haggie Road area. Although I'd have liked to hear their reports, I asked them to wait and talk to Walter Brock when he came in. Finally I rang Mark Ramsay the candidate and said I'd be out for a while but he could reach me at home after ten if he wanted.

When I got outside, it was drizzling again. It hadn't cooled the air much. There was a kind of soggy mist over the Bayhead, yellowish where the lights hit it and grey above the reclaimed land. Our office was bang in the middle of the constituency, with the fat-cat suburbs on the western hills, blue-collar to the east, shops on the north and Industria on the south. I took the quickest route to the centre of town where the *Gazette* has its new premises.

The editorial foyer was stockbroker's synthetic, but there was a smell that was genuine enough, wet newsprint and oil and acid, and the usual faint vibration underfoot that said the presses were rolling. I like that. My father was a printer and I spent a lot of time in printing works when I was a child.

I asked for Charlie at the enquiries desk. He came through at once and greeted me, and then stood rocking on his heels as if uncertain what to do next. He's a small thin man with the kind of blue eyes that look squint without glasses. His thumbs are long and flattened, some say because he's sucked so many stories out of them.

He said, "I'm sorry to drag you over here."

I shrugged. He stared at me some more, then said, "I'll stand you a drink. Or coffee."

"Coffee and food. I haven't eaten."

We set off along the block. Charlie was walking so fast I had to hurry to keep up. He mumbled something about having the jitters.

"That makes two of us."

"You?" He looked at me sharply. "Have you been threatened?"

"By every member of the team, including the candidate."

That raised nothing but an impatient grunt. We passed two coffee bars and stopped at a third, which was at the end of a chichi alley full of antique shops. The bar itself was brightly lit, and we were the only customers. It looked the sort of place that would pick up trade near midnight when the cinemas closed.

We found a table and ordered fried-egg sandwiches and cappuccinos.

"So who's been bugging you?" I asked. My voice came out snide, which I hadn't intended. I was tired and tense, and I've never been good at saying things the right way.

Charlie shook his head. "That's only part of it, the threats. What's getting to me, really, is the whole scene. Like when a nightmare comes true. From Christ knows when we've been telling people what would happen here, and now it is. . . ."

"And you can't quite believe it?"

"That's right. Crazy." He took a bite of food and chewed and stabbed a finger at me. "Why I asked you to come was because you know the way I work, Morry, I don't have to qualify my remarks all the time. Also it concerns you, as campaign manager it definitely concerns you." He hunched forward over his coffee. "I'm thinking aloud, see? This is all off-record, for both of us."

"Fine, Charlie."

13

"What I get given," he said, "is all the ulcer material. The Black Summit, urban terrorism, your election, everything the young tickle-tits can't cope with. I'd like to ask you some questions about the election."

"Sure." Watching him, seeing how his hands trembled, I reserved the right to reserve the answers.

"Are you going to win?"

I thought a bit. "We can win it. It will depend on a number of things. Issues can come up. We have to get more canvassers, trace more absent voters. Burman's a tough opponent. He'll smear us all he can."

"But you have a chance?"

"A good chance. Look, Charlie, this isn't an easy one to predict. It's a marginal seat, and the climate's very emotional. Gut feelings are what will count."

"When did you come into it? Before or after they chose the candidate?"

I smiled at him. "It doesn't happen like an invitation to the waltz. About six months ago the Party was told that Sid Heffner had a tumour on the brain and the doctors gave him a couple of months. We knew there'd be a by-election, which means that certain wheels turned. The constituency started looking for candidates. When Heffner died, they asked Mark, he said "No". They put pressure on me to change his mind. When he finally accepted, I became his campaign manager. If someone else had got the nomination, there might have been quite a different election team. I certainly wouldn't be down here losing money for anyone but Mark."

"Why did you pressure him?"

"Obvious. He's the best man for it."

"I'd have said he was totally wrong for Parkhaven. It's a conservative area, and he's left-wing. Maverick at that."

"Listen," I said. "You have to think about two aspects in an election. The first is the surface aspect. By that standard Mark is good. He's a solid worker and a brilliant speaker. He's well known in the city, he's lived both sides of the track, the press like him. He has more political insight than most. But I want to tell you that people don't get elected because they have the right surface aspect. They get elected because they match the gut feeling of the electorate."

14

"And you think Ramsay does?"

"Yes."

"How?"

"They're drowning," I said, "and they think he'll get them to shore. He's that sort of man. They recognize him."

"Bull-dust."

I said nothing. I wasn't going to tell Charlie that our canvass returns supported what I'd said, that Mark was pulling in votes against the predictable patterns.

"All right." Charlie leaned back in his chair. "Tell me in broad journalese, which I can regurgitate for my eager readers, how Ramsay will deal with Burman's smear tactics. Burman's already suggesting that Ramsay is a commie because he supports the Black Summit. How will he repudiate that line?"

"He won't," I said. "He'll ignore it. Mark is going to yank the voters right up into the problems of black power. Burman he doesn't see. Just doesn't see him."

"You get on well with Ramsay." It was a statement, not a question, and I laughed.

"Charlie, I don't get on well with anyone. With me it's bruises, bruises all the way. Mark didn't ask me to run his campaign because of my pretty ways. He thought I'd run it better than anyone else."

"Did he say so?"

"Yes, as a matter of fact." I closed my eyes. "He said, 'You're a quarrelsome sod, Morry boy, but you're inventive and tenacious. Will you do it?' How could I resist?"

"Would he stand the same chance without you as his agent?"

I considered. "There are other people who are better than I am, round the country, but they haven't worked with Mark. They wouldn't get quite as much out of him, and they wouldn't give him quite as much, as I will. If the angels take me to heaven tonight, it might cost us a few votes. Could be enough to make the vital difference."

I was puzzled by Charlie's attitude. He never asked random questions, but tonight, I couldn't catch the thread. I merely played along.

"You spoke about issues that could come up," he said. "You didn't name them. A little bird tells me it's the Transkeian labour problem that really bugs you."

15

"Not particularly."

"My story says you don't like the way your candidate is handling it. He's not sticking to the Party line, and he's making noises the voters don't like."

"I've already told you, Mark will make plenty of statements the voters don't like. Try and believe me, that is one of the reasons they are going to vote him in." I was thinking that Cameron was a shrewd journalist, and I was wondering whether he was making an intuitive guess, or whether someone had been telling tales. There were only two people who knew I disagreed with Mark on the Transkeian thing. One was Mark himself and he wouldn't have talked to any pressman about it. The other was Mark's wife, who took no interest in Transkei or any other political hot potato. In fact I sometimes thought she took no interest in Mark's career. But maybe it was just my presence that made her screw up her mouth like a pigeon's arse. He'd got under my skin enough to make me say, "All right, Charles, what's really on your mind?"

He blinked at me as if he was going to dodge; then said abruptly, "The white backlash . . . you must have noticed how it's increased over the past two months?"

"Yes."

"How badly is it affecting your campaign?"

"If you'd called half an hour later, I could have given you a better answer. We were canvassing Haggie Road tonight."

He nodded. It's a long, depressing street that runs from the city to Industria and contains a lot of municipal flats. Cameron knew well enough we'd already had three or four unpleasant incidents, dogs set on our canvassers, a car burned out and tyres slashed. It certainly went far beyond the recognized sport of tearing down the opposition posters.

"It's bad," I said, "but not as bad as it will be. And now tell me why the hell you're keeping me yakking here on a wet night when I've work piled to the ceiling back there? What's this about your being threatened?"

He put both hands flat on the table, looked at them and slid them slowly together. "In my job," he said, "I'm used to threats. Pressure from all sorts of quarters. I don't scare easily because I know that 99 per cent of that stuff is cranky and not worth a moment's notice.

16

"The *Gazette* is left of centre. We've taken a hard line on the labour disputes. We expected to reap the backlash and we have. You should see the letters we don't publish! What I'm saying, being hated is nasty but it's routine . . . or it was until the start of this campaign.

"When your Party chose Ramsay as candidate we were pleased, and we said so. Personally I don't think Colley Burman is a politician's backside, but the paper has given him a fair deal. Point is, what the paper has printed, what I've written, has been in accordance with past policy. Yet suddenly I'm being hounded. I'm being victimized."

His voice shook, and he looked at me almost pleadingly. "Honest, Morry, it's worse than I ever imagined it could be."

"What's happened?"

"Well, at first, 'phone-calls at the office. Anonymous letters. What's got me is the virulence of it. Loads of mail, the calls never letting up. Someone even posted me dog's mess. I had the 'phone-calls blocked at the switchboard. The yuks started 'phoning my home, talking to Eileen and even the kids. A couple of weeks ago I got home and found my youngest in hysterics. Someone's going to cut up her stomach, she says, can you imagine saying that to a six-year-old?"

"You told the police?"

"Of course, but you know the difficulties. It's almost impossible to catch nuts like that. They use a different call-box each time, the letters are typed. Why I 'phoned you—the thing that finally got to me—was this morning. About six o'clock, I went down to pick up the paper. Went out on the back porch where the roundsman drops it. The paper was lying there, and on top of it was my daughter's pet cat. Someone had strangled it, and skinned it, and tied a ribbon round its neck and left it there."

He raised his head and looked directly at me. There were tears in his eyes. "Christ, Morry, someone took the trouble to kill and peel an animal. I've seen a lot of things, but that really turned me up . . . I tell you. . . ."

"What did you do?"

"Picked the thing up in the paper and took it straight down to the police station. They didn't like it any better than I did."

"You made a statement?"

"Poured my guts out. I was bloody hysterical. It wasn't until

17

mid-day I had enough gin inside me to think straight."

That I believed. He was marginally sober now, but in another hour he probably wouldn't be. "So what's your theory," I said, "who are these slobs?"

"Vigilantes, I suppose."

"Come on, Charlie. You didn't drag me down here to chat about a few crackpots who've been around for years. Who's after you?"

He brooded, lips pursed. He seemed to be on the edge of talking, but then the old, cagey look slid back into place, and he shrugged.

"No idea."

So that was that. He'd changed his mind, I could go home and forget all about it.

I looked at him sweat and shake, and I reflected that rat though he was, in one respect Charlie had heroic qualities. He would put his neck at risk any time, any place, if the story was big enough.

Thinking back over our conversation, I played a hunch. "You still covering the Black Summit?"

"Sure."

"How's it shaping?"

"Okay, I think. Still scheduled for 19 March, still hoping the radicals will attend."

"You don't think this campaign against you could be connected with the Summit?"

"No, no." He screwed up his eyes in a smile that was meant to be ingratiating. "Listen, Morry, I just wanted to warn you there's something psychopathic loose. You should watch out for Ramsay and the rest of your bunch, know what I mean?"

We walked back to the *Gazette* office together. He was chirpy enough to make me wonder if all that stuff had just been the start of a gin bout. Charlie sometimes saw things through rose-coloured eyeballs.

It was ten minutes to ten when I went back to my car. The rain had stopped. I stood on the tarmac feeling the cooler air and the cold wet metal of the car door, and another spiral of cold that seemed to be moving inside my own spine.

If you're in politics in southern Africa, you become a bit paranoid. It has to do with violence, the massive international violence of Angola and Mozambique, Rhodesia and Zaire, the riots and urban terrorism near to home. It has to do with the men dying in detention, with the secret societies and corruption you know about and can't eliminate. You get to be desperate for change, you know you have to break a system and you also know you probably can't make it in time.

Living like that, you begin to pin your hopes on things like the result of a by-election, or the outcome of a conference. I wanted in every nerve to win Parkhaven. I felt the same way about the success of the Summit.

The idea there was to call together all the black leaders in South Africa, moderates and radicals. Once consolidated, they would demand a national convention to thrash out a new political format with the whites.

The obstacles were huge. Divisions within the African, Indian and Coloured power structures. Extremists who were opposed to any sort of unity. Elements in the Government who were trying to rush through legislation that would ban the Summit meetings altogether. Just about every explosive force on the sub-continent was being drawn into the Summit area.

Charlie was covering that area. And Charlie was being hammered into the ground.

I wanted very badly to know whatever it was that he knew.

Common sense told me the right thing to do was go home and get a good night's sleep. I started to drive to the holiday flat I'd rented for the duration of the campaign.

Halfway there, I turned back and made for Mark Ramsay's house.

III

ONE OF THE things that made Mark a good candidate was the
fact that he was born and reared in the constituency. His father
was a railway clerk and by all accounts bone idle, but his mother
was a tough little cookie with a good brain.

When her husband died, Dorothy Ramsay found work as a
book-keeper with one of the new factories in Industria. Her job
grew with the firm and by the time Mark was in high school she
was secretary of a very big concern, had a handsome income
and a nice big flat up on the Berea. Her money put Mark
through university, and her contacts got him a leadership-
exchange scholarship to study industrial relations in the States.
She died while he was over there.

On his return, he worked for some years in the Transvaal and
then came back to Durban to found his own industrial consult-
ancy, which has branches right through southern Africa. It was
there he became interested in the labour scene. He got into the
problems affecting a developing, multi-racial continent. He
wanted to put his views across, he wanted a platform. That was
how I persuaded him to stand for Parkhaven.

He had eloquence, but I don't think it was his power with
words that made him such a good speaker. He had a sort of
puritanical, driving logic. He would take an idea and force it
along right to its conclusion, no matter how uncomfortable that
might be. Most of us stop when our ideas get uncomfortable.
Mark never did.

I believe the reason we worked well together was because I
supplied the things he didn't have. I can be devious, and I
prefer to kick a guy in the crotch before he kicks me.

Mark and Bianca owned this house . . . not in the sauna sec-
tion, but in what was becoming even better. They'd bought an
old Natal homestead in a grotty area, got rid of the white ant
and the dry rot and made it look as it did in granny's day. Now
the district was improving all round them.

I drove up the driveway and parked my car under a big old

fig tree that had carpeted the ground with squashed fruit. When I think of that night, I remember the smell of rotten figs.

The house has a wide verandah, and a tall front door which was standing open. As I was about to get out of the car, I saw Mark and Bianca in the lighted hall. They were standing close together, and he bent his head round and kissed her on the throat and then the mouth. She didn't lift her arms, just moved forward so that her belly was touching him. The fire of light all around them could have been generated by their own bodies.

I thought, no dice for campaign talk tonight, and reached for the ignition key. But before I could switch on, another voice called from somewhere in the house. Mark lifted his head, and after a minute he and Bianca went through the door to the lounge. As they already had company, I decided I might as well join them.

They were sitting round the table in the bay window. In the middle, sprawled in a big leather chair with one leg over its arm, was Mark. He smiled and beckoned me over. He was telling a story, so I stood where I was to let him finish.

Looking at him I reflected that appearance plays more than its fair part in politics. I don't mean good looks. Study a photo of Ramsay and you'll agree that the word is not handsome. The eyes are full, almost prominent. The head is bullet-shaped, the hair thick, dark and springy. But there is an air of concentrated power . . . put that face among 50 others on a public platform, and it's the one you'll notice.

Sitting on Mark's left, listening in seeming repose, hands clasped, elbows on knees, was Bianca. She was wearing a long skirt of some silky yellow material, and a loose blouse, and her hair was pulled up on top in a way that made her cheeks look thinner than ever. Some guys say Bianca turns them on. I'd as soon cuddle a toast rack. She could never stand the sight of me, either.

The third person present was a man in a formal dark suit. Small, wiry, brown skin, brown hair that flopped around, and pebble glasses. Through lenses like that, it's hard to judge if a man is clever or stupid.

The story came to an end, everyone laughed, and Mark jumped up.

"Come in, Morry. This is David Tindall. What'll you drink?"

21

"Whisky, thanks."

Tindall was scrambling to his feet. "Look, if you people have work to do. . . ."

Bianca cut him short. "Sit down, Dave. Even a candidate is entitled to one night off."

Because that was aimed at me, because I agreed with her, it was on the tip of my tongue to tell her that in an election, a key election at a time of crisis, no one is entitled to anything, except to sweat his or her guts out. Then I remembered the second commandment : Thou shalt not fight with the candidate's wife, even though she be an idle-arsed bitch. I said, "Tomorrow will do".

Mark went over to the bar. "I'm glad you came. I've put some points down and I'd like Dave to hear them, too. We can use him, he's in television, plenty of good ideas for us."

I sat down wearily. Mark knew as well as I did that by the time this expert got his thesis on paper the election would be over. We'd set our campaign line weeks ago. But I was too tired to argue. All I wanted was a big slug of Mark's whisky.

"I am not precisely in television," said Tindall. "My business is electronics. I produce certain equipment for television studios. I also market video-tapes."

Mark handed me my drink, at the same time dropping a copy of the evening paper in front of me. The sheet was folded back to the headline, "Industria Unrest". He'd marked a couple of paragraphs.

"Police were called in to disperse a crowd of several hundred demonstrators at the Leith Metal works today. Tear gas was used when some of the men charged the main building, stoned windows, and damaged motorcars parked nearby. Five people were injured, two of them seriously.

"A police spokesman said the unrest appeared to be triggered by young men in their teens. Several were arrested.

"Last week 270 workers at Leith Metal staged a strike and on Friday these men were dismissed and ordered to return to their homelands."

I put the paper down. "Leith's management are a bunch of morons," I said. "They've a history of blocking negotiation by arbitrary dismissal and police action. Were you asked to comment?"

22

Mark nodded, resuming his chair. "I made some 'phone-calls first. Nearly all those who lost their jobs, were Transkeians. Those retained are Zulus. If you want to start tribal riots, that's as good a way as any."

I looked at him. "Are you going to use this on Wednesday night?" That was the date of his first big public meeting. What he said was going to count right through till election day.

"I think so. It's a flashpoint."

I said nothing. I didn't disagree with him about the subject. I wanted to discuss presentation, but not with other people present.

Tindall began fingering his spectacles. "In my humble view, Leith's actions amount to an incitement to violence. It is absolutely essential to use the issue."

The little man was almost bridling. I realized he thought of himself as taking Mark's part against me. Probably Bianca had been filling him up with a lot of nonsense. It was so silly I laughed. Tindall eyed me uncertainly, and Mark fielded the ball.

"You're right that violence is the gut issue of this campaign. I want to focus on violence in the labour field. How long since you lived here, Dave? Five years?"

Tindall nodded, and Mark said, "Then there are some new factors for you. Of course, some old ones stay constant. Blacks still face the industrial colour bar, lack of mobility, lack of training and job opportunity. They still can't join registered trades unions.

"But because the labour laws relating to blacks are no effing use to blacks, they will inevitably break down and be discarded. In fact, it's already happening. Barriers are going down, wages up, and opportunities increasing. We're in an era of rising black expectations that can't be satisfied—the black graduate has to take a job at a petrol-pump, the black doctor has no real vote, the black teacher can't buy land to build his home.

"Rising expectations that can't be met; the classic situation for unrest and violence, as any sociologist will confirm.

"The second new factor concerns black youth. You notice that cutting suggests the riots at Leith were started by teenagers? The Soweto riots of '76 threw up student leaders, young blacks who are sharp and militant. They have no families to consider, and no possessions to protect. They despise their elders as sell-outs.

23

They believe violence gets results. They're prepared to die if they have to. From now on, they will set the mood for blacks. The Summit, for instance, will only succeed if it attracts the young radicals.

"The third new factor is the Transkeian workers. Transkei became independent while you were abroad, Dave. There've been all sorts of wrangles between Transkei and the Republic about boundaries, land and citizenship rights. The net result is that thousands of Transkeian workers living in our major cities are technically foreigners. It's easy for an unscrupulous employer—like Leith Metal—to fire them ahead of other categories. There's growing insecurity among the Transkeians. Some hot summer night, they could turn on their neighbours in the townships . . . or move into Industria . . . into Parkhaven.

"And that's where you find the fourth factor, right here in this constituency. The white backlash."

Mark got up and moved to the window. "The whole of that area down there," he said, "borders on Industria. One quarter of my voters live there. Railway workers, harbourmen, truckers. Plenty of them are short on education, short on skills.

"In good times, they've got their bums in the butter. In a recession, that alters. The retrenchments start, jobs are hard to find, and the low-skilled white finds himself slugging it out with the high-skilled black. That's when the white backlash begins to hit.

"In the past, the Government coddled whites, but since 1974, that's begun to change. The white régimes in Mozambique and Angola have gone, those in South-West and Rhodesia are going. The message is there for South Africa. To survive, we have to throw out white privilege.

"That's being said, not only by opposition politicians like me, but increasingly by the Government itself. It's being said in the universities and churches and commercial strongholds of the Afrikaner volk. It's a welcome sound . . . unless you happen to be a low-skill white Government supporter living in Haggie Road. Then, it sounds like a death knell.

"The seeds of violence, the roots of violence . . ." Mark spoke these last words almost to himself. "That's my theme."

All the time we'd been talking, Bianca had sat half asleep in her chair. Now she roused herself.

"It's late. I'm going upstairs." Her hand brushed Mark lightly as she passed him.

We finished our drinks. Tindall, who was apparently a guest in the house, went off to bed. Mark walked out to the car with me.

I want to tell you, there was always a side of Mark that was darker to me than the far side of the moon. He had friends I never met, some of them jet-set and some from the slum quarters. They handed him facts and rumours he kept to himself. Sometimes he used what they gave him to build up a hand, and while he was building he didn't like to talk. He'd rather snap down the cards when he had the straight flush. It was a trick the press enjoyed, but as his election manager, I needed to know what was buzzing in his brain.

Now I said, "You think the police were right? That it was young people started the strike?"

He shot me a look. "Could be."

"Anything definite."

"Not yet. I'm working on it."

"Charlie Cameron hauled me down town tonight."

"Oh? Why?"

"Same topic as yours. Violence. He's been the victim of a hate campaign, pretty nasty. It's scared him more than I thought possible."

"Does he know who's behind it?"

"He tried to suggest the Vigilantes, on account of his support for your campaign."

"Do you believe that?"

"No. The Vigilantes are a bunch of cranks who couldn't organize a gang-bang in a brothel. I'm inclined to think the reason's connected with the Black Summit. Charlie's been covering that, which means he's been nosing around, looking for inside stories. My guess is, he's annoyed some of the heavies, black or white, and he's been warned off. Thing is, though he's scared, he smells a big story. He means to get it, even if he has to play the rôle of tethered goat. He probably tipped me off as a sort of insurance. If anything happens to him, then I'm duty bound to follow it up."

As I spoke, Mark watched me intently, as if he was matching what I said to something in his own mind. Then he said, "Morry,

25

I have some people coming to see me tomorrow afternoon, to bone me up on the labour disputes. Can you be here?"

"Sure. Who've you got?"

"Father Ignatius Tanda, Peck Mkise, Dr Zondi Simeyane, and Dudu Ndhlovu. Know them?"

"I've met Ndhlovu. Isn't he helping to organize the Summit?"

"He's the key man. Simeyane and Tanda are also involved. Simeyane is a Xhosa, doctor of medicine, works at Queen Elizabeth Hospital. Not likeable, but brilliant, and has a big following among the black élite, particularly the students. Tanda's a Catholic priest, and also a radiographer, in charge of the Mission's X-ray clinic out at Denville. He's a black-consciousness man. Spent several months in detention last year, was released without being charged. Peck Mkise is a trades unionist."

"Okay. I'll be here."

He nodded and stepped back from the car. As I turned down the drive, I saw Bianca standing in one of the upper windows. She had on a white wrap and her hair was loose on her shoulders, all ready for the big bedroom scene.

I drove back to my holiday flat. Those places are made to one pattern. The furnishings are mud-coloured so as not to show the dirt, and there's a smell of cockroaches. Mine always made me feel as lonely as hell. Drinking a couple of whiskies before I went to bed never made any difference.

IV

CAMERON'S WARNING stayed in my mind next day, but only as a background to a lot of other problems.

Anyone who has had anything to do with an election campaign knows that it's ten weeks in the salt mines. In South Africa we don't have TV elections and there's no official time on the box. The contestants slug it out in the bad, old-fashioned way, which takes three times as long as a campaign using television.

To win, or even to do well, you have to canvass the voters door-to-door which, with revisiting the "not-at-homes" can mean something like 30,000 calls. You have to use the Press and pamphlets and posters and billboards and word of mouth and every possible gimmick just so that the voters will know what your man looks like. You have to stage one or two house meetings every night, and three or four big public meetings in hired halls so your candidate can prove he's able to speak for 30 minutes without falling on his ass.

For the voters who have moved out of the constituency—and at least one in five will have done so—you must set up tracing systems that can chase him 1,000 miles, to Cape Town or Mata Mata. If you find him, and he's prepared to go to the trouble of lifting his wrist to sign the application form, you must arrange a postal vote for him. That section alone can break your heart.

You must have a big team of helpers, preferably political animals. You need canvassers who understand your policy and can sell it to people who'd rather stay ignorant. You have to have senior members who'll talk to those voters who consider themselves too important to be addressed by the ordinary door-to-door canvasser. You need ladies with voices of honey and skins of buffalo-hide, who will fix house meetings all round the constituency. You need young people to organize other young people, drop party literature, spend their leisure time putting up posters and almost immediately taking them down again. You need lawyers sometimes, and doctors to cauterize dog bites.

On election day you need God knows how many drivers and

runners and cooks and clerks, from six in the morning to nine at night.

You need money . . . far more than you've got . . . and physical endurance . . . far more than you think you've got . . . but above all you need those few picked people who can head up the key departments and staff them from the mixed bag of volunteers that flood into the campaign office as the election fever mounts.

Mark had a first-class team. It included people like Lisa Page, the perfect person to run a campaign centre; always cool and sweet-tempered. And Walter Brock at canvass-control. Wally was chairman of the Region, a successful engineer in private life, 45 years old and liked by everyone. I had no worries over personnel.

When I'd told Charlie Cameron we could win Parkhaven I wasn't bull-dusting. I knew from the canvass figures that we'd started the fight with the odds 60-40 against us, but we were pulling up fast. We were going to win if the swing continued.

That was the big If.

Rumours go through an election force like wildfire. A few canvassers coming in with long faces, the wrong word from a senior worker, and the morale can plummet. Then the press and the public pick it up, and the next thing, you're on the loser's greased pole.

That was what I was scared of. Things like vigilante violence, or the Industria strikes, could easily become gut issues in Parkhaven. They could cost us the precious marginal votes we needed to win; so I had to watch them.

Accordingly, I asked Wally Brock to keep a careful check on the canvass returns, and watch for any build-up of violence or intimidation. He reported that one or two canvassers down in the industrial sector had got the impression the voters were clamming up—"scared" was the word Wally used. But there was nothing we could act on.

Similarly, young Henry Beaumont, who ran our youth team, told me his poster-workers had met with some grief the past two nights. A gang of yobs had tried to wreck one of our trucks, and there'd been a rough-house outside the Riva café.

I warned Henry not to let anyone tangle with trouble-makers. "Clear out and leave them," I said. "I don't want incidents. And don't let the girls go anywhere rough, or we'll have a ton of angry mums coming down on us."

On the labour disputes, I spoke to Party headquarters in Cape Town, the caucus being there for the Session. I told them Mark was concerned about the victimization of Transkeian workers, and asked them to put some questions on the Order paper.

Also, Dick Tuttle and I set up some appointments for Mark for Wednesday morning, to go out to Industria and talk to certain employers there.

Since that time, I've gone over things time and again, wondering if I could have prevented what happened to Mark. I've never come up with any good answers. But I still feel guilty. I suppose I always will.

V

AT FOUR ON Tuesday afternoon, I went round to Mark's place.

Thinking there might not be room to park on the driveway, I left my car in the road and walked up to the house. Half-way there, I heard someone call my name. I looked round, but could see nothing, though I knew Nick must be hiding somewhere near. Then I heard giggling, and the boy came sliding out from under the bench in the summerhouse, and ran over and grabbed my legs.

Nick is five, the Ramsay's only child. He's not exactly a loner, but he knows a lot of games that one can play.

I swung him up on my shoulder and carried him indoors and dropped him over the stair-rail onto the middle landing. He sat there smiling down at me through the bars.

"Where's your Dad?" I said.

"In the study."

"Anyone with him?"

"A Xhosa." He gave the word its correct initial click. Mark spoke several dialects well, and was teaching Nick.

"Keep your powder dry," I said, and walked on past the stair-well to the study at the back of the house.

My first thought, as I walked in, was that these two men—Ramsay and Simeyane—had nothing in common.

Mark was in jeans and a T shirt and rope-soled shoes. He lay back in his chair, one foot pulled up on the opposite knee, a mug of coffee cradled between his hands. Opposite him sat Simeyane, bolt upright, immaculate in hand-tailored suit and silk tie. He turned towards the door as I entered. A strange face he had, the forehead high and narrow, the eyes almond-shaped, the mouth short but full-lipped. His expression was sulky and restless. When Mark introduced us, he gave me a brief nod and went on talking in a high, rather nasal voice.

"It's only a matter of time, Mark. Liberation is already taking place in Namibia and Zimbabwe. Soon it will be here."

I poured myself a mug of coffee from the pot on the hot-tray, and found a chair.

"You're postulating a liberation force," Mark said, "a liberation army, even. Would it include foreigners?"

"If by foreigners you mean our own exiles. . . ."

"I don't mean exiles. I'm asking you, would your radical followers here in this country accept aid from an army of foreign nationals—Marxists—Cubans, for instance?"

"Possibly. If the whites here continue to oppress us, then obviously the time will come when we will accept liberation from outsiders. When men are fighting for their lives, don't they take arms, troops, medical aid, money, anywhere they can find them?"

"Too bloody easy to discover, after the war, that it's merely been a change of masters."

Simeyane laughed. "You know what my students say? 'Better the devil we don't know, than the devil we do!'"

"And freedom comes through the barrel of a gun? Zondi—if they feel that way, that there's no room left for reconciliation—then why are you, one of their spokesmen, supporting the Black Summit? Isn't that an attempt to reach solidarity between blacks, to reconcile the moderates and the activists?"

"You can't reconcile sell-outs with militants, man."

"So you think they'll boycott the Summit?"

"I think they'll use it whatever way suits them. The young people don't get sentimental about the Summit, it's no holy cow to them. They know damn well, for the thing to succeed, it must have radical support. Without that, there's no life to it. If the students see a chance to establish some power for themselves, they will attend. If not, they'll stay away. They hold the balance. That is the fact of the matter."

Mark nodded, easing himself higher in his chair. "Tell me something else. Do you think there are agitators trying to abort the talks?"

The doctor gestured in sudden fury. "Agitators, Communists, why do you whites always look for these bogeymen? It won't be my people who wreck these talks, but yours. Don't you read your papers? Didn't you read, just the other night, there's a group in the Government wants to make black solidarity illegal?"

"They're in the minority."

"For how long? And if they can't bring in the laws in time, you think they won't just ban the whole thing?"

"I don't think they'll do that. They're sensitive at the moment, about their image, overseas."

"Oh, Mark, grow up! They're going to stop the Summit. Maybe this way, maybe that. You just don't know what we're up against."

Mark smiled suddenly. "Oh yes, I do. The Special Branch, Boss, Russia, China, the Vigilantes, and a good slice of my voters in Parkhaven. That's enough, without your young tigers joining in."

Simeyane was silent for a moment. There was a strange expression on his face, the half-ashamed look of a man remembering something he'd rather forget. He turned his head away.

"I know you have tried for us."

Mark considered him quietly. At last he said, "Something's going on, Zondi. I'm getting pointers all the time. Not just the labour unrest, something deeper. Corruption. Distortion. If you should hear anything. . . ."

Simeyane shook his head almost sadly. "I'm a rich bugger now. I don't hear the street cries."

"If you ever do. . . ."

"I'll call you." He stood up, holding out his hand. "I have to go now. I've a lecture to give. Goodbye, my friend."

When Mark had seen Simeyane to the front door, he came back and asked me what I'd made of him.

"A light-weight, isn't he?"

"What makes you say that?"

"Dunno. It's the impression I got. He gave me the feeling I was listening to a well-played record. You know, all the familiar clichés. I just don't see him manning the barricades, though. Not in that suit."

"Zondi has his following." Mark moved over to his desk in the corner of the room, shifted some papers in an aimless way. "He's an old-fashioned black radical, same as you and I are old-fashioned white liberals. The scene's not ours any longer, it's set for the new men, who don't waste time on theories. Through the barrel of a gun. . . ."

32

I said nothing, and presently he said abruptly, "Tanda is the man I need, and he's gone out of town."

"I thought he'd agreed to come?"

"Yes, but I got a 'phone-call this afternoon. He's been sent elsewhere by his superiors. They wouldn't say where, or why. It's very disturbing, in view of the fact—"

Before he could finish the sentence, the front door-bell rang to announce the arrival of Peck Mkise.

Nick must have answered the bell, because we heard his voice and then a much deeper one, laughing. That was followed by quick footsteps and a young man appeared in the entrance to the study.

He was medium height, compact and wiry. His hair was cropped close to his head. Nose, thin and almost Arabic, with flared nostrils. Thick flesh over the eyebrows, marred on the right side by a diagonal scar. A face that had taken a lot of pounding, but quiet, and obstinate as hell.

"Hey, Mark." The young man was staring at me with hard bright eyes.

"Hullo, Peck. I'd like you to meet my election manager, Maurice Faber, from Jo'burg. He's safe."

Mkise nodded, managing to make it derisive. He walked over to the hot-tray where the coffee was, poured a mugful, ladled in sugar with quick neat movements, came back. He stood looking down at me and still not liking me much.

"Morry is here by my invitation," Mark said, "because I rely on his judgement."

Judgement nuts, I thought, when nobody's even told me what I'm supposed to judge. Mkise echoed my thoughts.

"Of what?"

"Right now, of you."

Mkise gave a small grunt of amusement, and sat down. "Okay. First question?"

"The strike at Leith Metals . . . was it wildcat, or planned?"

"Good question." Mkise's voice was cool and dry, the English strongly accented. "We didn't plan it. Maybe someone else did."

"Did you get any warning it would happen?"

"None. There were some negotiations going on, about wages. Suddenly, they blew up."

"Didn't the works committee at Leith get any danger signals?"

"The works committee at Leith is a load of crap. But no, Mark, they did not see what was happening. They didn't have time."

"Do you know what sparked it?"

"I think the Leith management went mad. There were negotiations, like I say. Then on Thursday, the managing director came into the workshops. Starts firing men. The induna asked why; the manager said, because they are trouble-makers. So next day, Friday, the others started to strike. Friday afternoon, there were nearly 300 out. And all those men were fired."

"And yesterday?"

"You read the papers. A big crowd came, marchers from Umlazi and those places. They stoned the windows. The police were called. They tried to talk to the men, but then the demos . . . they fired a couple of cars. So then the fuzz used tear gas."

"How many were arrested?"

"Seventeen."

"The paper last night said five injured. How?"

"Three by stones, two shot. They didn't print that."

"If your people didn't organize the strike, Peck, who did?"

"I don't know, Mark."

"How wide is the labour unrest in Natal?"

"At the moment, only Durban area. But there are strikes at fifteen places, and it will spread. I'm telling you."

"What action are the police taking?"

"So far, it's low-key. It won't stay that way, if there are more demos like yesterday."

"Were you at Leith Metals at all?"

"I went there, after five. There were still big crowds, though not close in. People running about, and shouting. The police trucks were moving us back, and I kept out of sight. Didn't want to be mixed up in it."

"Do you support the police view that young people started the violence?"

Mkise sat quietly, shoulders hunched. At last he said, "There were some kids threw stones. Thirteen, fourteen years old. But they didn't start it. The trouble came from inside. When the manager started firing men, firing all the Xhosas on the payroll . . . that was the cause. The children came in afterwards."

"All the Xhosas. All the Transkeians," said Mark softly.

"Now why in hell do that, he must have known it would be inflammatory? Peck, do you think someone got at him?"

"Could be."

"And the kids. You say they came in after the riots began. Do you know that for fact, or is it just your opinion?"

As Mkise remained silent, Mark persisted. "Were they Xhosa kids, or Zulu?"

"I don't know. By the time I got there, they'd left."

"Disciplined? Organised?"

"They were just kids."

Mkise's face was expressionless. I thought, you can ask for a hundred years, he's not going to discuss them.

He talked a while longer about labour affairs. Everything he said darkened the picture of what was happening in Industria. He was uneasy, and also angry. As he was leaving, he said vehemently, "It's not my people, making this trouble. You want to find out who, you better go ask among the whites."

"I intend to," Mark answered.

VI

MKISE LEFT AT six and Dudu Ndhlovu arrived ten minutes later.

Sechaba Ndhlovu—Dudu was his nickname—was a national figure. I'd met him often at conferences and private gatherings. He'd been a teacher and a member of the old African National Congress, and now claimed to be retired. My guess was he still had a finger in a lot of pies, business and political. To look at he was short and thickset, very dark skinned. He liked to play the fat buffoon; but I'd no more have tried to tangle with him than I'd have fed my fingers to a power saw.

He brought Mark a pile of confidential reports about Industria, and the first half-hour of his visit, we discussed those. But when Dudu was into his second whisky, he leaned back in his chair and said, "So, tell me, how's your campaign coming? Can you win?"

Mark gave him a run-down of the facts and figures we normally divulge only to our key workers. Dudu listened attentively.

"That's a real swing," he said. "A winning one."

"If it continues."

"You think it can reverse?"

"The climate's hardened, the last two weeks." Mark gave a sly grin. "We're getting trouble from the white kaffirs." It was the sort of crack you could only make among people of like mind, and Dudu chuckled gently.

"Don't you always?"

"It's tougher than usual. Morry had a chat with Charles Cameron—*Gazette* man—last night. Charlie's been threatened by a bunch of psychos, and Morry thinks it could be because he's onto a big story, possibly about the Summit."

Dudu looked mildly surprised. "Didn't get it from me."

"But he's been digging?" I asked.

"He's had discussions with us, of course." Dudu's tone was guarded. "Routine stuff."

"So everything's okay?"

Dudu's shoulders jerked impatiently. "When you're trying to fix a conference for over 500 people, okay isn't enough. It's got to be good. We've ironed out the main problems. Venue, cash, speakers, we have. Also delegates from every interest group in the country, black, brown and yellow."

"How about the radicals?" Mark perched himself on the edge of his desk. "Simeyane was here an hour or two ago. He seemed to have doubts."

"Simeyane likes to make remarks to upset people."

"So what's the format?" I said.

"Friday night we have a big formal dinner on the roof garden of the hotel—that's the Southern Cross—the Leaders to preside. Open congress all day Saturday. Sunday, we break into small groups to plan the follow-up."

"Any idea what that might be?"

Dudu looked at me levelly. "Hard to say, Morry. I hope we'll evolve a planned strategy . . . economic, social, political."

"It's going to influence Mark's chances," I said, "what comes out of your meetings."

"I know that. You want to know, will they agree to negotiate with whites?"

"Yes."

"There'll be a faction that will never agree. But I think there'll be more who want negotiation. Why should we kill the nice white goose that lays the golden economy?"

"And when the talking's done," I said, "how will you implement your plans? What real power do you have?"

Dudu slowly spread the thick fingers of his right hand. "We have four powers, Morry my friend. The power of our labour, which we can withhold. The power to buy, which we can direct. The power of negotiation which is growing right there, in the big rich cities"—he closed the fingers into a fist—"and the power of violence. You must make your people understand this. If the whites break the Summit . . . if they refuse to listen to what comes out of it . . . then the last chance of peaceful change is gone. There will be violence, no one will be able to stop it."

Mark, who had been sitting in frowning silence, now raised his head. "You haven't answered my question, Dudu. Will the radicals attend? It's not good enough, relying on the Chiefs' support. You need the young, urban militants. It seems to me you're going to need Moses to bring that lot to the promised land . . . maybe even the Messiah."

"You may be right."

"I am right."

Dudu, seeming to debate within himself, suddenly smiled. "And if I tell you we have such a man in mind . . . that a few of us have invited him to come. . . ?"

"Who is he?"

"Amyas Mochudi."

While we were absorbing this piece of news, the sound of the supper gong rolled softly through the house.

Bianca had fixed a buffet meal, knowing we had to move on to a house meeting in three-quarters of an hour. Dudu refused to stay, saying he had too much work to do, but David Tindall joined us. He didn't seem to like me any better than he had the night before, which suited me.

It was an uncommunicative gathering. Mark, as always before he had to make a speech, was busy with a sheaf of notes. Bianca was in one of her withdrawn moods. Tindall addressed anything he had to say, to her. I ate my cold meat and salad, drank my chilled white wine, and thought my own thoughts.

There was plenty for me to addle over. So many issues could ball up the election: the labour unrest, the Summit talks, the white backlash. Now Dudu had brought in Amyas Mochudi, which I can tell you is about as close as you can get to drafting the Messiah, in these parts.

Mochudi spent five years on Robben Island, only being released a few months back, because his newly-independent Homeland put on the screws for his freedom. He was a hero to the young blacks in every township in the country. I'd read most of his political writings, including the banned items, and all his published poetry.

But the real reason his name got to me that night, was because he'd known Jess. I'd heard her speak about him. Jess was my wife, long ago, before the world ended.

After supper, I went upstairs to wash and change my shirt. As I reached the middle landing of the staircase, I happened to glance to my right. There's a kind of half-moon window there, that ventilates the study behind. It's deeply inset, and curled up on the broad ledge, fast asleep, was Nick.

Thinking he might roll off and hurt himself, I put out a hand and touched his shoulder. His eyes opened and he grinned at me.

"What are you doing up there?" I said.

"Listening."

"What to?"

"I can hear what they say, down in the study."

"Can you now? And how long have you been here?"

"Since after my supper. But I fell asleep."

"Come on. I'll take you up to bed." I lifted him, feeling the warmth and delicacy of his rib cage. He put an arm round my neck and I carried him up and put him into his bed.

"You promised me a car-sticker," he said.

"Yes. They aren't ready yet."

"But as soon as they are?"

"Yes. I won't forget."

"Mark Ramsay for Parliament," he said sleepily.

I put out the light as I went out of the bedroom.

The house meeting was in Preller Crescent, a white-collar area where Mark had solid support. The format was the usual one. The candidate arrived, got introduced to the 50 people crowded onto a patio designed to hold twenty; made a brief speech, and then answered questions for an hour or so.

It was my view that these meetings would win the election for us. Though Mark was great on a public platform, the people who attended the big public gatherings would be the political buffs. At the smaller meetings in private homes, we'd find the timid doubtfuls, who in that sort of set-up could find the courage to ask their questions.

Mark spoke well that night, pithy and humorous, and the guests kept him answering questions well beyond the scheduled time. I kept switching off. Very few people dream up anything new to ask a candidate, and I'd heard the answers a hundred times already. So while I registered that things were going well, that the fat lady on the swing-seat was going to vote Ramsay and bring her friends, that the bank clerk with bunions was still havering, my mind kept drifting off on flights of its own.

I stood at the back of the courtyard, fought off the insects trying to fly up my nose, and thought about Jess.

When the meeting ended at ten o'clock, I drove Mark home. I didn't go in for a drink with him. Instead, I took the car up to the top of the Berea and parked. Yesterday's drizzle had cleaned the air, and the city glittered like a Kimberley widow. I sat there telling myself all the reasons why it would be crazy to see Jess again, and at eleven o'clock I gave up and drove to her house.

VII

DON'T ASK ME to describe Jess. I don't ever see her properly. Someone like Bianca Ramsay, now, I can look at and say, "She's got a delicate nose and a square jaw, her hair is thick and fine and golden and her eyes are a dark greeny-grey like the sea just before sunrise". I can wax poetic, and not feel a damn thing for her beauty.

I suppose other people see Jess as medium-sized, with fair kind of frizzy hair, some freckles and too much tail. People use the word earthy to describe her, and say she is very amusing. All I can tell you is that for me she is an entire world, an entire experience. The very first time we met she took me right into her mind. That's something very few people do for anyone.

It was especially unusual for me. People put up a lot of mental barriers against an outsize half-Jewish metallurgist with a lousy temper.

On the occasion I mention, I was also slightly drunk. I was living in Jo'burg at the time, and I called in at an exhibition of Jess's sculpture, and someone introduced us. Jess stared at me out of screwed-up eyes. Then she said, "You look like a fighting man, Faber. Why don't you tell me the truth about my work?"

She really meant it. She took me round the room and made me look at all these objects. It was kind of a gauntlet she threw down, and I picked it up. The place was crowded with art foondis, which I am not, but knowing metals helped. I found she knew a lot about what you can do with metal in the way of refining it and shaping it. Later, when I watched her at work, I learned something else, that you can't understand anything about a work of art unless you know about its production.

I told her what I thought, that night, man I was possessed, hooked. I told her things I didn't know I knew, and she listened to it all with a half-amused, half-resentful attention. She also talked about herself. When at last we stopped talking, everyone else had gone home. The exhibition hall was empty, and there was a cleaner knocking on the plate-glass door, with a big round sun behind him.

It was three weeks before we went to bed together. From that time on, home for me was between her thighs. I don't make my love life a conversation point, but I'll say this : most times, sex is just sex, over as soon as the act's done, but sometimes you have it, and you lose the boundaries between yourself and another person. It's not so much being one flesh, as being one person. You enter into the glorious kingdom of your common humanity. It is a kingdom that can also be strange and frightening, and very, very hard to maintain. At least, I hope that it is hard, and that it was not just my stupidity that lost me the kingship. I hope like hell it wasn't just that.

When I was a kid, I was clumsy. I often broke things, and particularly the delicate, precious things. I'd get anxious, and somehow I'd bust them. So all through my adult life, I've been scared of the damage I can do the people I care about. That's why I left Jess. I've never stopped loving her, not for a single breath of time.

We were married for three years, and if it hadn't been for the child we had, everything would have been safe. I should say, the child we lost, although in my mind we didn't lose him, he got born. Don't think it's only women who dream about the kids they don't have. I have sons, in my dreams. I put my hand on their heads. I say, "son," to them.

But I cannot have sons at Jess's expense, and this is why I left her.

Queer though, on the last night before I cleared out, I ran amok, and broke things.

I went out into the garden at the back of our house in Johannesburg. I'd built a little shed, with a forge and kilns for Jess's work. One furnace was still glowing. She'd been working on an abstract composition in copper, and the piece, not a very large one, was lying on the workbench. I picked it up and put it quite carefully into the furnace. I threw in some tin shavings with it, and some saltpetre, and even dirty shavings off the floor, and then I stood back and allowed the whole thing to meld and fuse into an amorphous blob. I had the feeling that it was myself burning up in there, and Jess with me. I knew that was crazy. I walked out of the house and went to a hotel.

Next morning I 'phoned Jess and told her I wanted a separation. She fought the idea but after a while gave up and moved down to Durban.

That was three years ago. Since that time we've lived 500 miles apart.

Just before Christmas, when Sid Heffner died and the Parkhaven constituency fell vacant, our Party people got onto me to persuade Mark Ramsay to stand for us. I said No at first, but when I thought it over, I saw I had to agree, and when Mark accepted and asked me to be his manager, I had to do that, too.

Since I came to Durban—I'd taken long leave from my firm to cover the election period—I hadn't so much as 'phoned Jess. So I didn't expect a great welcome when I drove round to her place at eleven o'clock at night. When I got there I climbed out of the car fast and went and pressed the doorbell before I lost my nerve.

She had the upstairs flat. The windows were dark. I stood back and stared up at them. After a while one opened and Jess put her head out.

"It's me," I said. "Morry."

She didn't say anything, and I said, "Please Jess, could I talk to you?" She came downstairs and let me in.

It was a nice flat she had, with big rooms and windows all round. A lot of her work was on view. She went about the lounge switching on lamps, and came back and stood in the middle of the floor with her hands on her hips.

"You look bushed, Morry," she said.

"I'm tired," I agreed.

"Would you like some coffee?"

"Please." I followed her out to the kitchen and sat at the table while she made the coffee and heated the milk. She put the things in front of me, and then changed her mind and poured for both of us.

She must have been asleep when I rang the bell, because her skin was shiny and moist and her hair a bit flattened on the one side. She had on a blue silk wrap with short sleeves and her throat and arms were very brown, as if she'd spent the summer out of doors. I wondered if she'd been working with stone. Her palms were as calloused as a road-ganger's. Sitting there looking at her I remembered the whole feel of her. I mean, I remembered the texture of her body under me and the smell of her skin. The memory was so sharp I felt the tears spring up in my eyes.

She sat frowning at me and then said, "Bad trouble, is it, Morry?"

That was like her, to jump right over the recriminations and the What-do-you-think-you're-doing-here? bit.

I said, "Look, one thing. Everything was my fault. I know that."

Her eyebrows went up. "What good is it worrying whose fault it was? I never thought of that, much. Seems leaving me was what you had to do, you did it."

"Yes . . . but . . . as long as you don't think it made me happy. I wasn't chasing bluebirds."

"Happiness! Bluebirds! Morry, haven't you grown up yet?"

"What do you mean?"

"Oh, Jesus." It seemed she was going to get angry after all, she glared at me and pushed both hands up through her hair. Then she sighed. "So what's your problem now? Is it politics? The campaign?"

"In a way." On the way over to see her I'd tried to work out my reasons. Now that we were face to face I snatched the first straw that floated up to the surface. "Jess, how well did you know Amyas Mochudi?"

"Amyas?" She made a gesture of total incomprehension. "He's in prison."

"No, he's not. His release has been negotiated under the amnesty granted when his Homeland took independence."

"I didn't know. How long has he been free?"

"A couple of months."

"There's been nothing in the press, has there?"

"Virtually nothing. A few small paras. So far as I know, nobody has interviewed him, or even seen him since he left the Island. I can't find out where he's living. He's the invisible man."

"Are you suggesting he's in detention somewhere else?"

"I have no idea. His name came up in conversation today. It keeps coming up. Mochudi is news, he could have headlines any time he wanted, but there's nothing. If he's silent, it might be because he wants peace and quiet. It might be they knocked the

44

stuffing out of him, or offered him a deal too good to refuse. Maybe he's in Transkei, taking out citizenship. . . ."

"That's bull!"

"Okay, it's bull, but I don't know any better. You tell me what I should think, I'll appreciate it, I'll pay money!"

Jess leaned closer towards me. Her eyes, always very deep blue, go almost black when she's angry. "Amyas is a citizen of South Africa. He would never accept Transkei citizenship. That would be like accepting apartheid."

"How well did you know him?"

"Very well. I knew all the black leaders, when I was married to Ben. Amyas often came to our house. He was quiet. Sort of . . . implacable."

"When was this? The 'sixties?"

"The early 'sixties. Ben was still allowed to lecture. I was a student at the university, and Amyas was doing a post-graduate course in Commercial Law. He was . . . about 28, I suppose."

"Describe him for me."

"Oh . . . tall, for an African. Rather a long head, with high cheekbones and deep-set eyes. A good build, a beautiful walk. Tremendous energy. He was deft, deft with his hands and feet, a good dancer. Deft with his mind. He had a way of listening and smiling that knocked the phoney out of an argument. He laughed a lot. I think he found us all a little funny, our group, I mean. He called us the Salvation Barmy."

"A loner?"

"Not exactly." Jess frowned, trying for the right words. "He liked people, and they liked him. He was a great story-teller, when the mood took him. I remember one evening, he told us about his life when he first came to Johannesburg, when he was seventeen. He'd had a quarrel with his father, who wanted him to go to Fort Hare University. He skipped out and came to Jo'burg. Landed in gaol almost the first week, for a pass offence. After that, he learned the city the hard way. He had no work permit, of course, so he had to pick up what jobs he could. It was mostly manual labour. He slept anywhere : servants' quarters, outhouses, the single-man's hostels, the roofs of factories in town. Once he spent a month in a storm-water drain under Turffontein Race Course. He got to know the townships so well . . . he knew all the rackets, and how to get past the law. He told

45

me once, 'I'm an expert on the South African Way of Death'.

"He nearly did die. He got TB when he was twenty and was in hospital for nearly a year. When he got out, he cashed all he owned, about £100's worth. He bought a ticket home, and used what was over to throw a party for his friends. It was at Mama Shabalala's shebeen. It was an historic party. You can read about it in Vuzi's poem, it's there on my shelves, somewhere.

"Amyas went home, convalesced, and asked his family to stake him to a degree. Not at Fort Hare, though, he wanted Wits. They agreed. He got his LLb, and later went into practice with Nat Hlope, but he didn't really want to work as an attorney or conveyancer. He said, 'If I practice law, I'm dealing with the end-product of the baasskap system. I'll be helping to process people through the mincing-machine.' I said, wouldn't he be helping to keep them clear of the mincer, and he said, 'No, it gets them in the end, and especially it gets the people who work it. The most impartial judge on the South African bench is already on the road to Nuremburg, even if he doesn't understand that.' That was how Amyas saw things, he always drew ultimate conclusions. He never tried to evade them. It gave him the reputation of being far-sighted, but people didn't like it much.

"He used to say that blacks would never get their rights through the courts, or even through political movements. 'We'll have to fight in the streets,' he said. He wasn't dramatic about it, or anything. I don't think he wanted it to come to violence, he just thought . . . knew . . . it would. And now of course, it's happening as he said."

"What about politics? He was ANC, wasn't he?"

"Yes. He was active, politically, as a young man. He got a suspended sentence for his part in the Defiance Campaign of 1952. He was nineteen then. Towards the end of the 'fifties, before Ben was banned, Amyas began to come to meetings at our house. In 1961, there was all that anger building up. Remember? Sharpeville was very close. The blacks were using the ANC and the Congresses as platforms. There were strikes, everything was tense, everywhere you went there was this feeling of movement and anger.

"Amyas came to the meetings, but he never spoke much. He listened. He must have been aware of every facet of every problem. He probably heard plans that I never knew existed, but he was not—committed emotionally. One could feel that. He was kind of . . . waiting . . . and watching.

"I spoke to Ben about him, once. I asked if it was possible Amyas was a traitor. We were scared of police informers, because although Ben was within the law, we knew that some of our friends weren't. It was a strange time. Ben used to say that rebellion is always a relative thing, that what one man finds tolerable, the next may not, and so people are thrust over the boundary at different times. But he also said that to defy authority one must have two things : a deep fury, and sufficient strength to win. The fury was there, around Sharpeville, but not the strength. That was what Ben and Amyas both knew.

"Ben was certain Amyas would never betray his friends, and he said something I've always remembered. He said, 'In a colony of bees, there's a worker force and a fighter force. In particular there's one lot of fighters that is like a praetorian guard. It never enters a battle, even if the hive is under attack, until the last crisis, when the queen is threatened. Amyas is like that. It's not that he's outside the battle. He's merely waiting his time.'

"Ben was right. After Sharpeville, when a lot of the black leaders decided there was no more hope for peaceful change, and opted for sabotage, Mochudi didn't. He came round to talk to us one night. We had supper and sat talking out on the front lawn. Amyas told Ben he must stop fooling himself. 'It's no longer possible to mouth platitudes, my friend. We've lost this round. The ANC and PAC are banned. There is no legitimate organization for us any more. I can tell you exactly what will happen now. The leaders will try and hold meetings to bring their followers together, and they won't succeed. There are too many factions among us. We will all the time be under pressure from the security police. There will be demonstrations planned, and in response the Government will make new laws to bite deeper and deeper into our ability to make ourselves heard. In a few months, you will see all this, and you will have to choose, like the rest of us, whether to go underground and commit sabotage, and break the laws . . . or not. I know what you want to do. You want a compromise. You want peace with honour. That's not possible. If you know what is going on, then you will have to express yourself for or against those things. And even if you say you are against them, you may still be punished. You're a white man who is guilty by association with blacks. You can't condone the system, and yet in your heart you can't condone defiance of the law. So I advise you to cut adrift, Ben. In the same way, I advise my friends to do nothing for a while. If they take action now, they will be suppressed by laws. If they are suppressed, they will turn to unlawful action. Once that happens, the odds are too big for them. They will go into prison or exile. Either way, they will be political geldings. No. I am going to say to them, "Your best chance is to wait, and to use this time to build and plan." But they won't listen. Same as you won't listen, Ben.'

"He was right, as you know. The Treason Trialists were acquitted in March of that year, and there was all sorts of talk about how things would improve, now, but in fact the laws got tougher all the time. Nelson Mandela began his campaign for mass demonstrations round the country, and, immediately, there were intensive police raids—right through April and May, into June.

"Some of the black leaders quarrelled among themselves. Some went underground and began to plan Rivonia. Others left the country. Stories came back about how they were stranded in Dar-es-Salaam, no money and no jobs. It was an awful time.

"Then Ben was banned. I've told you how it was. He just couldn't stand the isolation. He got more and more depressed. I was 26 when he killed himself. He took sleeping pills. I was out all that day, and the people who found him . . . they threw water over him to try and revive him. When I saw him, he was lying all draggled, like a drowned moth. After he died, I wasn't in a fit state . . . I pulled right out of politics. By the time I was well again, I'd lost touch with my friends. They were scattered. Amyas had gone to the United States. He'd been refused a passport twice, then suddenly it was granted, and he went to Boston to study business management. He was away for . . . oh, about four years.

"I saw him a couple of times after he came back, but very briefly. We didn't talk about the past. We'd both made new careers. He had his own business, a consultancy based in Jo'burg, dealing with black advertising. He travelled a lot, he told me, to Zambia and Nigeria and places. He seemed happy.

"And then, about five years ago, I heard he'd been charged

under the security laws, and sent to the Island. I wrote to him. I don't know if he ever got the letter, he never answered it in any way."

Jess picked up the sugar bowl and tilted it so that a few grains slid across the surface. "I can't imagine we'd have anything to say to each other now." She glanced up at me. "Why do you need to know about him, Morry?"

"A hunch," I said. "A hunch that Mochudi might have come to the end of his waiting and watching. If he has, then it's going to play merry hell with my election campaign." I got to my feet. "Thanks for talking to me, Jess. I appreciate it."

When I was saying goodbye on the landing, a thought struck me. "Could he be traced through his family?" I asked. "Did he have relations, a wife?"

"I never met any. He had a half brother who was a lot younger, a boy call Hobeni, I think."

"Thanks," I said. "Goodnight, Jess."

She looked as if she might speak, but changed her mind. Perhaps she'd already said more than she wanted to, and was drawing back behind her barriers. We were all in our little compartments. She couldn't reach Mochudi any more, and I couldn't reach her.

VIII

NEXT MORNING AT six, I went to the kitchen and switched on the percolator, picked the newspaper off the doormat, and read it over strong black coffee.

The Industria situation was now the second-lead story on page one. There was a photo of blacks standing outside the Doyle Motor Components Plant. The story underneath said that an estimated number of 4,000 workers were now on strike at a total of nine Industria factories. There had been temporary stoppages at another eight places.

"The immediate cause" the report went on "appears to be low rates of pay, but an underlying factor is certainly the belief among workers of Transkeian origin that they are being re-trenched before workers from other parts of the country. The Fabricia Mills, which employ a high ratio of contract workers from Transkei, were the scene yesterday of angry demon-strations, and were forced to close down operations.

"The Minister of Labour is expected to make a statement in the House today. Meanwhile, the consul for Transkei, together with representatives of Ciskei and Kwa-Zulu, have met with white entrepreneurs in an endeavour to ease the trouble.

"The situation in the factory area, late last night, was calm. Police are maintaining a close watch, and loudspeaker vans have been patrolling the areas bordering on Industria, advising workers of the best routes to use to get to work today."

The seven o'clock news, which I heard on the way to Mark's home, added nothing fresh.

I found Mark having breakfast alone on the front verandah, Bianca having taken Nicky to school.

"You picked the right subject for tomorrow night," I said.

"Yeah." He lit a cigarette and held it so that the smoke made broad blue riffles in the sun. "Morry," he said, "what struck you most about yesterday's interviews?"

I'd spent a long time, during the night, thinking about that.

"The fact they've invited Mochudi."

"Exactly. Do you think they know where he is?"

"Dudu must know, but he won't tell."

"Do we have any way of finding out?"

I shrugged. "Someone mentioned Mochudi has a brother named Hobeni. We might trace him."

"Who told you?"

"I forget. Someone . . ."

"For God's sake, Morry. Remember." Mark peered at me intently, and then said abruptly, "Was it Jess?"

I sat there thinking what a fool I'd been to go anywhere near her, she was the last thing that I or the campaign needed. Aloud, I said, "Well, I did see her, last night. She can't tell us a damn thing about Mochudi, she hasn't seen him for years."

"She could find out. . . ."

"No."

"Well, you could ask her to. . . ."

"I'm hardly in a position to ask favours of her."

"Then I'll do it."

"You won't! Leave it alone, Mark, I'm telling you, just leave Jess out of it."

"All right. All right, Morry. Calm down."

I stared at him. "Jesus! Go on, go and fetch the car. I'll 'phone her."

She answered the call quickly. I asked if she would pull strings to help us find Mochudi, it was urgent. She said she'd do what she could.

She sounded friendly, and kind, and distant; as if she was talking to someone she'd known briefly, a long time ago.

When I came out to the car Mark was in the front passenger seat, and David Tindall in the back.

Mark said, "Dave's coming along. He wants to take some photos."

"Nobody's going to talk to us if you're clicking a camera."

"No-one will know." Tindall held out his hand. On the palm lay what looked like a pack of Texan cigarettes. "Developed by my firm," he said.

"What for? Industrial espionage?"

"Industrial counter-espionage." He sounded prim. I held my

51

peace. I'd already formed the opinion that Tindall was a nut, but if Mark liked having him around, that was okay.

We took the main road south to Industria. It's a good site for factories, from the point of view of infra-structure. Plenty of water, power, a huge labour pool in the southern townships. But from the point of view of the environment, then it's not good, because Durban has a long, hot, steamy summer, with no wind to move the pollution along.

We drove through the area of Indian stores, most of them already busy, the owners standing at the doors in their shirt-sleeves. There was a stink of food, vegetables and meat mixed up with the industrial smog.

My shirt and jacket were already soaked with sweat.

Almost as we reached the first factory, we heard the police loudspeaker van. It was churning out a message in Xhosa. Along-side it two motorcycle cops waited astride their bikes. The streets around were busy, but, as we moved further into the district, we passed places that looked as if they were closed down. At each of those, there were police trucks parked.

IX

OUR FIRST APPOINTMENT was with a man named Norman Camberley, owner of a fast-expanding paint factory. Norman was a member of our Party; aggressive, shrewd, and on the subject of the labour unrest, as uptight as hell.

"I've had problems, all right. If I tell you, it's not for publication."

"Understood."

"I'm being pressured by the police."

He waited while a secretary served us coffee, and when she had left, said grimly. "I shouldn't have trouble, here. I have good wage structures, pension plans, in-service training. My works committee is really effective. Until four months ago we were going sweet as a nut. Then the Special Branch came calling.

"They warned me there were blacks in my pay who were campaigning for trades unions. I told them I knew that, and it didn't worry me. Next thing I heard, my workers were being questioned, not here, but at their homes. Some of them were being cornered four, five times. I 'phoned and asked for an explanation. Got a lot of bull-dusting. And in the mean time my works committee just fell apart. You don't get ordinary men to serve, if they're scared the job's going to be a political hot-squat. I'm being pressured to stop backing the trades unionists. They can get stuffed."

"Any work-stoppages?"

"Not yet. But with my men nervous as cats, and no discussion taking place, we could be hit any time."

"How did the riots start?"

"Demos. Walks. You couldn't call them marches. That was about six weeks ago, groups of workers drifting about the streets like dust eddies."

"Young people?"

"A lot of them were young. First week or so, they seemed harmless enough. Then they started to be hostile. Stone-throw-ing, picketing. Three weeks ago it began to look really nasty. I think we could be heading for massive strikes, like the ones in '73."

"Would you say the young people fermented the riots?"

Norman shook his head slowly. "Queer thing. Six weeks ago, it was young people. Three weeks, even. Then they dropped out, quite suddenly. The strikers at Leith Metals and the other places are not specifically youngsters. They're just a cross-section of the whole work force. I took particular notice. It's my opinion that about three weeks ago—maybe a bit less—the youth brigade pulled out."

"A planned withdrawal?"

"I think so."

I intervened then. "Does the name Hobeni mean anything to you, Norman?"

"Not a thing. Want me to check with Personnel?"

"Please."

He rang through, and we waited for some minutes. Finally he replaced the receiver. "There's no Hobeni on our payroll. Never has been."

We left there with the feeling that we'd simply got deeper into the woods.

Our next call was at Leith Metals. The manager was a paunchy runt with bad teeth. He told us, between swallowing stomach pills, that he'd inherited the business from his uncle, hated it, and would sell out as soon as he could find a buyer.

"It's just one shitty thing after another," he said. "You can't get materials, you can't sell the crap when you've made it up, you got cash liquidity problems, labour problems. The buggers just walk out on you." He glared at us out of red little eyes. "You lot, you're all for the kaffirs. Anything black is all right with you. Well, I don't like blacks. I'm honest about it see? Half chance, a native'll bust up your plant and pinch anything that's not nailed down. Xhosas are the worst of the lot."

"Yet you employed a number of Xhosas, Mr Zeffrey."

"I did. Not any more. Fired the lot."

"That seems an extreme measure."

"Listen, I don't need you to tell me how to run my business. When I want advice, I go to the top."

"Did you, in this case?"

"Did I what?"

"Get advice from the top?"

"I got good advice, I can tell you. I got a straight tip-off from people who know what they're talkin' about when it comes to blacks, and the word was, 'Get rid of the Transkei lot, they're poison'. So out they went, and I'm not havin' any of 'em back, 'at's for sure. I told the press and I'm tellin' you, Mr Ramsay, because then you can't go spreading stories about me. I like to make myself clear."

"Who tipped you off?" I said.

"None of your bloody business."

"Was it the police?"

He shot me a look half venemous and half frightened. "I'm not discussing it with buggers like you. You go around tellin' coons they can have everything. Everything we've built up. You're the cause of all the trouble, I'll say it to your face."

We passed the main factory floor on our way out. Glancing through one of the big doors, I saw that nearly all the machines were standing idle. There was a big stack of crates in the loading yard, opposite a row of empty trucks.

Tindall, who'd been admirably silent up till then, gave tongue as we drove south.

"Maurice, I'd like to know what made you ask that question about the police?"

"I know Zeffrey," I answered. "Anyone in the metal trade will tell you, he's a greedy bastard. He employs unskilled migrant labourers because they're desperate for jobs and will put up with his lousy work conditions. Yet suddenly, he's fired nearly 300 men. You can see it's crippled his whole factory, it's going to cost him a bundle. He would only do that on a very strong warning . . . either from a source he trusts, or one that scares him."

"Are you saying the police would offer such advice . . . knowing it would almost certainly result in strikes?"

"Probably they wouldn't."

"Then why do you suggest it?"

I felt suddenly savage. "Tindall, do you understand what those strikers are doing? They own sweet Fanny Adams, but what they have they're putting at risk. And I want to know why, that's what we came out here for, remember? So I'll ask any questions that need asking, whether you like them or not."

Mark said hastily, "Where next, Morry?"

"Filey, Lofts," I said. "Dick Tuttle set this one up. Four companies in this road have had men out on strike, but for some reason Filey, Lofts, escaped. They make high class kitchen ware, everything from non-stick pans to stoves. They're very big. Factories in Pinetown, Richards Bay and on the Rand. Top boy is Alexander Condor, born in Hungary but hasn't lived there since the revolution. He spent a number of years out east, then central Africa, then here. Likes warm climates, supports the Government, has a holiday home on Corfu where he goes for three months every year."

"I've met him," said Mark. "Pleasant guy to talk to, more than can be said for Zeffrey."

It was along this road that we began to pass long queues of men and women outside the factory fences, hoping to find work where others had been dismissed. With close on two million unemployed, people weren't waiting for dead men's shoes, they were tearing them off the living.

It was too quiet in Industria that morning. The idle yards silent, the job-seekers silent, the young police recruits silent in the riot trucks.

Another thing I noticed. Several walls in the area had been daubed with paint. A big M.

X

THE WORDS "Filey, Lofts & Co. Ltd." were spread across a modern brick façade that occupied a whole block. Behind stretched acres of corrugated iron roof, new, painted brown. There was security fencing right round the property, a guard-box at the main gates. In the shade beside the box, tethered to a long chain, lolled a dock-eared Doberman.

I stopped the car and the guard, a big Irishman with pale red hair, stepped out and checked the card Dick Tuttle had given me.

"Through there, sir, the courtyard on your right."

"You have good security here."

"Need it, these days. What I say, be ready for trouble, and ye'll niver find it." He waved us forward.

We turned into a wide square planted with grass, trees and cannas. The buildings round it were white with brown fixings, and on the left a flight of steps led up to a double door marked "Office and Enquiries".

We parked the car and made for the entrance. The reception area was air-conditioned. We handed Tuttle's card to the receptionist and sat back in big soft armchairs until a messenger arrived to take us through to Alexander Condor.

I suppose I'd been expecting the standard tycoon : equal parts of alcohol, avarice and after-shave. Condor wasn't like that. He was of medium height, with the spare torso and powerful wrists you find in good horsemen. Skin very brown, eyes dark and velvety as old port. There was a purple birthmark on his left temple.

A travelling chess-set stood among the executive clobber on his desk, and the walls were decorated with photographs of fast cars and presumably fast horses. Condor did not appear in any of the pictures.

He greeted us genially and asked how he could help us.

Mark went into his spiel about wanting to get at the root causes of the unrest. "I don't believe the public is getting the full truth. The papers mentioned nine factories idle. My own assessment, just driving through this morning, is fourteen in this sector alone."

"I'm afraid you are right." Condor's voice was as deep and soft as his eyes. "It is bad, and will grow worse if things are not handled correctly."

"Are they being?"

"Why do you ask?"

"Well, for example, at one place we visited, the management has dismissed all Transkeian workers, apparently on the strength of a tip-off that they might make trouble. Have you had any warnings of that sort?"

"No. If I had, I should report the . . . what do you call it . . . tipster? Immediately."

"To the police?"

"And to the Labour authorities."

"Do you employ Transkeians?"

"Some."

"Could you tell me, are you proposing to retrench them?"

"We are in a period of recession, Mr Ramsay. I may have to retrench. If so, I'll cut back on the men who come from outside of Natal. After all, isn't that good business practice, that foreign labour is the last to be taken on, and the first to be retrenched?"

"Foreign? Many of these Xhosas were born in this city. They have a greater claim to be South Africans than . . . well, than you do."

"I am naturalized citizen," said Condor mildly. His face creased suddenly in a smile both diffident and charming. "But this is ideology. And business as we know is not so strict. I admit I have Xhosas who have worked for me many years. They are skilled men, they are valuable, I do not wish to lose them. A good worker is perfectly safe with me. Agitators . . . that is another matter. But perhaps you don't believe they exist?"

"Oh yes, I do," said Mark bluntly. "I've seen them do their stuff in several parts of the world."

"Then you understand me. Men who are incompetent, go out. And men who make trouble, make fights, beat up other workers at the bus rank . . . those also I dispense with."

"One last question, if I may . . . did you ever employ a young man named Hobeni?"

"Hobeni?" Condor lifted one of the chessmen, turned it

58

absently in his hand. "I don't think so. I employ so many in these works. But you could check it with my Records Department. And now, I wish to ask you something. Why did you select my company to visit today?"

"Because my PRO regards it as a model company, and because you seem to have escaped strikes."

Again we got the pleasant smile. "I touch wood when you say so. Well, I have assumed you want facts and figures, not idle conjecture. I think it will be best if you talk to my Records Controller. That is Mrs Tonkin. I have already asked her to look out certain material for you."

With which he eased us to the door. Mr Condor's PR style was, I considered, as efficient as his security measures.

A cute little secretary with an articulate backside took us to the Records Department. We passed along a corridor, (more photos, of the Minister of Economic Affairs at an Assocom luncheon, of Corfu, of the Condor Electric Dishwasher), and went down two flights of stairs, which brought us out near the main factory area. The clang of metal and the smell of hot oil came to us even through closed doors.

The office itself had a biggish floor-space, open plan with the usual desks, chairs and filing cabinets spread around it. Three people were working there : a white typist with fat arms, and two clerks, one Indian and the other African.

In the far corner, in a little cubicle behind asbestos partitions, we found Mrs Tonkin. The cubicle being too pokey to hold more than one visitor, Mark went in and I stood at the door. Tindall wandered off and started chatting to the black clerks.

Mrs Tonkin was a woman of medium size, fairly plump, with a pale square face and heavy brows. Her thick, greying hair was docked and secured behind her ears with Kirbigrips. She sat with her forearms flat on the desk. She looked the sort of lady you find in most big concerns, dowdy and reliable, been there for ever and with a memory like an elephant.

Condor must have 'phoned her while we were on our way downstairs, because when we arrived she already had a stack of papers on her desk : wage schedules, work programmes, a copy of a pamphlet dealing with pensions and health insurance. She pushed them across the desk.

"Mr Condor didn't mention who you are representing."

"Myself." Mark picked up a page and began to read.

"But who recommended you to come here?"

Mark remained silent. I said, "Mr Dick Tuttle".

"I never heard of him." Her tone suggested that was our loss.

When we'd checked through the material, Mark asked about Hobeni. Mrs Tonkin got up and went over to a filing cabinet, returning with a handful of index cards.

"I can help you if he's a permanent, or on contract. If he's just a temporary, then it will mean hours of work to trace him, and unless you're sure he's worked here . . . and I take it you're only interested in current records? I can't go searching through old stuff. . . ."

"Say, over the past year."

She began to flick deftly through the cards. In a short while she'd extracted three, which she gave to Mark. I read them over his shoulder.

Two of the Hobenis were over 45 years old. Mark laid those cards aside and studied the third.

"Hobeni, Don," he said. "Shift controller, aged 27. That could be the one."

Mrs Tonkin compressed her lips. "He's left."

"Oh? When?"

"Last month."

"What sort of man was he?"

"He was in charge of the fork-lift operators."

I looked at her to see if that was a deliberate evasion, and decided it wasn't. Mrs T. was the sort of woman who would define a man by the work he did.

"Was he an educated man?"

"Yes. He could have done clerical work but he didn't like it. He acted as interpreter, sometimes. He was a clever boy, too clever, really. He started to get big ideas."

"In what way?"

"Oh, money and that. He had debts."

"A family man?"

"He wasn't married. But they all have women. He was buying furniture and clothes. He borrowed from his friends, all the time. That's why we let him go. When they get into debt, then there's fights. It causes a lot of nuisance."

"Was Hobeni fired?"

"Yes."

"Would you say he was a good employee?"

"No."

"Why not?"

"He made trouble, I told you. He had too many debts. Since he left, we've had letters from all over, all sorts of shops, you wouldn't believe."

"Was he politically active?"

"I don't know about that."

"Could you give me his address?"

"He's left where he was. We sent on some bills, and they came back. The shops have been onto us, too, about him."

"Have you any idea where he could have gone?"

"Back to Transkei, I suppose. He had his leave pay, and that."

I picked up the sheaf of papers that still lay on her desk. Probably they'd been ready for us ever since Dick Tuttle made the appointment for us. They were the sort of stuff a good PR man would get out for, say, a visiting pressman. Which gave me an idea.

"Mrs Tonkin," I said, "has a guy named Charlie Cameron been to see you?"

For the first time she looked directly at me. It was an unpleasant experience. Her eyes were big and luminous and somehow greedy. I felt she was trying to get hold of my brain and squeeze out all the things I kept secret, like the way I felt about Jess. I felt she was smelling out my antecedents, my mistakes, my lies, like a witchdoctor smells out evil. My flesh crawled.

Then someone laughed in the outer office. Mrs Tonkin shifted her gaze, and came back into focus as a dumpy, sour, efficient old bag who didn't like having her routine interrupted.

"Nobody of that name ever came here," she said.

It was nearly noon when we started back for town.

When Mark had first suggested we go out to Industria, I'd thought he was wasting time, we'd get nothing we didn't already know. Well, I'd been wrong. I'd known for weeks that Industria was a potential bomb, but I hadn't been there, I hadn't watched the fire moving up the fuse.

I hadn't been scared enough. I was now.

Aloud, I said, "I will bet you any money you like, Cameron has been around these parts".

"You think the Tonkin woman lied?"

"About Cameron, yes."

Mark waited for me to go on, watching me the way he did sometimes when I was playing a hunch; a quiet, attentive look.

"I think she lies by sticking to superficial facts. I mean, like Hobeni being fired, and running up debts. That could be true. But she knows a lot more that she isn't telling."

"For example, that Hobeni was fired because of political agitation?"

"The thought crossed my mind."

Mark said softly, "Man, but I'd like to find Hobeni!"

"You won't do it." Tindall spoke from the back seat, and Mark twisted round to look at him.

"While you were with Mrs Tonkin," Tindall said, "I took the opportunity of speaking to those two clerks. They both knew Hobeni, and they both said categorically he's skipped out to avoid debt-collectors. You'll never trace him now."

"Did they tell you anything else about him?"

"Very little. He's Xhosa, of course. His friends think he's 'gone across the river', which I take to mean, back to Transkei. They say he has important connections there, who may be persuaded to settle his bills for him."

"Did they mention names?"

"Yes. A brother. Amyas something-or-other."

"Mochudi," I said, "and we won't find him, either. What's more, none of us is going to waste time trying. We have an election to win, it's enough already."

I dropped Tindall off in Umbilo Road. He wanted to develop the pictures he'd taken that morning.

But on the way to the campaign office, Mark returned to his hobby-horse.

"We could ask Charlie about this Hobeni."

"Listen," I said. "If you recall, we were given Mochudi's name in confidence. If we so much as mention Mochudi or Hobeni to Charlie, he's going to wonder why. If he already has wind of them, it'll sharpen up his appetite, and he'll be snapping round Dudu and us, like a hyena. Stick to your job, Mark, which is to catch votes."

He fell silent, then, leaning back in his seat with his eyes shut. After a while, he said, "Well, I've got a strong line for my speech tonight. Those tip-offs Zeffrey mentioned. Highly inflammatory."

"You won't find out who's responsible, in time."

"Don't need to. That's not my job. I shall challenge the authorities to find out, and to put a stop to it. The press will like it, and we may get enough follow-up to justify questions in the House. I'll work on it."

XI

WE'D BOOKED A church hall for the meeting, in the best part of the constituency . . . best, I mean, in terms of voter-support. The suburb was an old one, and the occupants well-to-do and orderly, so we didn't expect fireworks. But in view of the climate, I'd warned Henry Beaumont to bring along some of his rugby friends. They arrived at seven o'clock and we arranged that three or four of them would stay near the main door, and a couple at each of the side doors, to frighten off drunks and rowdies.

The hall looked good. Dick Tuttle had got it decorated with banners and posters until you saw "Vote Ramsay" wherever you looked. During the afternoon, David Tindall had come to the campaign office with the pics he had taken that morning, shots of Mark at Industria. They were first class, with the kind of clarity and immediacy you only get from an expert, and when Tindall offered them to me I jumped at them, saying I could use them as press handouts.

"I could have a dozen blown up big, if you liked," he said. "You could use them on hoardings, if you can find the sites."

"Great," I said. "Keep clicking, boy, you've got a job for the duration."

We mounted the originals in the foyer, above the tables where Bess Hooper and her girls would be handling voter-enquiries.

At seven-fifteen, Dick went backstage to get the final balance for the mikes, and to start the taped music. People were already trickling in, our own supporters and a good leaven of faces I didn't know. I looked them over carefully, to see if Colley Burman had sent any of his die-hards. There were a couple of them at the back, with prepared questions in their hot little hands.

I did a tour round the building. The caretaker had a cottage directly behind the hall, and we exchanged a word or two. I went round to the front entrance, after that, and switched on the arc lights above the lawn. There were a few small groups of people standing talking on the grass. I didn't recognize any of them, but that wasn't surprising, Durban not being my home ground.

The press came early, about seven-thirty. Timmins of the *Evening Standard* brought a photographer with him, and Charlie Cameron was there, and a new guy from the *Chronicle*. Dick Tuttle dealt out extracts from the two main speeches. The printing deadline for the morning papers was 9.00 pm, so their reporters would only catch Mark's speech. Anton van Rooyen, our guest speaker, would have to rely on the *Standard* for coverage.

By a quarter to eight, the hall was full, most of the seats taken and a good crowd standing at the back.

It was at this point that Dick came over to me and said quietly, "Trouble, I think."

"Where?"

He nodded towards the far aisle. Several men were pushing along it, moving with that mixture of doggedness and swagger that marks the thug coming into a political meeting. I counted seven of them. They separated and took seats in different parts of the hall.

I went outside again. Mark had arrived with Bianca. They were halfway up the path, with supporters thronging round them. Anton van Rooyen was there too. I could see his mane of fair hair shaking as he called an answer to someone in the crowd. Right at the back was Walter Brock, edging the whole circus towards the hall, like a good sheep dog. I drew him aside and told him there were probably some Vigilantes in the hall. As chairman of the meeting, it would be up to him to see things didn't get out of hand, and he asked me if I'd spotted the ringleader.

"I'm not sure. Perhaps a big chap in a blue T-shirt, sitting in the middle row, on the left."

"I'll watch it, thanks Morry."

We started the meeting at five past eight. Dick Tuttle turned up the music, and boosted the platform lights, and the speakers' party went marching up the centre aisle to a nice burst of applause.

I noticed that both the *Standard* photographer and David Tindall were busy taking pictures.

XII

THINGS WENT WELL at first.

Wally Brock made his speech of welcome, cracked a couple of jokes, introduced the platform party, and said nice things about the candidate.

Mark came forward to the speaker's mike.

As soon as he started talking, I knew he was on peak form. He seemed to be generating energy rather than using it. That is the mark of the true orator . . . not just well-found arguments, not just an expressive voice or a command of language . . . but that packed-down, spilling-over power that electrifies a crowd like the growl of a tiger.

He began by describing the economic situation in southern Africa . . . how in Angola, Zaire, Zambia, Rhodesia and Mozambique, the political crisis ran side-by-side with an economic crisis, so that the continent was spanned by a belt of régimes desperate for viability. He showed how, as the world cut back on its aid programmes, the flow of military hardware was increasing; and that to millions of people, it was beginning to appear that not only power, but jobs and food came through the barrel of a gun.

As long as he discussed other countries, the audience remained quiet. Then he turned to South Africa itself, beginning to expound his main theme, that industrial relations lay at the heart of South Africa's problems. Here, he said, were the greatest injustices, and the greatest opportunities for reform. It was in our factories, mines and harbours that we would spawn a revolution, or create the economic upsurge that would make us the pace-makers and peace-makers of the whole of Africa.

I'd read the speech many times, and yet it held me because of what Mark was putting into it, the force of his own vision and belief. That was what he had, and that was what was going to make people vote for him. I knew it. So did the Vigilantes.

At twenty minutes to nine, Mark started on Industria, and the heckling began.

Now heckling is part of politics, you expect it, and a good

speaker actually benefits by it. It gives the political diet a sharper flavour, and it wins sympathy from the audience. Moreover, a man with a mike can always out-shout the man down on the floor of the hall. But sometimes heckling goes way beyond acceptable limits, and becomes an organized attempt to break up the meeting, and that was what we got, that night.

The yobs we'd spotted earlier began to shout, at first separately, then in unison. Within minutes they'd built up a barrage, mindless, raucous. All the old hate words were there—kaffir-lover, hotnot, coolie—laced with four-letter words. Mark responded by turning up the amplifier on the mike. His voice rode the uproar, but no one sounds his best when he's yelling his head off. Wally Brock, in the chair, made repeated calls for order, without effect. Dick Tuttle came over to where I was standing in the main doorway. "This is bloody nonsense, Morry. We're entitled to throw them out."

"Not us!" I remember feeling an actual jerk of apprehension in my stomach. "We mustn't throw the first punch. That's what they want."

"They're wrecking Mark's speech, and it's important it gets heard."

"The press will cover the main points."

But then I heard a new clamour behind me, and looking round I saw a whole new mob thrusting into the foyer. They were singing and shouting, and sounded half drunk. All their faces had the same expression, a kind of stupid lust. I glanced at the two side doors. They were coming in there, too. No question about it, we were in for a punch-up.

I said to Dick, "Do me a favour. Get to young Beaumont, and tell him to move his boys up to the stage steps. These buggers may rush the platform. I'm going to call the police."

To do that I had to go outside the hall and round to the back, to the public call-box fixed to the wall. When I reached it, I found the wires had been jerked loose. I ran to the caretaker's door, banged on it, and when he stuck his head out, asked him to call the cops. Then I ran back to the hall.

By then, you could hear the noise all over the block. A good many people in the audience, either infuriated or scared, were shouting back at the hecklers. Others had started to push their way towards the exits. But the rowdies there had linked arms and were swaying back and forth. I had to strongarm my way past them.

It wasn't possible to reach the platform. The whole floor was a mass of surging, screaming people. I climbed on a chair, cupped my hands, and yelled to Wally Brock that I'd sent for the police. He nodded, and began to repeat that news into the mike. It got across to part of the crowd, and for a moment there was relative quiet. We might even have restored order, if the damn-fool *Standard* photographer hadn't decided at that moment to take pictures.

I saw him jump up onto the edge of the platform and I shouted, "No!" but the next minute the flash-bulb popped. The uproar began again, but sharper, with a high note in it like the whining of bees. Someone grabbed at the photographer's legs, dragged him down. His camera went smashing against a wall.

Near me, an elderly man aimed a blow at a young thug in a red lumber-jacket, and the thug immediately lashed out backhanded and swatted the old fellow over half a dozen chairs into the aisle. He lay there, flat as a little rag, and the woman with him set up a wild croupy screaming, her lips blue.

Then every light in the place went out.

I acted by fear rather than reason. I pushed my way up the side aisle, dodged round the press table and bellowed for Henry Beaumont. I heard his voice on the steps and headed for it. Next minute, a solid wedge of bodies hit me from behind and lifted me towards the stage.

There were people lashing out in the darkness. The press table went over with a crash. A burst of swearing turned suddenly into a scream of pain. Something whistled past my neck and caught me a glancing blow. I got one foot on the lowest step and then was blocked by a tangle of stumbling, kicking legs.

I put my hands on the edge of the platform and heaved myself up. A foot smashed into my cheek. I put up a hand, grabbed the ankle, lifted and shoved. The man toppled past me.

The console of switches for lights and mikes was over on the left. I blundered forward, and met the velvet curtaining. As I struggled to swing past it, I heard the police siren, rising and falling, sweeping nearer. And then, as suddenly as they'd dipped, the lights came on again.

Dick had pulled the main switch. He was half leaning, half

crouched, against the side wall, both hands pressed to his face. Blood trickled between his fingers. As I got to him he slithered down to a sitting position.

"A bottle," he said. "Some effer hit me."

"Stay still," I said, and swung round to look at the platform party. Mark was the one I was scared about. The candidate.

It was strange. The whole thing had happened so fast, they'd hardly changed position. Mark had left the speaker's rostrum and was standing with his arm round Bianca. Anton was just setting down a chair. Walter still had the chairman's mike in his hand. He started to talk into it, asking people to sit down, to be calm. Some of them obeyed. The hecklers had vanished like smoke in a high wind.

I turned back to Dick. Whoever had rammed a broken bottle into his face had meant business.

"It missed my eye," he said, and I knelt beside him and lifted him into a more comfortable position, while the sirens homed in on the shreds of our meeting.

XIII

ON THE ADVICE of Lieutenant Kray, we closed the meeting at once. A doctor in the audience offered to take Dick Tuttle to hospital in his own car, and Mark went with them. Anton van Rooyen drove Bianca home. Walter Brock and I stayed at the hall.

Kray was a quiet man; sandy hair bleached grey at the cap-line, light-blue eyes ringed with bleached lashes, a down-turned mouth. He cleared the crowd in rapid time, once I'd told him the bovver-boys had left; and then came back to us.

Walter thanked him for answering our call so fast, and Kray shook his head.

"I didn't answer your call, sir. I'm from the patrol car. A lady in the flats over the road 'phoned in about the noise from here. Lucky for you we were in the vicinity. Did you contact the station? If so, they'll be along shortly. Tell me, were you on the platform right through the meeting?"

"Yes, I was," said Walter.

"Did you recognize any of the people who started the fighting?"

"I didn't recognize any of them, but I'd be able to describe them, and identify them if I saw them again."

Henry Beaumont and his friends were straightening out the hall, picking up chairs and collecting our banners and what was left of our party literature. Kray glanced at the press table. "Was there a photographer present? Did he perhaps take a picture of the crowd?"

"No good," I said. "The camera was smashed and the film exposed. If you have records of the members of the Vigilantes, you'll find them easily enough."

Kray's gaze shifted to me, cold, showing neither belief nor disbelief. "You're saying it was Vigilantes, sir?"

"Yes."

"But you don't have proof?"

"Finding proof isn't my job," I said. I was tired and angry,

70

and I didn't like Kray much. "The ringleader should be identi-
fiable. About six-two, 190 lbs, dark hair cut very short, long ears
with heavy lobes and an asymmetric face."

Kray blinked rapidly.

"Asymmetric," I said. "Lop-sided. The bone structure on the
right is heavier than on the left. I should think it's a congenital
malformation."

Kray shrugged. "Sergeant Masson will maybe know him."

"Who's Masson?"

"There, in the foyer."

The party from the police station had arrived, three of them,
twenty minutes after the fight ended. They were talking to the
caretaker, no doubt getting his name in triplicate. As I started
sucking in my breath, Wally put a hand on my arm.

"Cool it, Morry."

"I'll leave you two gennelmen," said Kray, and walked away,
quick and light on the balls of his feet.

Slowly, the few of us who remained converged in the middle
of the hall. Sergeant Masson came over and sat with us and took
statements. He was young, with a Border ribbon on his jacket.
He showed all the concern that Kray had lacked, and I began to
hope that the thugs wouldn't get off scot free. When I men-
tioned the Vigilantes, he nodded.

"Ja, there's some bad elements there; and they don't like you
liberals. Trouble is, sir, you can't charge a man with heckling.
And the assaults you speak of, those happened after the lights
went out, not so? So there's no witnesses."

It took a long time, getting statements from all of us, and
when I'd given mine, I asked permission to make a 'phone call.
There was a café still open across the road, and I went there
and called Charlie Cameron.

When he came on, he sounded both tired and cagey.

"Charlie," I said, "did you recognize any of those yobs in the
hall tonight?"

"No."

"They could be your tormentors."

"Possible."

"Do you have photographs of any of the Vigilantes?"

"They won't pose for us." His voice sounded dry.

"But any mob scenes? Car-rocking? Anything like that?"

71

"I'll check for you . . . tomorrow."

"Thanks Charlie."

"Listen," he said. "That friend of yours, who was taking pics tonight. . . ."

"What friend?"

"No dodging, Morry. I saw him. A word from a friend. If he has photos of what happened, tell him to put them in the safe. And tell him to watch his back. This lot is very nasty indeed."

"I'll tell him."

"We pay good rates for clear prints."

"I'll tell him that, too."

I hung up and rang the hospital where they'd taken Dick. He was in the operating theatre, being stitched up. His wife had arrived from the country. Mark Ramsay was staying with her until Dick came round.

Back to the hall, again.

It was past one o'clock when the police packed up and allowed us all to go home.

XIV

THE PAPERS NEXT day gave the meeting good coverage, in the sense that they described the rough-house in detail. The *Gazette* also reported Mark's speech as far as he'd been allowed to make it. But the two main points, the two most newsworthy and important points, had not been made.

I drove Anton van Rooyen out to the airport to catch the early plane for Jo'burg, and he said we mustn't let it rest there. "Mark's campaign theme is Industria. His opponents don't want to let him speak about it, because they know that it will win him votes. Why don't you get one of the papers to print his speech as a feature article?"

Mark agreed it was a good idea, and at ten o'clock I took the text to Charlie.

He didn't look pleased to see me. He sat hunched behind his desk like a sick bird and did no more than glance at the first couple of pages of the speech.

"I'll see what we can do," he said. "It's a hell of long and probably won't cut well."

"Look," I said, "there are two good stories in that thing. The victimization of Xhosa workers, and the fact that employers are being conned into sacking them. Sniff around, you know damn well you'll find something good."

Charles shook his head. "Too late, Morry." He rummaged through a stack of paper on his desk and found a telex message, which he tossed over to me.

The gist of it was that urgent discussions, on the subject of the Industria unrest, were to be held by the relevant ministers, the Trades Union Council, the Chambers of Commerce and Industry, and the Durban City Council. Transkei was also being consulted. While this was happening, the press was kindly to keep its opinions to itself.

"Who's it from?" I said. "The Minister? Security?"

Charlie shrugged.

It was no use arguing with him. I knew the minefield of laws the pressmen had to tread. Infringements could mean, at best, a brush with the Press Council, and at worst, police or court action, with severe penalties attached. And Charlie didn't have the ultimate say-so about what got printed.

I tried Timmins of the *Standard*, and got the same response.

"It stinks," I said. "The public should know about these tip-offs."

"The only safe way to raise the issue," he told me, "is in the House of Assembly. Why don't you fix that?"

"I will."

Tindall did have one picture showing the crowd at the hall. He brought it to the campaign office, and we agreed that he should take it to the police . . . but that the negative and a couple of prints I would stash with the Party's legal advisors.

That afternoon, when Mark was through work at his own office, he and I went to see Dick. He looked terrible. His face was swollen and bruised, with black stitches everywhere, and he talked with stiff lips.

"It was my own fault I got slugged," he said, "I walked right into it. See, when the lights went out, I jumped up onto the platform to reach the console. The bugger was there waiting for me. Must have been the one who turned 'em off."

Mark said, "Did you get a look at him?"

"No. I ran into him in the dark. He put a hand on my shoulder, I suppose to get his range, then he jabbed the bottle into my cheek. I went down, and he stepped over me and scarpered."

"Did he knock you out?"

"No. I was hell of whoozy, you know, but I didn't actually pass out. I could hear all the chaos going on. I started to try and crawl towards the console. Then I heard the police sirens. That kind of spurred me on, and I got to the switches."

Mark hissed between his teeth. I knew what he was thinking. If it hadn't been for the sirens, the man with the bottle might have got stuck into the people on the platform. We could thank God some little old lady in the flats had 'phoned the flying squad; and that there was a car close by.

That evening at the meeting of the campaign committee, we came to some decisions. The white backlash must be regarded as a serious threat to our workers. No women would go out on

74

evening-canvass, or on day-canvass in bad areas. The men would work in pairs, wherever possible.

Mark had already asked the Leader to raise the Industria issues in the House. We decided to get out a pamphlet, quoting extracts from Mark's speech, and distribute it to every voter in the constituency. The number of meetings in private houses must be stepped up.

As Walter Brock said, "We're not going to win this election on Party policy. We're going to win it on Mark Ramsay, his personal charisma and impact. We've got to get him to the people. Nobody is going to stop us."

"The violence last night," said Bess Hooper, "was a kind of urban terrorism."

"Good phrase. Put it in the pamphlet. And we need letters to the press, lots of them. Ordinary people detest violence. We can turn what happened to our own advantage."

True enough, but it ignored one vital point. If Mark was the key to our success, he was also the prime target for attack. Walter urged him to look out for himself, and he promised he would, but I didn't set much store by that. Mark always stuck his neck out, and he had that thing about liking to act on his own. I knew we'd never stop him from taking risks.

Could we have saved him, somehow? I don't know. Violence may be a part of modern politics, but you don't expect it. The very essence of urban terrorism is that it is beyond the pale, and normal people can't predict it, or defend themselves against it.

During the week that followed, the labour unrest escalated. The government was still exerting its plea for silence, so not much appeared in the press; but the press boys told us privately that nearly 30 firms were now affected by the strikes, and that the dock workers were being drawn in.

Extra police started coming into Durban from other parts of the country, with Hippo trucks and riot equipment.

The top-level talks among the industrial leaders were referred to briefly in Friday's *Gazette*. That same afternoon, our Leader spoke in the House about the Industria strikes. He cited the victimization of Transkeian workers, calling it inflammatory discrimination, and urged the Minister to check up on the rumours that employers were being incited to dismiss these men.

The Minister, in his reply, reminded the House that he had repeatedly requested employers not to retrench Transkeians. "People who put about false and malicious stories are infringing the law, and damaging race relations. I am aware of the rumours which are circulating, and I can assure the honourable members that they are being fully investigated. When they are traced to source, any offenders will be dealt with very severely indeed."

This exchange got headlines on page four of the *Evening Standard*. Mark read it when he came in from canvassing.

"We've drawn blood," he said. "The interesting thing is, I'm sure the Minister means what he says. Yet Zeffrey implied his tip-off came from an official source, and Camberley said he'd been visited by the Special Branch. If they're speaking the truth, then someone local, someone in Government employ, is acting clean against the Government line. Trying to get Transkeians dismissed, when the Department expressly wants them retained." He thrust the paper aside and began to wolf his supper of curry and rice. "What we need," he said between mouthfuls, "is someone on the inside."

"Waste of time," I said. "That crack-in-the-Government stuff is nice for the Sunday press, but it's no use in an election campaign."

Mark shook his head. "Those tip-offs are important, Morry. They're a pointer. A pointer to something big. A scandal—no, that's the wrong word—a threat to this city. Underlying everything, the unrest, the violence. I want to get to the bottom of it, but the people I know can't help me. You think of some names."

After a while, I thought of one. "There's Ocky Heubner."

"Who's he?"

"On one of the Admin. Boards. I could talk to him, if you like."

"Sure. How well do you know him?"

"Well. Since I was a kid. He loves roses, and my father grew them, once. I'll call on him tomorrow afternoon."

XV

HEUBNER LIVED IN Cato Rise, a new suburb. The bungalows
were painted maize, terra cotta, pale green, but those places
always have the same atmosphere, only the colour-schemes
change. I was brought up in a suburb like that, and as I drove
past the gardens where people were washing the car or mowing
the lawn, I felt like six-year-old Morry Faber, coming back from
town with his dad. I could even smell the paper bag of bagels on
the back seat.

I could have picked out Heubner's house by the blaze of roses
showing above the fence. The old man was in the garden; big and
paunchy, with a lugubrious nose and drooping, sun-burned jowls.

I'd known him in Jo'burg, and had a good working relation-
ship with him. Our friendship came from many things; the fact
he'd known my father, the fact my mother was Afrikaans-speak-
ing, and something more, that had to do with the way he looked
at life. He'd been poor, the son of a poor-white farmer. The
National Party had pulled him out of that poverty, and nothing
would ever change the way he voted; but he was a Nationalist
of the old school, before ideology became more important than
human beings, and sometimes he would plant his hooves and put
his head down and buck the Government boss into the dust.

He saw me as I crossed the road to his gate, and raised a hand
in greeting.

" 'Naand, Morry."

" 'Naand, Ocky."

He held out the flat of his palm, on which lay a big black
and yellow beetle. "That's what I want to be in my next life,
Morry. A gogga that eats only roses." He smiled at me over his
glasses. "Will you have a beer?"

I said I would, and we sat out on his little strip of lawn, with
the last of the afternoon sun on our backs, and drank iced lager.
We talked a little about old times, and about the election, but
not much. We'd never needed commonplaces. I told him I'd
come to him about the unrest in Industria.

"Ja," he said, "it's bad. But we're dealing with it."

77

"Who's 'we'?"

"The labour authorities. We are having top-level talks, you've read in the newspapers. . . ."

"Yeah. But what I haven't read in the newspapers is the full, uncensored story of what's happening out there. Why are Transkeians being retrenched? Who is advising employers to retrench them? Come on, Ocky, you know there've been tip-offs. Where do they come from?"

"I can't tell you that."

"Can't, or won't?"

He squinted at me out of his shrewd little elephant eyes. "I tell you one thing," he said grimly, "they don't come from my Department."

"Do you think they could have come from the Security Police?"

"No. That's ridiculous." His answer was a little too vehement. "The Cabinet line is perfectly clear. The Minister has said, he's very angry about the dismissals, they are very disturbing at such a time."

"Then why has the press been asked to play down the story? Why weren't the tip-offs exposed, why did it have to wait until Mark went out to the factory area, and poked around, why was it left to my Party to raise the matter in the House?"

He shook his head. "Nobody likes to wash his dirty linen in public."

"Even when it's in the public interest it should be washed?"

"You don't understand, Morry. It's not so simple." He shifted his weight in his chair, and sighed. Over by the fence, the roses seemed on fire. "I'm retiring next year," he said.

I understood what he meant. He would like to live in peace, and enjoy the pension he'd worked for, but it wasn't going to happen that way.

"Morry," he went on, "don't think I'm blind. I can see what's happening at the factories. This week we talk, and maybe next week the police will have to use tear gas, and the week after that, someone gets shot. I can lie awake at nights, like you. But man, there's very little I can do about it. I'm on the way out. The people I could talk to in the strikes of '74, the strings I could pull . . . they're gone. My friends have died or retired, and the new people don't know me, they don't care to listen to me. I'm being frank with you now. I'm telling you there are things happening

78

that frighten me. These Vigilantes, these animals who brawl and burn and are not arrested . . . the tip-offs you spoke about . . . yes, they frighten me, but I'm not such a fool as to think I can wave my wand and they'll disappear. They are symptoms of a disease, an incurable disease. You know what that is?" He leaned towards me. "It is history, it is time that passes and brings change. It is the change that you have been shouting for, for so long, you and your liberal friends. And now it comes, what do you feel about it?"

"I feel you're bull-dusting."

"Oh, ja?" He watched me across the tankard he held.

"You're telling me there's a power struggle in the National Party, right against left . . . which everyone knows. And you're trying to tell me that the tip-offs came from someone who'd like to swing a bit of power into his own hands . . . which I don't believe. Because if this was just a straight party fight, then you would know the names of those responsible, and they'd have been fixed weeks ago. No, Oom, try again."

He shook both hands at me. "Wait now, wait now. A moment ago you asked me, did the tip-offs come from the police. Why did you ask that?"

"Because at least one factory has had visits from the Security boys over the past four months. The owner happens to employ a high percentage of Transkeians."

"What factory is that?"

"I can't mention names. Another factory-owner we spoke to hinted that his tip-off came from a very reliable source. We got the impression it could be a police source."

"I've told you, that is ridiculous. It doesn't make sense, man. Why would any security policeman commit an action that is going to have an adverse effect on labour right through the city? Why would he undermine security?"

"Perhaps because he was ordered to."

"By whom?"

"I've no idea. I thought perhaps you could find out."

The old man squeezed his face into lemon-wrinkles. He sat quietly for a while, and then said, "Look, Morry, if what you tell me is true, then it is my duty to find out about it. But you must remember that we are human beings. There is a great deal of confusion. Orders are being misconstrued, in some cases. It need not be a question of deliberate malice. Like I said, we are prisoners of history. We are swept along by the torrents of time."

I got to my feet. "Will you try and find out the source of the tip-offs, Oom?"

"Ja. I'll do that."

I said goodbye and left him. When I glanced back from the gate he was still sitting in his chair, with the empty tankard in his hands.

Saturday night is night off in an election. I had dinner at Mark's place, and afterwards Bianca and Dave Tindall went off to watch television, and Mark and I sat talking on the verandah. I told him about my meeting with Heubner.

"He doesn't know what's going on," I concluded. "He's as foxed as we are."

Mark lolled back in his chair and his voice came lazily out of the dark.

"The old boy's right," he said. "Change, confusion and violence, it's our period of history. We can modify it, but we can't make it disappear. The next phase will be an intensification of urban terror. In fact, it's already begun."

"I don't care for the fatalistic attitude," I said. "Not in a liberal, white, Christian candidate, I don't care for it."

He laughed. "So what must I do?"

"Bend the something-or-other closer to the heart's desire, like the poet says."

"Okay. I'll remember."

Sunday evening I stayed home, to work on the draft for our second election mailing.

Soon after ten, the 'phone rang. It was Jess, and she sounded flustered.

"Morry? I'm sorry to 'phone you so late."

"That's okay, I'm up and dressed."

"The information you asked for. I have something, perhaps."

"Want me to come over?"

"Could you?"

"Right away."

Crazy man, I thought, as I climbed into the car; but I tell you, the summer bees that shrilled in the tree on the corner were playing Beethoven's Ninth.

80

XVI

WALKING UP THE stairs behind her, you know I felt very strange? Nervous and excited. I put my feet down very quietly and decorously, I concentrated on not being clumsy. Faber come to visit his ex-wife, can you believe it?

When we reached the living-room I saw she'd put out a lot of food, a cold steak-and-kidney pie, biscuits and cheese and fresh lettuce, and a carafe of red wine. It was laid out on a good cloth, with silver knives and forks.

"Help yourself, Morry," she said, "make yourself comfortable."

I poured wine for the both of us, no spots on the cloth, and then I tackled the pie. I felt hungry for the first time in days. I sank my teeth into a great big slice of happiness. She sat on the other side of the table and watched me. After a while she began to talk.

"I've asked around, about Amyas Mochudi. I haven't learned much."

"Elusive," I said.

"Yes, he is." She drank some wine, slowly, as if she was testing her own thoughts. "Perhaps that's the most important thing, right now, that he is elusive. He never used to be, in the old days. When I knew Amyas, he was always very much present. He was right in the centre of his society. People talked about him, they always had a new story to tell about him. He was colourful, he made people laugh, he made them act, he was there."

"And now, no one even knows where to look for him."

"That's right. They say he's not in Transkei."

"Who says?"

"A couple of my friends. People who know Transkei. Live there. I think you can take it Mochudi is not in that territory."

"So what's the story?"

"Well . . . one is that he's ill. They say he was released early from the Island, so he could go home quietly and die."

"Do you believe that?"

"I suppose it's possible he's been ill. He had TB as a young man. Anyway, it's one theory. Another is that he's gone out of the country."

"Illegally?"

"Yes."

"Where to?"

"Russia or China. And that I don't believe."

"Why not?"

She hesitated. "He's too much his own man, to turn Communist. Or at least . . . he was. I suppose he might have changed since I knew him."

"Do you think he might have gone to one of the African countries . . . to study or train . . . maybe join up with one of the exile groups?"

"I suppose it's possible."

"But you don't believe it?"

"I don't want to." This time she paused longer. At last she said abruptly, "I don't think I'm a very reliable witness, Morry. I'm a failed liberal, remember. I see people as they were ten years ago."

"Your guess is as good as mine. Probably better."

"I'm out of politics, I pulled out by choice, and frankly I don't really want to be involved again."

I said nothing.

"That's despicable of me, isn't it?"

"No. You had a rough time. You don't have to come back for more."

She set her glass aside and looked at me. "I did find something. Whatever his friends say, the common people believe Mochudi is in the country, and not only in the country, but in this province. There's a sort of mystique growing. Know what I mean?"

I did know. Africa is a place where legends grow. So many people are illiterate, and, having no written records, they are talkers and story-tellers. It can happen that a character—he may be hero or villain—becomes the centre of a folk-lore while he's still alive. Go into the townships and you'll hear about him. Everyone knows him, though no one has actually met him. He's in the work-a-day gossip and the songs they sing on the road gangs. His jokes, his warnings, are passed round eagerly. He can become so big, he's on the police files.

"What are they saying about him?"

"That he's the new liberator. That he's taken on the cloak of Sisulu and Mandela, and will come to lead them, when it's time. There will be a time of bloodshed and burning, and Amyas Mochudi will come out of the fire to lead his children. The sangomas have thrown the bones, and say it's so."

A sangoma is a witch doctor; not a dispenser of medicines, but a diagnostician, often a woman, who interprets dreams, casts fortunes, divines whose evil influence is causing the sickness in a patient. There's a lot of psychological insight attached to being a sangoma, and a lot of empathy. There's also a measure of hocus-pocus, and a very sharp nose for news. If the sangomas backed the Mochudi rumours, then they must be taken seriously.

"You think he has a big following?"

"Very big, and growing very fast. I've seen his name spray-painted on walls and bridges. Sometimes the full name, sometimes just a big M."

"That's right," I said, "I remember, I saw one in Industria."

"I think you'll see more."

Somewhere at the back of my mind was an idea I couldn't catch hold of. It had to do with something Jess had said.

" 'Mochudi will come to lead his children,' " I said. "Are those exact words?"

"I think so. Two or three people used them, to me."

"And the word 'children' was used literally? Meaning kids, young people?"

"Perhaps." Jess frowned. "I took it to be kind of a biblical phrase. Why?"

"I'm trying to weave some threads together, that's all. I've listened to a lot of people over the past few days, informed people who don't talk out of turn. Nearly every one of them has had something to say about young people. The Summit can only succeed if young blacks attend. Trouble in the townships is sparked by school kids. The police blame young militants for the strikes at Leith Metals. It all adds up to power. Child-power, if you like. And now you say, Mochudi will come to lead the children."

Jess moved her hands uneasily over the surface of the table. "I don't think it's that. Amyas isn't a Pied Piper. He wouldn't exploit children."

"If children are the decisive factor in a struggle for liberation. . . ." I was thinking aloud, now. "If Mochudi sees them as decisive . . . then he might take steps to control them. He might appoint a lieutenant . . . a sort of youth commander. On Tuesday, you told me he had a half brother, Hobeni. We've been asking around. On Wednesday we came across a Don Hobeni, who worked at a firm called Filey, Lofts. He was sacked from the job a couple of weeks ago, and since then, he's disappeared.

"Another thing. We visited a factory-owner named Camberley. He's had a lot of trouble over the past few months. He told us that at the start it was the young people who were fermenting it, but that three weeks ago they pulled out."

"So?"

"So about the time that Don Hobeni was kicked out of his job, and vanished from his home, the young militants pulled out of the strikes. It could be because they'd lost their leader."

"Do you want me to try and follow that line?"

I looked at her. She has dark blue eyes that seem darker when she's worried.

"No," I said. "The water's getting too deep and too cold. Our business is the election, not black-power politics. Forget it."

She nodded, and I could see she was relieved. So that was my cue to leave. She'd given me supper, answered my questions, and she'd also made it quite clear she didn't want any more political hot-seats. I had no reason to stay, except that I wanted to. I wanted to think of something compelling to say so I could stay a little longer. While I sat there, dumb as a bump on a log, she suddenly said :

"It's time you started taking your own advice, Morry."

"What?"

"Forget black-power politics. Stop trying to carry the world on your shoulders."

"Me? I'm not worrying !"

"Like hell."

So then I found myself talking like a teen-age dolly in the gipsy's tent. I told her everything that had happened that week. Cameron and his flayed cat, the way our canvassers had been waylaid by thugs, the meeting, Dick Tuttle's face. All of it came spilling out. She listened without interrupting. At the end she said, in a kind of exasperated way, "Morry, can't you see what it all adds up to? Things have gone way beyond the point when you can do any good. All the work you're doing, all this canvassing and planning, it's too late. Can't you see that?"

"It's never too late."

"Oh, yeah, Faber must go down fighting."

"You sound like Heubner."

"Who's he?"

I didn't trouble to answer. After a while Jess said, "What does Mark think will happen here?"

"Says the urban terrorism will get worse."

"And if he's right? If there's violence . . . riots . . . black against white . . . what do you intend to do?"

I looked at her. "Intend is a big word. Are you asking me which side I'll be on? What do you expect me to say, that I'll side with the blacks, because they are the true victims of apartheid? They won't be the only ones. That I'll side with the whites, to preserve law and order? What law and order, the old crap, that I loathe? I don't know what I intend, Jess. Come the revolution, I'll have to play it by ear."

She was watching me with a bright, intent look, as if she was willing me to say something. She looked beautiful, and warm, and I wanted more than anything to please her.

But sitting there opposite her, I remembered what she'd said. She didn't want to be involved. She was clear about that. I did want to be involved, I was involved, in the election and the whole political war. I wouldn't pull out, even for her.

"From half a husband," I said, "comes only half an answer. Forget it, Jess."

The eagerness died out of her face. She stood up. "It's after one o'clock. You'd better go."

When I got home, I looked at myself in the hall mirror. I looked at my heavy nose and jaw, my dark skin and hair, and I thought, that's it, boy, you're stuck with your genes, now and forever. Maurice Faber, who can't decide whether to be a white man or a black man, Morry the political animal, the pig-in-the-middle.

During that last week, I often came close to 'phoning her. I wanted to. Only she'd laid down her terms, and if I 'phoned her, I'd have to meet them, or pretend to. So I never called her.

85

The real tragedy about people, all of us . . . we can love people and trust them, we can be right there with them in the same city or the same room, and we can't say the few words that make the difference between win and lose, or life and death. We can't even say that much.

The count-down week passed. On the final weekend, we settled the appointment of various election agents and officers. Each of us had to sign forms before a competent witness.

At five o'clock on the last Sunday, the kids started putting up Mark's nomination posters. When all the trucks had gone out, he and I drove round the constituency, checking how things looked.

By ten, the work was done, and the teams came back to the campaign office for curry and rice and beer. There was a great spirit among us, a winning spirit.

I watched Mark carefully, and I felt he was in exactly the right frame of mind. He was thinking about the election, narrowed down to that one objective, all his energy concentrated on it.

I went home very happy, that night.

Yet 7 March came and Mark was lost to us, at the time when he was most needed.

XVII

I CAN BE specific about the events of Nomination Day. The police questioning has fixed details of time and place in my mind.

I got up at six-thirty, bathed, shaved, dressed in my new light suit, and fixed myself coffee and toast. I looked through the *Gazette*. There was good election coverage, pictures of Mark and Colley Burman, the usual stuff.

My briefcase was already packed, and contained the forms already completed for our election officials, as well as the ones to be signed by Mark. We'd decided he would sign his nomination papers in the court. Timmins of the *Standard* had told me that Burman had opted to lodge his application in advance. Later, when I realized these facts could be significant, I tried to remember whose decision it was for Mark to sign in the courtroom. But at the time I didn't give it a thought.

I called in briefly at the campaign office, and picked up a pile of telegrams for Mark. They'd already been opened, and were from Party divisions round the country . . . the Leader and caucus, provincial chairmen, and friends. Many of the names, I knew. I rolled them all into a sheaf and put them in my briefcase. At eight forty-five I left the office and drove over to pick up Mark and Bianca.

There was time for us to drink coffee at their house. Bianca looked very good in a plain cream silky dress. She was all set to be nice to me, and asked a lot of damn fool questions, like did I have the deposit money. She asked me why we couldn't just give a cheque, instead of having so much cash—the deposit is R600— and I explained that the Returning Officer was entitled to refuse a cheque, and it was better not to run that risk.

Mark was very quiet, and very tense. I got the feeling he was puzzling over something, and wanted to be left alone.

At nine-fifteen we went out to the car. As we were standing beside it, one of the upper windows of the house swung wide, and we saw young Nick standing there, in his pyjamas. Bianca called to him to get back to bed.

"I'm not sick any more," he said. "I want to go with you."

"I told you, you can't."

His face creased up. Mark moved forward. "Listen, Nick. This evening a lot of people will be coming here, and if you're well enough, you can come down and listen to us talking. But you must stay inside today."

The child see-sawed on the window-ledge, playing for time.

"Are you going to the court now?"

"Yes, I am, and if I stay chatting I'll be late."

"Are you going to win?"

"Yes."

"Because all the sleepy people are waking up." Nick dropped into sing-song Zulu. "Abebelele sebevukile. Abebelele sebevukile." He giggled delightedly.

"Shut the window, now, son."

Nick did as he was bid, and then leaned against the glass, fingers and nose splayed flat. Mark waved to him and he waved back. We climbed into the car and drove down to the city.

"Who taught him that?" said Bianca. "The sleepers are waking? I hope he's right!"

It was a hot day, but there was a breeze on the Esplanade. I found a parking place not far from the Government offices. The Burman cars were already lined up in the parking bay.

Walking along the road, we met up with Mark's proposer and seconder, Louis de Villiers and Bess Hooper. Bess, who must have attended a dozen nominations, teased me about my new suit, saying I looked like a cabinet minister on telly. "Sure," I said. "Press my belly button and I sing 'Die Stem'." There was a good feeling among us, that we were on the winner this time.

When we reached the ground-floor lobby of Bay Buildings, we found it full of men in Cleansing Department overalls. Also, one of the lifts was being serviced. There was a printed notice beside it, "Lift Under Repair".

We went up to Mr van Eyck's office, number seventeen on the fourth floor. The door was almost opposite the bank of lifts. A young woman greeted us and told us the hearing would take place in the inner office, which led off number seventeen. Van Eyck was in there, talking across his desk to old Colley Burman. Colley lifted a hand to us in greeting.

Walter Brock had already arrived. He was standing in the outer room, talking to Timmins of the *Standard* and another reporter. There was a photographer, too, the same one who'd been at our public meeting. Mark and I went over and joined the group, while Bianca, Bess and Louis walked into the court-room to find seats.

Timmins asked me if I thought there'd be any surprise nominations. I said I'd give him a case of whisky if there were. The photographer said he'd like a pic. of the two candidates together, but he'd get it later, after their papers were lodged.

Then Timmins said, "Mark, you got anything good for us today?" And Mark said, "Very good. Front-page stuff. I'll tell you about it when all this is over."

At that point, a whole batch of spectators appeared, among them David Tindall, and they came up to Mark and stood around taking the mick out of him.

There was a clock on the wall, and I kept my eye on it.

A couple of minutes before ten, I touched Mark's elbow, and said we should go in, now. The whole bunch of us started moving towards the door. I was the last through it, and, as I reached it, I heard the sound of a lift coming up, and I looked out into the corridor and saw the indicator was working, on the lift that had been out of action. The light stopped at four, but the doors of the lift stayed shut.

Inside the courtroom, there were about 30 people. Van Eyck was still standing behind his desk, with a male and female clerk. Behind them were three long windows that gave a wonderful view of the Bay.

Mark walked over and shook hands with van Eyck, and then went to sit next to Colley Burman in the front row of chairs. Walter and I stopped at the small table just inside the door, where I put down my briefcase, and opened it so I could get out the nomination forms and the deposit money. I remember, I was just opening the case when ten o'clock began to strike on the Post Office clock, way over in the centre of town.

I've been asked a lot of questions about what happened next. I know the whole thing took less than five minutes.

Ten o'clock struck. Mr van Eyck stood at his desk, declared the court in session and spoke a few brisk words of welcome. Then he made the formal announcement that there was an election pending in Parkhaven, quoted the relevant Government proclamation. He announced that Vincent Colley Burman, having been duly proposed and seconded, and having accepted nomination in the manner and form required by law, was duly nominated as a candidate for the division of Parkhaven. And he asked if there were any further nominations.

Walter Brock said "Yes, sir," took the nomination forms from me, and moved forward with them and the deposit money. Mark stood up and approached the desk. Van Eyck moved back, towards the windows; took the money from Walter, handed it to the woman clerk and asked her to count it and issue a receipt.

That left four people close to the desk. Mark, Walter, the male clerk, and van Eyck. The clerk was the only one of them facing the door. The others, like me, had their backs to it.

I never saw the gunman clearly. I heard a movement in the doorway, and at the same moment I saw the clerk leap sideways, slamming against van Eyck, who stumbled and fell. There came a harsh stuttering that seemed to explode right inside my head. I saw Mark lift up in the air and crash down across the desk and roll off it. I saw the clerk, still on his feet, but spinning, I saw him claw at the window, and then glass and blood sprayed out into the sky. I saw Walter go down like a tree.

I started to turn, but someone grabbed at my legs, dragging me down. As I went sprawling, I caught a glimpse of the man with the gun. He had a stocking pulled over his head. He wore white overalls, with the words Cleansing Department in red letters across the chest. The gun looked like a machine-pistol.

He stepped back slowly, almost in slow motion; and then he turned and bolted for the corridor, and I heard the lift doors close.

The room was full of screaming, and a hot smell. Some of the people were on the floor, crouched among overturned chairs, and others were in boiling movement. Their faces looked blank and vague, or distorted. I began to crawl towards where Mark lay, at the foot of the desk.

Bianca had already reached him and was trying to lift him in her arms, screaming all the time. He'd been hit in the head and the neck and the spine, and he was dead. I leaned across his body and caught Bianca by the shoulders. She struck out at me.

I put my hand under her chin and forced her head up so she

had to look at me. "It's no good, Bianca. Listen to me. It's no good, he's gone." She stopped screaming and her mouth pulled wider and wider so that all her teeth showed, and her eyes shone white all round. Somebody came up behind her—Tindall I think —and lifted her away from Mark. There was blood all over her dress and her hands and when she saw that she began to scream again.

I started to turn Mark over. Then I realized that if I moved him, his head would come clean off, so I let him be, and took off my jacket and spread it over him.

While I was doing that, I heard another bang, and there was a flash of light. The *Standard* photographer was trying to take pictures. Colley Burman reached over and grabbed the camera out of his hands. The photographer tried to snatch it back, but van Eyck was there first, shouting that this was still a court of law, that he would have order, that everyone was to sit down and be quiet.

The words began to take effect. I heard groaning over in the corner. I walked round the desk and almost fell over the body of the clerk, slumped under the windows. He was dead. Beyond him, lay Wally Brock, with Bess Hooper kneeling beside him, holding a wadded handkerchief to his shoulder. Wally was half conscious. A bullet had creased his skull, and another had hit him high in the right arm. I tried to help Bess check the bleeding.

Above us, at the desk, van Eyck began making telephone calls. Ambulance, police, other officials in the building. A couple of customs officers arrived from over the road, and stood guard in the corridor—the pressmen, I noticed, had already slipped away —and a doctor and two nurses came up from the Immunisation Department. Walter was given a shot of morphia, and they carried Bianca through to the outer office, and gave her a sedative. It didn't seem to have much effect. I could see her hands lifting and falling, as if she was pulling invisible bell-ropes.

Van Eyck finished speaking to the police and pushed the 'phone aside. I got up from the floor and went to him.

"Mr van Eyck, can I please make a couple of calls?"

He stared at me in a blind sort of way. His hands were shaking violently, and his mouth was flaccid.

"I must get in touch with my Party," I said. "I must tell them, before the news gets out. There's the leadership, my campaign

91

office, Mrs Ramsay's home . . . and Mrs Brock. . . ."

"Yes. Of course." He stared down at the clerk's body. "I'll have to speak with Johan's mother. Almighty God, this is so terrible."

I 'phoned the Party's main office. At first, when I tried to tell them Mark was dead, they wouldn't believe me, thinking I was some kind of nut. But they accepted it after a while, and said they would inform the top echelons. I asked them to 'phone Lisa Page and ask her to send one of the women round to Ramsay's house, to pick up Nick and take him somewhere safe. I didn't want the press talking to him. I warned them to lock the office doors against enquirers. Finally I put a call through to Walter Brock's wife, and explained that he was hurt but I didn't think in danger, and that he'd be taken to Addington Hospital.

While I was making this last call, the ambulance men arrived. Walter and Bianca were put onto stretchers and carried away.

There was a strange sort of quiet when they'd left. The people who'd come as spectators had shrunk towards the back of the court, like cattle seeking shelter from the storm. Tindall and old Louis were sitting close to where Mark had fallen. Bess Hooper came over to me, picked up my hand and pressed it to her cheek. I could feel her tears warm on my skin.

Then we heard the sound of the lifts coming up, and the corridor and the outer office were full of police, uniformed and plain-clothes. The man in charge introduced himself as Colonel Gerardt Buddler.

I looked at my watch at that point, and saw that it was half-past ten.

92

XVIII

BUDDLER STOOD JUST inside the door of the courtroom. He was tall, spare as a thorn tree, with a yellowish tan and pale brown eyes under thick lide.

He spoke to van Eyck in Afrikaans. "We'll have to shift these people somewhere else, meneer. My men will have things to see to, in here. Can you provide another room, on this floor if possible?"

"Of course, certainly." Van Eyck was garrulous with relief. "But Colonel, must all these poor people be delayed? The women, especially?"

"If we can move everyone out, Mr van Eyck, then we can decide what comes next."

"Very good. I think I can arrange for room 23. . . ."

"Will you do so, please? Don't go out, use the 'phone." Buddler walked slowly over to where Mark lay. "Whose coat is this?"

"Mine," I said.

He leaned down and lifted it carefully and laid it on the desk. "This is Mr Ramsay?"

"Yes."

"And your name, sir?"

"Maurice Faber. I am . . . I was . . . his election agent."

"We may require you to make a formal identification, later."

I had a sudden vision of what might happen. I could be kept answering questions till nightfall. I spoke off the top of my head.

"I have to get out of here, Colonel."

His eyes, neither friendly nor unfriendly, scanned my face.

"Why, Mr Faber?"

"The chairman of my Party is in hospital. The vice-chairman was beaten up last Wednesday. God knows what's going on at central office, at this moment. There'll be enquiries coming in from all round the country, Parliament, the press."

He considered me, chewing the inside of his lip. Before he could say anything, Colley Burman stepped forward.

"Morry, you can't leave yet. I'm sorry to speak at a time like

93

this, but there's things that have to be settled. You can't just brush them aside."

I didn't grasp his meaning. He turned red, and mumbled "I was nominated, man! I've got a party to think about, same as you. I have to know, is there an election or isn't there?"

I felt a huge disbelief. The dead men on the floor, the crowd bunched at the back of the room, the police; these had nothing to do with what Colley was saying. Van Eyck, too, sank down into his chair and sat staring. It was Buddler who broke the silence.

"I think you'll have to give a ruling, meneer."

Van Eyck shook his head numbly. "I don't know . . . there's no precedent. . . ." He clasped his hands together and rested his forehead on them. At length he raised his eyes.

"I think Mr Burman is correct. In law, the court has not risen. In law, it remains in session until eleven o'clock."

Buddler made a sound between a grunt and a sigh. He turned and faced the people at the back.

"I want everyone who is not officially concerned with the business of this Nomination Court to go along to room 23. I hope we will not keep you waiting too long." He leaned his head through into the outer office and called, "Sergeant!" A uniformed policeman appeared. "See these folk are made comfortable in number 23. I want names, addresses, and they must wait there until I say they can go." He stood watching while these orders were set in motion. In a few minutes, the court was almost cleared. Three of Burman's supporters stayed behind; and on our side, Bess Hooper, Louis de Villiers, and David Tindall. Buddler faced van Eyck.

"Now, meneer."

Van Eyck had a copy of the Electoral Act open on his desk. He swung it round towards us.

"Yes. I think the situation is this: If a candidate dies after he has been duly nominated, then there is provision in law for the election arrangements to be withdrawn, and started afresh. If Mr Ramsay had been nominated before he . . . before this terrible thing happened . . . then the case would be that the Attorney-General would withdraw the proclamation of election made in this division. We would have to start the whole process again. But as it turns out, Mr Ramsey was not officially nominated. In those circumstances, I think that the electoral process already begun, and Mr Burman's nomination, must stand."

Louis de Villiers said, "But my dear sir! A murder has been committed. A crime. Surely in view of that, you can adjourn the court?"

"I don't think I can. A Nomination Court is precisely defined. It sits at a fixed time, ten o'clock to eleven o'clock, on a proclaimed date. I think—I believe—this court must remain in session until eleven. I and my staff, must remain here until then. I know the idea is bizarre and horrible, but I think that is what must be done."

A voice spoke behind me. "Can we put up another candidate?" I glanced round and saw it was Dave Tindall.

"No!" I said sharply. He came closer, peering at me through those thick lenses.

"Why can't we?"

Van Eyck intervened. "Mr Tindall, a candidate is chosen by a political party according to its own constitution. There is a proper procedure to be observed, and the approval of certain committees has to be obtained. It is not an arbitrary matter."

Tindall swung round on him. "The circumstances are hardly normal. Surely there must be other people whom we could. . . ."

"Listen to me," I said. "It is not possible to replace Mark. It is not possible. Accept that." I looked at van Eyck. "Whatever happens here . . . whatever this court or any other decides to do about Mr Burman's nomination . . . whether or not he is declared elected . . . I will not let it rest there. If the election is allowed to stand, then my Party will petition against it. If there's no provision in law for us to petition, then we'll get the law amended. No matter how long it takes or what it costs . . . you tell them that, understand?"

I looked across to where Mark was lying. "When can he be moved?"

I could hear my voice high and rough, like a power saw going out of control. The floorboards were surging under my feet. Buddler's hand gripped my forearm.

"Luister, nou, Mr Faber. We don't allow people to profit by crime. You can leave it to us." He leaned over and took my jacket from the desk, folded it neatly inside out and handed it to me.

"If I let you leave now, sir, you understand I will need to talk to you later? Where can I find you, say in two hours from now?"

"I'll be at the Party's central office."

"Very well." He beckoned one of his men over. "Mr Faber has permission to leave. Get his name and address from him, and then see him down to his car."

The man he'd detailed was a municipal traffic cop, named Mason. I was to realize later that within minutes of the shooting, people started pulling in any sort of uniformed official they could see. The whole area seemed to be crawling with them. I remarked that the police might be better employed looking for Mark's killer.

Mason shook his head. "No need, we already got him."

"What d'you mean, arrested?"

"Shot. He's dead. He came runnin' out of the buildin' with the gun still in 'is 'ands, and one of our officers got 'im."

There were big lapses in my behaviour that morning. For instance, it wasn't until I was driving to Addington Hospital that I realized I'd left Bess Hooper and Louis de Villiers without saying goodbye, or giving them any instructions.

I didn't think, I simply reacted. It wasn't until hours later, maybe days, that I was capable of putting facts together in a reasoned way, let alone planning. The bullets that killed Mark, blew my mind too.

When I reached Addington, Walter Brock had already been taken into the operating theatre. An intern in casualty told me he'd been lucky. "The scalp wound is only skin deep, and the other bullet went through the fleshy part of the upper arm. A couple of inches higher, and the shoulder blade would have been shattered. You know, when a bullet hits bone the bone fragments scatter, like a sort of internal shrapnel. Does frightful damage to the surrounding tissue. Your friend lost a lot of blood, but he seems in good physical shape, he should be all right—though of course he'll be out of action for some time."

"And Mrs Ramsay?"

"She's heavily sedated. Also, there is a policewoman sitting beside her bed." Curiosity gleamed in his eyes, but he controlled it.

"How long will she need to stay here?"

96

"Not long. She's badly shocked. We'll discharge her as soon as we can, but she shouldn't be alone."

"I'll see there's someone with her." It would mean getting Bianca's sister to Durban. She lived on a farm in Dordrecht. I'd have to arrange something.

From the hospital I drove to the central office, getting there about twenty minutes past eleven. I found it under siege. The corridor outside was jammed with people, and our African messenger, Noble, was standing guard at the main door. As I pushed through the crowd, three pressmen grabbed hold of me. I told them that no one was allowed into the office, but I'd fix for them to be 'phoned every hour, on the hour, with the latest information.

Inside, I found our three organizers dealing with a torrent of enquiries. The 'phones were ringing without cease, and the telex belting out messages from Cape Town, Pretoria, Jo'burg. At my suggestion we closed the Parkhaven campaign office, and brought Lisa Page and some of the hard-core workers into town to help us.

I found an office and a telephone and got busy. My first call was to our Party's legal advisor, a senior advocate. I asked for his opinion on our position as regarded the election. His reaction was that van Eyck was correct. Mark had been killed before he was nominated, and that appeared to make Colley Burman the new MP for Parkhaven. "I'll have to check it, of course. The situation is not straightforward. If the police investigation leads to the laying of criminal charges. . . ."

"The killer's dead," I said. "The police shot him."

"Leave things in my hands. I'll come back to you. In the mean time, I think we should say as little as possible."

Leave it to the police, leave it to the lawyers, leave it to Heaven. One dead candidate, passed to you, please.

I went out to the switchboard. The operator had listed scores of incoming calls, local and out-of-town : pressmen, diplomats, party members, friends, even a couple of nuts who said they were glad Mark was dead. Now the senior organizer had closed most of the lines, keeping them for outgoing calls. There were dozens of people who had to have notice of what had happened ; members of the campaign committee, of the regional and provincial executives.

While I was still out there, Dick Tuttle arrived. He looked ill and shaky, having left hospital only the day before, but as vice-chairman he wanted to be around, and doing something. He had a portable radio with him, and undertook to set up an information room, monitor the telex and decide what to hand out to the press.

I put calls through to a number of people. Bianca's sister was out at a church meeting, and I left a message for her to 'phone me. The Leader of the Party and the chief whip were not in the House, yet. Again, I left messages. I spoke to Stan Vermont, who's a top admin. officer of the party in Cape Town, and asked him to see the echelons round the country were informed. Stan used the word "assassination". Somehow it sounded more accurate than "murder".

At 11.50, the Leader came on the line, in great distress. He'd known Mark well. He asked me to tell him how it happened, and I did my best. I told him Bianca and Walter were in hospital, but not in danger, and reported what I'd done so far at the main and the Parkhaven offices.

"Would you like me to come to Durban?" he said. "I can fly up at once, you know."

"I don't think you should. There's nothing to show this is an isolated attack, there could be others. I don't think you should put your neck on the block."

"You think it's some sort of gang action?"

"I don't know. It could be. It could be terrorism. How many people have access to rapid-fire machine-pistols?"

"That what he used?"

"Yes." At the time I hadn't been conscious of seeing the gun, but, thinking back, I got a picture of it in my mind, quite clear. It looked like a Scorpion gun.

"Morry?"

"Yes, I'm here."

"Listen, for God's sake if you think there'll be other attacks, warn our people to take care. Don't let them meet in large groups, for instance. And Maurice? You'll stay with the campaign?"

"For Christ's sake, Simon, we don't have a campaign!"

"We can't assume that, until it's been established beyond doubt. I'll get the constitutional-law boys onto it. If there's a

98

chance of a re-proclamation and a new election, we'll have to field a new candidate."

I said nothing. I was thinking they wouldn't find anyone to fill Mark's shoes.

Simon picked up my silence. "I understand how you feel, Morry. He can't be replaced, as a friend or as a candidate, but we're in politics. We have to win Parkhaven if we can. We need it. I don't have to tell you. But what I am telling you is this, if there's an election over there, I want you running it. Now, I count on you to keep the campaign office open as long as there's the smallest chance of our getting back in the fight."

"A big 'if'."

"We must wait and see. How about the region? If Brock's in hospital, who's in charge?"

"Tuttle, as vice. There's a good executive. Dick's calling them in for an emergency meeting this evening."

"Well, get police protection. And tell Dick I'm available to fly up any time, will you? I'm going to talk to the Minister for the Interior now, and anyone else who can give us a ruling on the legal position. I'll come back to you as soon as I can."

He said goodbye and rang off. I sat for some time with the receiver in my hand. I didn't want to replace it, or move, or listen to any more voices. I was still sitting there when I heard footsteps in the corridor. There was some muttering, and then a tap on the door, and Bess Hooper came in, with David Tindall at her heels.

Bess walked over and stood in front of me. She looked exhausted and distraught.

"Something important . . ." she began. "After you left, Morry, we decided. . . ."

"Well?"

She seemed to be fishing for words, then they suddenly came out in a burst.

"Mr Tindall is standing as candidate for Parkhaven. Louis proposed him and I seconded. So there is a contest, after all."

I sat staring at her. Tindall bent towards me, his hands linked together like a nervous girl's.

"Maurice, understand, I'd have preferred to discuss it with you . . . but you left, you know, and there was no time. We only had six minutes to make up our minds, before the court closed."

Bess took out a pack of cigarettes and fumbled one loose. "It's quite legal. I asked the Returning Officer."

"Luckily," said Tindall, "I am registered as a voter, and a P-Party member, though of course I appreciate I don't stand as a Party candidate. An Independent merely, that's undersood." He reached into his pocket and drew out an envelope, which he extended to me. "I fear I had to use the cash you had provided, as my deposit. I have made out my cheque for the same amount, in favour of the Party."

He was smiling. There was actually a look of triumph in his eyes. I thought, this little prick is telling me he's the candidate, and I could feel a crazy sort of laughter coming up in my throat, like bile. God knows what I might have said to him. Only at that moment, the switchboard operator buzzed me on the inter-com. Someone had 'phoned from the electoral office, to say that Colonel Buddler was on his way over to see me.

I went out into the corridor, and yelled for Dick Tuttle. When he came, I asked him to go into my office, lock the door, and try to talk some sense into the two half-wits in there. Then I walked to the lift foyer, to wait for the police.

XIX

IN THE BEST of circumstances, I don't like policemen. The records may show that they are a brave and resolute body of men, but I happen to support left-wing policies in a right-wing State. I invite blacks to dinner and have friends who are banned. The police, for me, are those people who punch home the apartheid laws.

On that first day, Buddler was just another cop, not a man whose personality, whose thinking, could be vitally important to me. I had a slot marked for him, just as he had one marked for me.

He brought a Sergeant Prins with him, a thin little guy with a stuck-on pencil moustache. Prins looked as if he'd make a good dog-handler.

During those early interviews, Buddler was courteous and even chatty. He seemed eager to nail down the Ramsay case. I discovered, when I checked through the *Gazette* files, that he was ambitious—the sort of policeman who gets his name in the papers. He'd made some spectacular arrests, which I suppose meant he'd taken his share of risks. He was usually referred to by his nickname, Colonel "Cherry" Buddler.

His first questions were indirect, almost random. He spoke about Mark, and asked about his business, his status in our Party and his relatives. I think he saw I was punch-drunk, and was trying to let me down slowly.

He talked about the election, and my job as Mark's campaign manager, wanting to know why the Party had "imported" me from Jo'burg.

"Don't they have good men here, Mr Faber?"

"Yes, of course. But I've known Mark since army days. He was a personal friend."

"Mr Ramsay chose you himself?"

"Yes."

"Would you say you were thoroughly in his confidence? I'm speaking now of politics."

"I suppose I know . . . knew . . . more about him, politically speaking, than anyone else."

"Even his wife, sir?"

"Mrs Ramsay doesn't much care for politics. A lot of women don't."

"Tell me. Did Mr Ramsay have any premonition that someone might have a go at him?"

"You mean kill him?"

"Well, attack him in any sort of way?"

"I don't think he did."

"Did he ever mention he had enemies, anything of that nature?"

I shrugged. "He didn't have to. We all knew he had enemies, anyone in the top echelons of our Party, does. Mostly they stop short at abuse. In this campaign, they have not."

"You mean there's been violence, before today?"

"You know damn well there has been. We've made reports to the police. Our canvassers have been beaten up, two of our cars have been burned. On Wednesday, thugs broke up our public meeting and jabbed a broken bottle into the face of our vice-chairman. If one of your prowl cars hadn't come along, more people might have been hurt."

"Isn't this just part of the—what d'you say—election fever, sir? People get worked up. That's not new. Where I was born, every election meeting was a punch-up."

"Colonel, I've been in eleven campaigns, some of them in rough areas. I know all about election fever. But the violence is usually spontaneous. On Wednesday, it was premeditated and well organized. We formed a very clear opinion about who led that mob, we gave a description to the police. We even provided photographs. I haven't heard you've made any arrests."

Both policemen were looking hard at me. Buddler said, "If we can come back to that, Mr Faber? I'd like you to tell me now what happened this morning. Anything you can remember, anything you saw or heard."

I went over it with him. Collecting Mark and Bianca. Our arrival at the building. The men from the Cleansing Department, the broken lift. The scrambled conversations in the outer office, and our entry into the courtroom. The shooting itself.

Buddler went back over that ground very carefully. When he asked for a description of the gunman, I couldn't tell him much. A big man, in Cleansing Department overalls, with a stocking pulled over his face.

"And his hands? Did you see them?"

"No. He had gloves on. I saw the gun. A machine-pistol."

"Can you describe it, sir?"

I did so. "It looked like a Scorpion."

His pale, percipient eyes widened slightly. "You know guns, sir?"

"Yes. I did a course, in the army. I've handled Scorpions. This looked like one. It wasn't one of ours and it wasn't a Sterling or an Uzi." As I spoke, I became certain of myself. Then I remembered something. "You have the gun," I said. "The man was carrying it when he tried to escape. . . ."

"How did you know that?"

"That traffic-cop—Mason—told me. Was it a Scorpion?"

"Yes, it was."

"A Russian gun," I said. Scorpions had been used in two examples of urban terrorism in Jo'burg, and they've been found several times in secret arms caches.

Buddler didn't answer me. He was taking a large envelope from his pocket. He extracted a sheaf of photographs and handed them to me. "Do you recognize any of these people?"

They were head-and-shoulders shots of some dozen men. I leafed through them, handed one back.

"This is the man who led the trouble at the meeting."

"Are you sure of that?"

"Certain. The face is asymmetric, you can't mistake it."

"And this?" Buddler handed me a smaller, square print, of the sort that is developed in a couple of minutes. I studied it. It showed the same face, but this time the eyes were startled rather than gloating, and the mouth trickled blood instead of obscenities.

"He shot Mark?"

"This is the man we intercepted and shot as he was leaving the building this morning." Buddler's eyes watched me carefully. "Our ballistics experts will check if it was bullets from the gun he was carrying that killed Mr Ramsay and the clerk."

103

I could feel the blood coming up in my face. "You're saying this man killed Mark, the man who was at the meeting, the man we warned you about, four days ago?"

"Mr Faber. . . ."

"If you'd done something about it . . . if you'd arrested him then. . . ."

"On what charge could we arrest him?"

"There was violence at that meeting. Christ, you sit there and tell me. . . ."

"We did take it up, sir. We did act. Unfortunately, the photograph you sent in to us was not very clear. We attempted to interview Calgut but he was not at his home, since the meeting. He was away, until last night."

"Calgut? Is that his name?"

"Ja. Joseph Reiner Calgut."

"Is he a Vigilante?"

Buddler's mouth turned down. "Well, now, I don't have a list of their membership. Let's say he runs in bad company, sometimes, but I don't think he's a Vigilante. See, Calgut was always a loner."

"You seem to have known him well."

"I knew him, yes."

"He had a record?"

"No. He was suspected, two, three times, of being concerned in incidents like the one on Wednesday night. Another time, there was an assault on an Indian taxi-driver, and the man accused Calgut, but there was no evidence, and the victim himself had done time. We couldn't make it stick."

"So he ran around loose."

"Ja. Like a lot of others who should be in the tronk. This one, this Calgut . . . he hated blacks. He hated anyone who didn't think like he did. He belonged to one of those crank churches, that preach hell-fire, and he liked to dress up smart on Sundays, and visit his friends and tell them, 'You gonna burn'. He was a mad bugger, but he never belonged to any organization that I knew."

"How come he had a machine-pistol?"

Buddler did not answer at once. At length he said, "Seems he smuggled it in. He was a mercenary, you know. Fought for the Arabs in the Middle East, six years ago. And we think he was

104

in Mozambique, too. Then Angola. He picked up the Scorpion some time, up there. Last year he came back here, and he got the gun in."

"How do you know?"

"He told his mom. He lived with his mom, believe it or not. She's a nice old woman who doesn't allow drink in the house, and she didn't like weapons either, but she let Joseph keep it because she said he was proud of his army service. She doesn't know what army that was, she's . . . well, thick, you know? Calgut had his identification on him. We sent someone round to his home right off, and the old woman said he slept there last night. This morning about half after nine she went out to buy bread, and when she got back, he'd gone. Must have taken the gun with him. He had a leatherette tool-case he used on his job, it must have been in there."

"What was his job?"

"Cleansing Department. He did emergency shift-work."

"Convenient."

"Yes. Mrs Calgut said he'd been threatening to have a go at you people ever since the election began. He had a real hate against Mr Ramsay. Talked all round, in the pub and everywhere. Nobody took much notice, because he often said he was going to donner this one or that."

I didn't say anything. I was thinking that between the lot of us we'd muddled Mark's life away, and I couldn't put all the blame on the police, even if I wanted to.

Buddler gathered up the photographs. "So that's it, Mr Faber. This case will be closed fast, don't worry. When you know who the killer is it saves everyone a lot of trouble and a lot of pain. You can take my word."

"Because Calgut pulled the trigger," I said, "can you assume he was the only one concerned? There could have been others."

"I don't think so. He was a loner, sir, a psycho. Of course, we'll investigate that very thoroughly. The Special Branch will do some checking up, too, because of that gun. But I think you'll find your friend was just the victim of a psychopath."

Useful word, psychopath. It had been used to describe the man —or men—who terrorized Cameron, and the same cap could be fitted to this man Calgut. I was too tired to point out that describing a type of behaviour didn't nail the criminal, or put breath back in a dead man.

There was one point I wanted cleared.

"What will happen now? There'll be an inquest?"

"Ja, that's right."

"Will it delay the funeral?"

"I shouldn't think so. You can get permission to bury him, once the post mortem is through. Will you . . . er . . . be seeing to all that?"

"I don't think so. Mrs Ramsay has relations. I've sent for her sister, and her husband will probably make the arrangements."

I walked to the lift with the two men. The crowd that had been blocking the corridor had been dispersed, and a policeman was on duty at the lift foyer. Seeing him triggered a thought.

"When I called at Addington this morning," I said, "the doctor told me there was a policewoman on duty at Mrs Ramsay's bedside. Why?"

"As protection."

"Against what? If you're right, Calgut's dead, there's no further danger."

"I believe that's so. However, we won't take chances. For the next few days, Mrs Ramsay and the child will be under surveillance."

Buddler's voice was too loud, and, looking at him, I saw there was sweat on his forehead. It came to me suddenly that he was afraid. On the way back to the office, I wondered about that.

In this country, the public fear the police. They have such power. They can detain you without explanation, and without informing your family or your lawyer. They can keep you in solitary confinement for months. They can help to ban you, silence you, suppress your writings, confiscate your passport, banish you to some point hundreds of miles from your home. They can deny you access to the courts. Any sane man fears those powers.

Yet they were not great enough to keep Buddler from sweating, and I wondered why.

When I got back to the office where I'd left Tindall and Bess, they'd left. Dick Tuttle was in there alone, with a plate of sandwiches and a bottle of brandy at his elbow. He poured two doubles and handed one to me.

"How did it go?"

"The police theory is that Mark was killed by a psychopath, working on his own."

"Calgut? There was a news-flash, saying a Joseph Calgut was shot dead, while attempting to escape."

I sat down and drank some brandy. Someone had put a list of names on the desk, people who wanted me to 'phone. Dick shook his head.

"None of those is vital," he said. "I took the urgent ones myself. The Leader 'phoned again. The snap verdict down there is that the election goes ahead. So he's flying up tomorrow, to talk."

"About the candidate?"

Dick blinked at me in his tortoise way. "Take it easy, Morry. Tindall's nominated, but we don't have to deal with that today. We can take a little time."

"Sure. A day, two days." I finished the brandy, and poured a second.

"Eat something," Dick said.

I sat back in the chair and looked at him over my glass. "Let me tell you some things, Dick. The first is that Tindall is a tit. A prime tit. That being so, we have to get the Party out from under him. That will take two or three days, because there is going to be a reaction to that last-minute nomination. People are going to see him as the blue-eyed boy who stepped into the breach. Our job is to make it clear he is not a Party nominee. He is an Independent. He is not financed by the Party. He is just a nut who went and stuck his neck out, and it is no part of our job to save him from his folly. We have to convince the public of that, and we have to do it so nicely that we can't be accused of ditching one of our own members. Later we can persuade him to withdraw, before Burman massacres him at the polls. At least this needn't cost him more than the deposit money. He gave me his cheque for that, because he used our cash, did he tell you?"

"Umh." Dick put up a hand and smoothed his lip. "I don't think the cash bothers him much. He mentioned private funds."

"What are you trying to tell me? He doesn't imagine he can actually fight this campaign, does he?"

"My impression is he takes himself very seriously."

"Then he's crazy."

"Maybe. He must have something, though. He persuaded Bess

and Louis to put him up."

"At a time when they were half out of their minds. . . ."

"Yes, but he's quite shrewd. Seems he told Bess that Colley Burman shouldn't be allowed to profit through Mark's murder. You know how Bess loathes Burman."

"Jesus, Dick, you're not suggesting Colley had any hand in that shooting? He's a racist moron, but he's no murderer!"

"The fact remains, if Tindall had not put his name forward, Colley would have been returned unopposed, and his Party would be one seat richer right now. Unlikely as it sounds, you should consider the possibility that Mark was killed for political gain, though not necessarily by anyone in Colley's party."

I closed my eyes. That day was like walking down a hall of mirrors. Endless vistas, endless images, creating confusion and despair.

"Dick, listen. You're not kidding yourself that Tindall could beat Burman, are you? With Mark as our candidate we had a chance. With this frog, none."

"We may have to accept the frog, if the Party echelons want him."

"They won't. After Mark? There's no comparison."

"Of course there isn't. Mark was in a class by himself; but you have to admit, if Tindall stands, he'll get a certain sympathy vote."

"Five hundred, at most."

I was troubled by something else Dick had said, his reference to Tindall's having private funds. Did Tindall have any idea what an election cost? He could be putting in his chip for thousands, rather than hundreds. Someone was going to have to explain that to him.

At five o'clock, I telephoned the Ramsay house. Bianca's sister, Elizabeth Jonker, answered. She and her husband had flown up from East London, and would stay a few days. They had Nick with them, and expected Bianca home next day. There was a police guard on the house. I asked how Nick was.

"He's all right. He's been told, but he doesn't understand. He's too little."

"He's not scared?"

"No. I'm going to sleep in his room tonight, though."

"I'd like to come and see him, some time."

"I think he'd like that, Mr Faber. I'll tell Bianca." It was a brush-off, but a kind one. I was glad Nick would have her around. Dick had called the regional executive for 5.30, and asked me to sit in on it, though I wasn't a member. It was a short meeting. There were personal things to be said and done for Mark's family, and an election campaign to be closed down . . . or so I thought. But I was disturbed to find Dick had been right. There were a couple of people on the executive who felt we must consider Tindall seriously, and get a decision on him from the candidates' committee.

Dick shelved that one adroitly, pointing out that Parkhaven constituency had to be consulted first, and that the Leader would be with us next day.

It was half-past seven when I left the central office. The newspaper boards carried the words: "Ramsay Shooting Latest". I bought a newspaper and threw it onto the back seat of the car.

Up in the Parkhaven area, I passed a team of Henry Beaumont's kids, taking down Mark's nomination posters. I stopped and spoke to them.

"Henry said to get them all down tonight, so that Mrs Ramsay won't have to see them."

"Tell Henry thanks, from me, will you?"

The boy's face screwed up. "Everyone's said they're sorry, tonight. I mean, the people on the street, nobody's against him now."

I went home and bathed. Then I spent a couple of hours on the telephone, speaking to people I thought were entitled to know what was happening.

I also drank a lot of brandy, and called Jess several times. Her 'phone didn't answer, so I guessed she must be out of town.

Somewhere around three o'clock, I added a sleeping tablet to the skinful of brandy I already had, and fell into a half doze on my living-room couch.

XX

NEXT MORNING AT seven, the 'phone went. I got to it fast, hoping it might be Jess, but it was Elizabeth Jonker.

"Mr Faber. . . ."

"Maurice."

"Yes, thank you . . . Maurice. I wanted to let you know. . . ." She stopped, as if she was having difficulty finding the right words. "We went to see Bianca last night, at the hospital. She's . . . all right physically, but she's half out of her mind. You can imagine."

"Yes."

"She seems to feel . . . she blames politics . . . for losing Mark. I know it isn't fair, or just, but that's how it is."

"You mean, she'd rather not see any of us for a while?"

She gave a sigh. "I think it would be better if the Party people keep away, just now. I am so sorry, Mr Faber . . . Maurice. I know you must be feeling, the way we all feel." Her voice started to slide into tears.

"It's okay," I said. "They'll understand. I'll pass the message along, no visitors."

"Later, perhaps."

"Sure. Thanks for letting me know."

I meant it when I said we understood. Bianca had never wanted Mark to stand, or even shared his political views. I could see how she didn't want any of us near her, to remind her.

Those days, I thought about Mark a lot, the way you do when a good friend dies. Adding up the good memories and the bad. Thinking about things I could have done to prevent what happened. In the end I realized that that sort of self-blame didn't do much good.

What I couldn't forgive myself was that I'd never pulled finger and made my peace with Bianca. We didn't get on, we never would, but it must have been hard on Mark, hearing us wrangle. So I wanted to talk to her and tell her I was sorry. Even after her sister warned me off, I still hoped to have this chance.

Let's be honest and say I needed to talk to someone close to Mark. When I spoke to the Party people, they knew part of what was going on in my mind, because they'd liked him and worked with him, but I needed more than that.

I tried 'phoning Jess, but there was never any answer.

Dick and I spent the morning at central office. One thing about a political party is that it's geared to meet the unexpected. We could call on people to help dismantle Mark's campaign. At the Parkhaven office, there were a lot of humdrum tasks, like cancelling the print orders, and taking thousands of manifestos out of their envelopes.

At central office, the enquiries were now pouring in from all round the world. The foreign press and television people wanted not only stories, and photos, but information on all sorts of issues like the constitutional position.

We bought the full range of newspapers, most of which carried the assassination as the main story. There were dozens of eye-witness accounts, pictures, tributes to Mark from all the political parties. One or two of the editorials made reference to urban terrorism, but most took Buddler's line, that the shooting was the work of a crazy man, acting alone.

For some reason, that line was beginning to annoy me, and I was interested to see that the Afrikaans press didn't like it. The words "sameswering" and "komplot" occurred. Conspiracy.

At noon, I went down to Addington to see Walter Brock. He was in a lot of pain, but anxious to talk. He said Colonel Buddler had been in earlier that morning and taken a statement from him.

"Not that I could tell him much. I had only a sidelong look at the guy. But as they got him, I suppose identification doesn't matter so much. Buddler seems to look on it as act of a madman."

"And everyone accepts that. . . ."

"Don't you?"

"I don't know."

"You have another theory?"

"No theory. Nothing positive." I couldn't even be sure what I felt, except this uneasy resentment. "It's too facile," I said. "I'd be happier if the police expressed doubts, if they were . . . asking questions. There are a lot of those, you know."

"Such as?"

111

"Well . . . the timing of the attack. Anyone who wanted to kill Mark could have gunned him down when he was alone in his car, or in his garden, or out canvassing in a dark street. Why shoot him in a multi-storey building, from which escape would be damn-near impossible? A Government building, where you'd expect to encounter cops or security men? Why do your killing in a crowded room so that you'd be bound to be seen by somebody?"

"If Calgut was a psychopath, as the police say. . . ." Walter eased himself into a more comfortable position, "he may have had a lunatic's reason to shoot Mark when he did. The dramatic effect. Even the need to be caught."

"There was careful planning. Calgut was dressed in Cleansing Department overalls, and there was a team working in the lobby. The lift opposite the courtroom was labelled out of order, that must have been done so he could use it to get away. I heard it go down."

"A man can be psychopathic and still be capable of organized action."

"I don't believe he pulled this alone."

"Have you got any reason to disbelieve it?"

"I feel it. I feel there was a purpose in killing Mark. Someone stood to gain. People did gain."

"Who do you mean? Poor old Colley Burman? Morry, for God's sake. . . ."

"All right, it's improbable, but it is a question, and it's a question that the police should be asking, that we should be asking. Listen, if you ask yourself who gains by Mark's death, then you come up with a lot of answers. Burman very nearly got elected unopposed, so his party gained. The racists gained. You could argue that everyone that wants violent change, gained. And David Tindall gained."

Walter shook his head in derision. "Tindall is a light-weight, you know that."

"I know it. Thousands of voters don't, yet. The cold fact is that Tindall is now in a good position to capture Party support and make himself the official candidate for Parkhaven. He's serious, Wally, he wants to fight the seat."

"Wait a moment. Are you trying to say that Tindall arranged for Mark to be assassinated, so he could. . . ?"

"I'm saying it is a question that should be asked, and answered."

"The man's a close friend of the Ramsays."

"Is he? Does anyone here really know much about him? Oh, the curriculum vitae . . . but his politics, that's what counts here. What does Tindall stand for?"

"He's a member of the Party."

"A name on a card, and a yearly sub. Wally, you think about the timing of this murder. Mark was killed in the courtroom. He had not been nominated, Burman had. The gunman shot Mark as soon as the court was in session, but before we'd managed to enter the contest. That precise set of factors determined that the election had to go ahead, but that we couldn't find a substitute candidate. And, literally over Mark's dead body, Tindall gets himself nominated."

Wally frowned. "What happened there?"

"I left the court. I told Tindall we couldn't put up any successor to Mark. As soon as my back was turned, he asked Bess and Louis to nominate him. There was six minutes to go before the court closed, and they did as he asked."

"But they nominated him as an Independent, didn't they?"

"Are you ready to bet he doesn't mean to end up as the Party candidate?"

"Frankly, I think you have to stop that sort of talk. Don't even think that way. Tindall is a friend of Mark and Bianca, he's a Party man. If what you've been saying gets about, there'll be hell to pay. You have no reason to accuse him of wanting Mark dead."

"I don't. I'm saying that these are questions that should be asked. Mark's dead, but there's no reason to shovel him into a hole and forget him."

"Nobody intends to do that." Walter tried to sit up, wincing. "I will say this much. Until there's an official verdict on Mark's death, the Party must be careful. Tindall mustn't be allowed to claim he has our backing, and certainly we must offer no support, in cash or in kind."

"Can I pass that advice on to Dick?"

"Yes. And take it easy, Morry."

At that point a nurse came in and said I had no right to excite Mr Brock, and would I please leave.

I walked along the sea front to where I'd parked my car. The surf was warm and sluggish, and a heat haze blurred the sidewalk. I leaned on the wooden rail for some time, looking down at the beach.

I thought about the questions that should be asked. Not only Tindall. There was Calgut, too. Why hadn't they nailed him, after the meeting? And how did it happen that a policeman, an armed policeman, was waiting to shoot him as he left the building?

At that time, I didn't feel rage, or fear, those came later. I had no plan.

I saw the dark, round snakehole in the ground, and like a child, or a madman, I felt the need to thrust in a stick, and stir.

XXI

AFTER LUNCH, DICK and I drove out to the airport to collect the Leader. We took him to his hotel on the Marine Parade, and spent the afternoon there with him, going over what had happened, and talking through the most urgent problems.

Simon agreed the priority was Tindall. "We have to check his background. How long has he been a member?"

"Ten years. But he's been out of the country most of that time. He only got back here a few months ago."

"Then we must check his record abroad. He must be cleared of any Marxist sympathies, because old Burman will be watching that like a hawk. We'll probably find that Tindall is a perfectly ordinary little man who happened to blunder into an extraordinary situation. We'll have to be discreet. I can make some enquiries with our British and American contacts. Leave that part to me. Has anyone spoken to him since yesterday?"

"He 'phoned me this morning," Dick said. "Told me he wouldn't come into town at all, today. He wants to play down his candidacy, until after the funeral."

"When is that?"

"Tomorrow," I said. "No friends, by request. Bianca doesn't want to be reminded of politics."

Simon said drily, "Seems she makes an exception of Tindall. Well, no matter. I'll try and see her privately, before I leave." He turned back to Dick. "What else did Tindall say?"

"He emphasized that he appreciates our position. He doesn't expect to carry our colours, or use our funds. He said he hoped some of our workers will support him, and he asked if he could take over our campaign office in Parkhaven. I told him I'd put it to the Party authorities. Letting him have it would save us some cash. We've eight weeks still to go on the lease."

"Did he ask for access to our card systems?"

"The mannikin doesn't know enough to know he needs them."

"But we must treat him as a serious contender?"

"Yes."

115

"When does the Parkhaven committee meet?"

"Tonight, seven-thirty."

It was at that meeting that the trouble we'd foreseen began to develop. Parkhaven had a strong committee, with a passionate desire to win the seat. Nearly half of them saw David Tindall as a saviour, and wanted him adopted as our official candidate.

Bess Hooper was one of these. She pointed out that Tindall was a dead duck unless he had access to our Party card-systems, and records.

"It's no good thinking we can sit back and let him go it alone," she said. "He won't get off the ground. He is a member, and he'll be seen by the public as our man, whether we back him officially, or not. If we withold our records, our cash, and our workers, then he's going to lose his deposit. That defeat will be seen as our defeat, you mark my words. What's more, it will look pretty dirty of us, not to support him, when he's stepped into the breach."

It took all Simon's talents to convince them we must wait, at least until there'd been some check of Tindall's history. "After all," he said, "it's not merely a question of whether he wins or loses. The real question is whether he should stand at all. It may be best to persuade him to withdraw."

I didn't enter the argument. I wasn't a member of the region, so I had no right to get involved, and anyway I didn't wish to. I looked round the circle of faces, absorbed in their argument, already excited at the prospect of a new candidate, and I felt light-years away from them. If they wanted to set up a sitting target for Burman to shoot at, let them.

I left before the end, and went back to my flat.

When I got there, I found a late-delivery telegram in my letter-box. The caretaker must have signed for it. It read: "Deeply distressed news Mark's death. Returning Durban immediately please Maurice be careful love Jess."

There was a big pile of letters, too, a lot of them from blacks. Peck Mkise had written, "We have lost our friend, who fought for us. We are crying in our hearts for him."

I watched the late news on television, which included a lot about the Ramsay case. We had pictures of Calgut, of the house where he'd lived, and of his mother, telling about how he'd always been a difficult boy, often in trouble. We had a picture

116

of the Minister, explaining that, despite the dreadful circumstances, the election must proceed. There was a photo of Tindall and Burman, standing together outside the electoral office. And there was one of Lieutenant Kray, the man who shot Calgut.

I recognized Kray as the man from the patrol car that was called to our meeting on Wednesday night.

XXII

THE NEXT DAY, the day of the funeral, I wakened to the sound of rain, the steady downpour that Durban gets in summer.

The Party offices were closed as a mark of respect, so I didn't need to hurry to get up. I 'phoned the Ramsay's house and spoke to Nick. He asked when I was coming to see him, and I said soon. I 'phoned Jess's number, too, but she was still away. There was no point in going out to the airport to meet her, since I didn't know what plane she'd be on.

I was eating breakfast in the kitchen when Colonel Buddler and Sergeant Prins arrived, could they have a little of my time? I asked them in and gave them coffee. Buddler was spruce and affable. He was glad to tell me, he said, that enquiries were moving ahead very nicely.

"For instance, we've established that Joseph Calgut was under psychiatric care as a teenager. The doctor told us he had a paranoid personality. It's a pity he wasn't certifiable then."

"How was his bank balance?"

That got me a blink of the thick eyelids; but he didn't try to stall. "He didn't have one. Post office savings."

"Any large deposits, recently?"

"No."

"You've checked it?"

"We have made very careful enquiries, sir, and we can find nothing to suggest that Calgut gained materially from the killing."

"Maybe he was paid in cash, and stashed it somewhere."

"We'll watch for that, naturally."

"But you won't find anything, because of course Calgut is dead. Like Lee Harvey Oswald."

Buddler said nothing.

"Dead as a doornail," I said. "Plugged by a cop, a Lieutenant Kray. One of your men, Colonel?"

"Blitspatrollie."

118

"It was Kray who broke up Calgut's mob at our meeting, last Wednesday."

"What's your meaning, Mr Faber?" There was no bonhomie in Buddler's voice now.

"It's a coincidence."

"They happen."

"Indeed. When's the inquest?"

"Next week, I'd say."

"And the verdict will be wilful murder, by Joseph Calgut. The thing is finished and klaar, in the police book. So why are you here, Colonel?"

He had been sitting back in his chair, palms flat on the table. Now he leaned forward.

"Mr Faber, you've rubbed it in you don't like our theory of this killing. You believe Calgut didn't act on his own. . . ."

"I think it's a possibility."

"Of course it is. And we are investigating that possibility."

"I'm glad to hear it!"

"Then, sir, why don't you try to help us, instead of trying to teach us our job?"

"I don't understand."

"You remember when I spoke to you on Monday, I asked you, did Mr Ramsay have any enemies? You mentioned the Vigilantes. We are following up that suggestion, but you can put out of your mind that they have any real organization. They're a bunch of crackpots, nothing more, they couldn't feed hay to horses. Now I want to ask you something on another tack, so to say. Last Wednesday, you and Mr Ramsay and Mr Tindall went out to Industria, isn't that so?"

"Yes."

"You visited certain factories, and questioned some of the owners and people out there. Later, Mr Ramsay asked for two questions to be raised in the House: the one was, Why are Transkeian workers being victimized?; and the other was, Who tipped off these employers to retrench Transkeians? And Mr Ramsay made the implication that it was someone in authority—someone, that is, in the Government or in the police force—who made those tip-offs. Do I have that correctly?"

He had turned his head a little sideways, and the pose was somehow tigerish. I tried to think quickly.

119

"The facts are right. But the implication you speak of—that didn't come from us, it came from one of the factory owners. It seemed serious enough for us to ask the minister to look into it."

"Who made the implication?"

"A man named Zeffrey, at Leith Metal Works. It's a firm that's had a lot of labour disputes."

"Yes, I know Mr Zeffrey. Now, I'd like to hear everything you can tell me about that morning in Industria. Who Mr Ramsay saw, what was said."

I guessed he wanted confirmation of what he already knew, rather than fresh information. I reported as much as I could recall of the interviews with Camberley, Zeffrey and Condor. At the end, Buddler nodded.

"Anything else, Mr Faber?"

"Not that I remember."

"At Filey, Lofts, you also spoke to a Mrs Tonkin, didn't you, in the Records Department?"

"Yes, we did. I'm sorry, that slipped my mind."

"What did Mr Ramsay want to know, meneer?"

If I lied, he'd check with Mrs Tonkin, and there was Tindall, who'd probably already been questioned. I said, "Mark wanted to get in touch with a young man named Don Hobeni".

"Why was that?"

"I think because Hobeni has the reputation of being an activist in labour matters. Mark wanted to talk to him."

"Who gave him Hobeni's name?"

"I did."

"And who told you, sir?"

"I can't remember. It's fairly common knowledge, I'd say."

"And did you talk to Hobeni?"

"No. We couldn't. He's left that job and no one knows where he is."

"You haven't traced him, since?"

"No."

Buddler spread thick fingers on the table, considering. "Mr Faber, since Monday, I've spoken to a lot of people about Mr Ramsay. I get the impression he was a stubborn man. If he wanted something, he went after it?"

"Yes."

"He wanted to get in touch with Don Hobeni, do you think

120

he might have gone on trying, without your knowing about it?"

"It's possible. Not likely, though. He wouldn't have had the time. He had a job, you know, as well as being the candidate, and we were working on the run-up to Nomination Day."

"Did you know that Don Hobeni is a half brother to a man named Amyas Mochudi? Who served a sentence on Robben Island?"

"Yes, I had heard that."

"From whom?"

"Read it in the paper." I reached for the coffee pot and refilled the cups. "Mochudi's something of a household name, among blacks. There's a cult for him in the townships, I'm told."

"Was Mr Ramsay trying to get in touch with Mochudi?"

"Not that I knew. Look, Colonel, we had our hands full. We were fighting an election."

"Was Mr Ramsay concerned in black politics?"

"No." I spoke sharply. "That was something Mark believed very strongly, that whites shouldn't try to think for blacks."

"But your Party does that all the time."

"No we do not. We believe that blacks will have to claim their share of power by their own initiative. We can't do it for them."

"And how will they make this claim?"

"Same way as you or me. Peaceably if possible. Forcibly, if not."

All this time, Sergeant Prins had been silent, but now he suddenly spoke up.

"You think a lot of blacks, don't you, sir? It's like you felt you belonged more with them, than with us."

I looked at him. He was smiling, and there was a load of malice in his thin little mug.

I touched my curly hair, held up my dark-skinned hands. "Well, maybe I do, Sergeant. Maybe I'm just another cheeky kaffir who doesn't know his place." I turned back to Buddler. "I'd like to know one thing. You've been asking me questions about politics. Does that mean you think there could have been a political motive for Mark's murder?"

"It's an angle we have to consider, in the circumstances."

"If it's the right one, does that mean you'll turn the case over to the Special Branch?"

Something flickered in Buddler's eye, annoyance, disquiet.

121

"Politics doesn't necessarily mean subversion, does it, Mr Faber? If there turns out to be subversive elements in this, then it comes in the territory of the security boys. Until then, it's my case."

After the two of them had left, I sat down and thought over what had been said. Someone had obviously told them about our wanting to get hold of Hobeni and Mochudi. It could be someone out at Industria. I tried to remember whether Mochudi's name had come up, there. I thought not. Someone close to Mark might have spilled it . . . Bianca, or Tindall for instance. Then again, the police could have picked it up from the township informers, or sources I never even heard of.

One thing I'd learned that morning, was to watch out for Colonel Buddler. He was sharp and thorough. He'd learned a hell of a lot about us in the past two days. He'd been shrewd enough to see how obstinacy was the flaw in Mark's make-up, and we could count on his looking for the flaws in each of us, so he could put the pressure on, crack us open and pick out the meat.

I don't know exactly when I decided to go to the funeral. Probably I'd been building up to it ever since Elizabeth Jonkers warned me not to.

Lisa Page 'phoned me about noon, wanting to talk, very upset. "I just can't stop crying," she said. "Now there's no work to do, everything just hit me. I sent flowers for Mark from all of us. The notice in the paper said donations to the Cancer Fund, to hell with the Cancer Fund, he didn't die of that. I think that woman is a bitch to say she doesn't want us."

"I'm going," I said.

"Honestly?"

"It's a free cemetery."

"Great. I'd come with you, only I can't pull myself together."

"I'll say one for you, Lisa."

At three o'clock I drove up to the graveyard, that's right on the crest of the Berea, with views of the sea on the east, and the inland hills to the west. There are trees up there, too, cypress and cedar that glittered with wet, but the rain had stopped.

They told me at the gatehouse where Mark was to be put, and I walked up there, up a hillock with a clump of trees on top, and down the far slope. It faced the blue-black sea, with the black

122

rain clouds lifting back, and one far-off burst of sun.

The funeral party was already at the graveside. There was Bianca, her sister and brother-in-law, and five or six people I didn't recognize. The parson was standing with his book open. He smiled at me, the rest didn't notice me. Bianca's eyes had a blank look and her skin had gone kind of loose round the jaw and eyes.

The parson started to talk. I listened carefully to the words of the service. Most funerals I've been to have been Jewish, or those phoney cremation deals at a mortician's parlour. I thought this was a good service with good words. I wondered if he could hear them. I don't believe in any after-life, but he always did.

I wasn't there to prove any point, I was there for myself. There are some things like laughing and making love you do because you want to or need to. I needed to be at Mark's burial service.

An idea came to me, listening there, that now, no matter how clumsy I was, I couldn't do or say anything that would hurt him. Mark always understood that I didn't mean to trample anyone, it's a defect in me I can't help, and he always gave me space to retrieve my blunders. Thinking about that, I got a jab of pain that went up from my heart to my throat, so the tears jumped into my eyes. It was like Peck Mkise said, we have lost a friend who fought for us, and we are crying in our hearts for him.

They came too. The blacks, I mean. I left the service a little before the others, and as I turned I saw that the crest of the hill was lined with black people, standing quietly among the trees. I walked up to them.

They were all very carefully dressed, some of them in the regalia of their Zionist churches, green or blue, with big white crosses on the chest. The sangomas were there, too, hair plaited in a thousand little snakes' tails, necks hung with charms.

One old woman caught hold of my arm and peered at me with blue-hazed eyes.

"Are you his friend?"

"Yes, mother."

"And the other one, did he come?"

"Which one?"

"Mochudi. They said, Mochudi will come."

"No, he's not here."

123

She shook her head dumbly, and stepped back.

I walked over the crest of the ridge and started along the path that wound down to the main gate. As I went, I passed other black and brown people, scores of them, either standing quietly at the pathside, or moving up towards the burial site.

There must have been over a thousand people in the cemetery that afternoon. They flowed together, they moved onwards, they began to sing and their voices rolled softly to me, like rain.

If I had been clear in my mind, I'd have understood that they were weaving Mark into the new cult. He had been the voice in the wilderness. Now he was dead, and they waited for Mochudi to come.

XXIII

IT WAS HALF-PAST four when I left the cemetery, and drove back to my flat. I was bone-tired and yet I couldn't settle. My brain was churning with ideas that I knew weren't rational, and at the same time I knew I shouldn't dismiss them. After a while I went out and walked in the streets. The rain had cooled the air. I walked fast, up the hill, along the ridge, anywhere.

About eight o'clock it started to drizzle again. I went into a corner café and sat at a table and ate a couple of meat pies. There was a pile of evening papers on the counter, but I didn't even bother to buy one.

At eight-thirty I went back to the flat and gathered up a parcel of things Mark had left at the campaign office. I took them over to the Ramsay's house.

I didn't think what I was going to say when I got there, I simply marched up to the front door and rang the bell. Elizabeth Jonkers answered it. When she saw me, she stood with the door half open against her, and bit her lip. I held out my parcel.

"I brought these, they're Mark's. And I want to talk to Bianca."

It was hardly diplomatic language, but Elizabeth seemed not to mind. She shook her head gently.

"I'm afraid she won't see you, Mr Faber."

"Will you ask her?"

"I told you . . . she resents you."

"Listen. David Tindall is standing in Mark's place. She doesn't seem to resent him. He's still here, isn't he?"

"As a guest in the house."

"Will you please just tell Bianca I'm here?"

She continued to gaze at me in a half-sad, half-frightened way. She was a plain version of her sister, flat in the breast and buttock, with a wispy face; but her eyes were kind. After some more lip-biting, she sighed and said, "All right, I'll tell her, but I don't think she'll come down".

She led me into the living-room. I sat at the table where we'd been sitting ten days ago, talking about the labour situation. I

125

put the parcel down on the table. The house was very quiet, a lot of flowers standing about with the little florists' cards still attached to them. Upstairs I could hear someone walking back and forth with quiet, measured steps. Probably they were packing away Mark's clothes.

After a while Bianca came into the room.

She was still wearing the black dress she'd had on that afternoon. Her hair was kind of flat against her head, as if she'd pulled off her hat and never combed her hair. Her face instead of being vague and flaccid, was pulled tight, lips, eyes, skin pulled into sharp lines. She came and faced me across the table.

"I consider this to be in the worst possible taste."

"I know. Your sister told me."

"Can't you get it into your head, I don't want to see you? I don't want you or any of the rest of them near me, ever again. Is that plain enough?"

"I'm sorry, Bianca. I know how you feel. You don't like me, that's okay, I won't trouble you much longer, but there are some things we have to talk about."

Her mouth twisted, but she didn't say anything. I leaned down and pushed the parcel towards her.

"I brought back what I could find at the office. There's a sweater, some photos, everything except the notes for his speeches. I want to go through those. They may throw some light on why he was killed."

"He was killed by a madman. The police have said so."

"It's a theory, Bianca, not a fact."

"I'm afraid I'm not interested in your opinions. Thank you for returning the things, and if you don't mind, I now have a wish to be left in peace."

"Bianca . . . please spare me a moment."

She had already started to go out of the room, but she turned back with that patient expression that's intended to be a rebuke.

"Well?"

"Couldn't you go away from here?"

"Why should I?"

"It might be safer, for you and Nick."

"We're perfectly safe There's no further danger."

"There could be."

"Nonsense!"

"Please listen to me. You could know something, without realizing it, that could endanger you."

Her neck arched in irritation. "Oh, this is too silly! I've told you. Mark was killed by a maniac. The man is dead. I'm not in the least afraid of being harmed, and Nick is quite safe in my care. Now, will you please leave?"

I moved to block the doorway. "Did Mark ever speak to you about a man named Don Hobeni?"

"No, he did not."

"Or Amyas Mochudi?"

"No."

"Think carefully. Did he have any visitors, in the past few days, apart from people you know?"

"The police have already questioned me, and I have answered them. I don't propose to let you repeat the process. Now, please——"

She tried to push me aside. I stiffened my arm against the door jamb, and she suddenly lashed out, catching me a blow on the mouth.

Everything I'd felt since Mark was shot, everything I'd been unable to express, seemed to pack together in my brain and then explode. I smacked aside her flailing arms and I shouted at her: "Don't you need to know why he died?"

"I know why! My husband's dead because he agreed to stand in the election, he's dead because of politics, he's dead because of you!"

"That's a bloody lie!"

"You got him into it. You persuaded him. I heard you, night after night, all that big talk about your country needs you, the blacks need you. What about me, what about Nick, don't we need him?"

"Mark stood because he believed he had to."

"No, he did not. He did not believe it. He was in doubt. He didn't want to stand, I begged him not to and he was listening to me until you came down here, and got round him!"

"Bianca, every candidate has doubts, it's part of the job. But you're wrong about Mark."

"I am not wrong. I'm his wife, I shared his life, I knew him. I got the home truths that you and the rest of them never got. He'd gone way past you and your precious Party. Do you know

127

what he told me, he told me that even if he won the election, it would be a waste of time, because it was too late for white politics to matter. So it was all a waste. He's dead, for nothing." She thrust her face forward. Her eyes looked half-demented. "Your Party, all the other parties, you know what they are, they're a place for sick people. I've watched you all, strutting about, puffed up like turkeys with your stupid little plans. Why, when I look at that office you're so proud of, all those silly women scrabbling through boxes of cards, and writing envelopes, all those people knocking on doors and saying 'Vote for us', do you think you can change anything, do you think anyone cares? You're just a sick joke. You're not ordinary human beings, you don't want a decent home life like other people, you get your kicks from fighting. That's all it is . . . all these meetings . . . speeches . . . this election. It's a chance to fight. It's fighting, and lying, and breaking up lives . . . my life . . . my life. . . ."

She was shouting between clenched teeth. I tried to put a hand on her shoulder and she wrenched away from me.

"Look at you. You bloody failure. You couldn't keep a wife. You couldn't keep a home. You bloody coloured man. Do you think I can't see what you are? And you know something else?" She swayed in the doorway, finger pointing. "You know what Mark said to me, once. He said, 'I'm in this because of people like Morry Faber'. Mark's dead because of people like you. And you come here to give me . . . sweater . . . nothing. Nothing, nothing, nothing."

She leaned against the wall and slid down towards the floor. Footsteps came pelting down the stairs, and Elizabeth Jonkers ran past me.

"God." She kneeled beside Bianca, glanced up at me. "Please go, go!"

I got out of the house somehow, and into my car. As I went down the drive, I saw Nick running across the lawn. His spindly arms beat on the dark like moths and he called to me, but I accelerated away.

I drove straight to Jess's place. The lights were on upstairs. I got out of the car and started to hammer on the front door, and yell. I was shaking like a wet dog and my teeth were chattering. When Jess opened the door to me, I just stood there shivering, until she put both arms round me and pulled me inside.

JESS FABER

South African citizen
Aged :   36 years
Occupation : Sculptress
Race :   White

XXIV

WHEN I SAW Morry standing on my doorstep, I thought he'd been physically hurt. There was blood on his shirt, his face was running with sweat, and his eyes looked out of focus.

He pushed past me and went blundering up the stairs; at the top he wheeled round to face me.

"Can I stay here tonight?"

"What is it? Are you hurt?"

"I'm all right. Can I stay?"

"You can have the spare room."

He walked in there and dropped down on the bed and put his arm across his eyes. When I asked if he needed a doctor, he swore at me and said all he wanted was to be left alone. It was plain he wouldn't—or couldn't—talk to me.

Morry never did have any safety valves. Where other people, far less vulnerable than he is, can find some ease in talking, or drinking, all Morry can do is endure. Sometimes this dumb-ox suffering builds up to a kind of frenzy. He went berserk, once, and broke up a lot of my things. That was on the night he left me.

If I'd had any sense, I'd have come back to Durban as soon as I heard about Mark's death. The shock of seeing him butchered must have been terrible for anyone in that room, but for Morry it was a special sort of loss.

Morry often said that without Mark he'd have become a porter on Boksburg station. The two of them met up during army service, and when they were discharged, Mark persuaded Morry to apply for a bursary from Cape Town University—which he got—and drew him into a circle of energetic and creative people.

It was the first time anyone had shown confidence in Morry, and as a result, Morry would never allow any criticism of Mark. I'll admit Mark had brilliant gifts, a shrewd political insight, the power to attract people, a superbly articulate tongue; but he was also stubborn, erratic, and vain, and it was his faults, as well as his great virtues, that brought about his death.

130

Well, we were all in the same boat, that week—people of no great significance, who had to make significant decisions, and live or die by them.

Taking Morry in was one such decision, though I saw it as something that concerned only the two of us.

I wanted Morry back. That was the most important fact in my small world, and I judged everything, even Mark's murder, by whether or not it would bring Morry back to me.

I will admit that I am a woman who needs a man in her life, not only for sex though that is important, but because I don't feel alive unless there is a man to share the whole pattern of living.

I was married to my first husband, Ben Fraser, when I was seventeen, and I was very happy with him for ten years. I was never attracted to any other man while Ben was alive. After he was banned, and committed suicide, there was a spell when I didn't want company, but it lasted only about a year. Then I started to need my work, my friends, and what welfare workers call a stable and lasting relationship. I tried two or three men, or perhaps they tried me. Anyway, it ended each time in wrangling and boredom.

I began to worry about myself, because I felt that living as I did was . . . not immoral, I didn't think much about that . . . but spendthrift. I was buying people I didn't like with energy I couldn't afford.

That was the mood I was wearing when Morry walked into an exhibition of my work that Finn Cremer was staging. I noticed him standing with a group of art critics that was arguing over one of my metal abstracts. He was the clumsiest-looking man I'd ever seen : very big, with hulking shoulders, a heavy broken nose, heavy brows, and the sort of curly black hair that no barber can shape.

I asked Finn who the big lummox was, and Finn said, "That's Maurice Faber. Don't insult him, he's rich, and he lent us this gallery, free." I went up to where he was standing. The critics were bandying words like "latent power", and "deliberate ambiguity", and just for fun I asked Morry what he thought of the sculpture. He gave me a sideways glance of the bright black eyes; picked the masterpiece off its stand; turned it over in his blodgy

131

fingers; and said, "You're using too much manganese".

After that, I was lost.

He told me later that he "recognized" me, that was the word he used, as soon as I spoke to him, and being Morry he also told me it was the first time he'd ever fallen for a woman with duck's disease.

And so, good morrow to our waking souls!

Morry's business was metal. It took him to the big mining centres and ports scattered around the country. He'd built up a good reputation as a consultant. A lot of the people he enjoyed were in the mink-and-manure set, new rich and busy keeping up with the Dow-Joneses.

I was a sculptor. My stuff was selling well in southern Africa, and beginning to go in America and Europe. I held regular exhibitions, I had to maintain my sales links, and fit in life-sittings, and some teaching. When I met Morry I was spending one day a fortnight at a black high school in Soweto, and running a night class twice a week at my studio.

Our attitudes to work differed greatly, because a business consultant has to operate within the establishment and as a part of society, whereas an artist is alone, and stands outside of society, to observe, criticize and interpret. When I felt bitchy, I'd call Morry an exploiter, and he'd answer by saying I was a con-woman, selling my work to suckers who thought it gave them status.

Our backgrounds had nothing in common. Morry was half Jewish, quarter Afrikaner, quarter God-knows-what. I could trace my line back through five generations of plump, white Anglican money-grubbers.

Yet in spite of being so ill-suited, we managed to find delight concord and love. Both of us had had a rough time getting where we were. (Morry had had to manage without a family since his teens. I had had to cut myself off from my family, when I married Ben; and then I lost him.) Both of us liked fending for ourselves, and we liked the same sort of people, busy and vociferous. We had the same taste in music, food, and of course politics.

After Ben died, I stopped being a part of any formal political group. I never joined Morry's Party, but I supported his views.

Finally, Morry and I suited each other in bed. I don't have

132

romantic view of sex, but neither do I have a clinical one. People nowadays talk about having sex, or making love, or screwing, according to their taste in words, as a series of isolated acts. I think sex is as continual, in every person, as breathing or developing blood cells. If I like sleeping with Morry, it is not merely for a temporary excitement or satisfaction. That I've had with other men. It is this. When his body enters mine, I am making him free of my whole life, as I am made free of his.

This was not something I ever found with Ben, happy though I was with him. Ben never really loved me, or any other human being, as much as he loved ideas. He was faithfully married to ideas, and when they let him down he took poison, not being able to go on without them.

Morry and I seldom fought, and when we did, it seemed to start from something I couldn't control, some deep resentment in him which he would never discuss with me.

It was only after we'd been married for more than a year that I realized that this resentment, along with Morry's temper, and even his clumsiness, came from being scared. It wasn't a conscious fear. On the surface, he wasn't scared of anything. Underneath, he was very much afraid, and when his devils got after him, he'd bluster, and over-react, and land himself in trouble.

He had always been reticent about his early life. He told me he'd been very happy as a child, but didn't give details, except to say that he'd been brought up in Benoni, which is an industrial town on the outskirts of Johannesburg. I had to glean the facts from other people, putting scraps together to make some sort of picture; and that I did only after he left me.

Mihail Faber, Morry's father, came from the Lebanon as a young man, in 1930, and spent the rest of his life here, though he was never naturalized. The depression of the 'thirties having begun, he took quite a menial job with a scrap-metal merchant. Later he joined a small printing works in Benoni. He was a clever man, quiet and hard working, and he got ahead. Because he was a diabetic, he was never called up in the war.

By 1941, when Morry was born, Mihail owned the printing works, and was building it into a promising business, with a clientele across the Eastern Rand.

Mihail married a country girl. Her name was Elizabeta Cornelia Clemens. She was quite pretty, from the few pictures

133

Morry had of her, with the heavy-boned, fair good looks you see in a lot of Afrikaner families. She was also rather stupid, certainly not the mental equal of her husband. She made a good home for him, though, and Morry was happy.

Everything went all right so long as Mihail lived, but in 1952 he went into a diabetic coma from which he didn't recover. He left his widow comfortably off, with ownership of the printing works, the house in her own name, and money in the bank. There was a small trust fund to look after Morry's schooling.

In a very short time, Elizabeta Faber managed to muddle away both the business and the house, selling them both for peanuts. Although I don't know exactly how she lived for the next three years, it's clear she started to drink heavily, and she also took up with a man who was no good to her.

This was a Swede, name of Bo Knudsen, who left the whalers in Durban and headed for Johannesburg. He lived in a derelict house with a rag-tag of hoboes. He called himself a salesman, but in fact he was just a bum, and had been arrested a couple of times for being in possession of stolen goods.

Mrs Faber moved into this household, and took Morry with her. He hated his years there. I think what horrified him was not the crummy life his mother led, but the fact that she was happy leading it, happier than she'd been in her life with his father. In months of boozing, of night-long gavine-parties that ended in brawls, of days spent idling on the stoep, she seemed entirely content. "It was as if she'd shucked off a corset and was relishing the sag," Morry said.

When things got too rough, he used to light out and spend a couple of days with the Lutheran minister, down the road.

They lived like that until 1956. The reason for their leaving I found when I searched old newspaper files, after we separated. There was a report of an inquest, dated 24 October of that year. The inquest was on the death of the six-weeks-old daughter of Elizabeta Cornelia Faber. Apparently there'd been a shindig so violent that the police were called. When they went into the house to haul out the trouble-makers, they found Mrs Faber sprawled on her bed, drunk, and the dead baby lying under her. She must have rolled over in a stupor, and suffocated it.

It was a sad enough story, but I doubt it would have made the news pages, except for the way Bo Knudsen reacted. He

134

stated in the court that he was not the father of the child, and told what seemed to be a trumped-up tale about Mrs Faber's "going with twenty other men". He even hinted that she had deliberately overlaid the child, and he refused to have anything more to do with her. He proved his point by slinging her possessions out into the street during a rain-storm. When Morry tried to stop him, he belted Morry across the back with an iron bar.

That brought the welfare authorities into the matter. They wanted to declare Morry in need of care, but, at fourteen, he was full-grown, and having none of that. Instead, he got his mother into a shelter for alcoholics. When she was dried out, he took her south, to a little village called Perdevlei, near Cape Town. She found work there, in a trade-store.

I suppose Mrs Faber was cured in the sense that she gave up drinking, but then she went overboard for religion. The sect she joined was a branch of the Dutch Reformed Church, one that frowned on anything that was any fun at all. There was a photograph of the elders, standing in their Sunday blacks. The people of Perdevlei seem to have been nasty, bigoted, racialistic yokels who made Morry's life a misery. The only good thing they did was straighten out Mrs Faber's money affairs, so that she could at least live on her income.

She lost all interest in Morry.

Luckily he had his educational trust. He finished his schooling in the Cape, and as I've already said, went to university there. He saw less and less of his mother. She died in 1969, so I never met her.

Morry didn't tell me all this, but I don't believe he ever forgot those years. They certainly conditioned him. His strength of will and his tolerance, his attitudes towards race and religion, his hatred of drunkenness, his love of his friends, must have come from that time. And that other legacy of fear, that he concealed even from himself.

Morry could never accept happiness as it came. There was always anxiety in him, and it affected the people close to him. You can't be carefree with a man who bites every coin.

Perhaps we'd have got by if we'd met no big problems . . . if such a thing is ever possible. What broke us up was that I fell pregnant.

That was something I had not believed could happen. I'd been

135

married to Ben for ten years without conceiving. The doctors said that as a teenager I'd had a tuberculous infection of the fallopian tubes. Then, at the ripe old age of 33 when I'd got used to thinking I was sterile, I found I wasn't.

The day I got confirmation from the doctor, I sailed home on cloud nine. That whole day, I savoured the thought of telling Morry. He was down in the Free State on business, and didn't get home until about nine that night, by which time I had rehearsed my big scene in my mind a dozen times.

Well, it didn't go according to the script.

When I got to the line, "I am going to have a baby," Morry stared at me for a moment, and then walked out of the room. I followed him, still talking, and it wasn't for some time I grasped that he wasn't glad. His face, as they say in the Bible, was set against me. He didn't even want to talk about the baby. I could see he was struggling to act the way I expected him to, but he just couldn't make it. That night we lay awake, not touching, not talking, light-years apart.

Next day he put on a different manner. He acted the part of the pleased father-to-be, which was worse for me than his first reaction, because it was phoney as hell. When I tried to get at what was worrying him, he kept saying, "I'm glad, naturally I'm glad," and giving me the bright, flat look.

I tried to understand. I talked it over with my doctor, who put it down to jealousy, but finding a name for the disease didn't cure it. I tried to get through to Morry, every way I could. I hid my hurt. I let it show. I was patient. I picked quarrels, in the hopes that that way we might blast our way through, but in the end I just had to accept that Morry did not want my child. I made up my mind he'd change his mind once the baby arrived.

The accident happened when I was two months gone. It was summer, and after a long drought we had a week of torrential rains along the Reef. Morry and I lived in a hilly part of the city, and to reach the local shops we had to use a road that was shored up by high brick walls. The rains must have undermined their foundations, because, one day when I went to pick up some groceries, there was a cave-in, and 40 feet of brickwork came down, burying me and two other women.

They pulled us out as quickly as they could. One of the women was dead, the other only lightly injured. I was taken to hospital with broken ribs and a cracked pelvis, and I lost the baby. They kept me under drugs the first two days. When I came round, Morry was sitting beside me. It was late in the afternoon, and I could just see the big outline of him against the window. I put out my hand and he took it and pressed it hard against his cheek. He looked tired and very sad, only I knew he wasn't sad for the baby we'd lost, but sad for me.

I wasn't in hospital long. When I came home, it was like a reversal of the previous few weeks. Morry tried to make up to me, and I couldn't respond, no matter how hard I tried.

All this time, we loved each other. That made it so hard—that we loved each other, and could neither of us understand the other.

I felt dull and grey right through. I could see Morry growing more and more desperate in his efforts to comfort me, and I didn't care. I needed to be left alone to recover in my own way, and I expected Morry to give me as much time as I needed. I thought I could rely on that, at least, but I was wrong.

I can't even remember what sparked the final explosion. We got into a terrible row, and I said something to the effect that he was glad I'd lost the baby. He looked at me in a mad kind of way, his eyes glittering and screwed up; then he went out to my studio at the back of the house, and destroyed a whole lot of my work; and then he left me.

He went to a hotel in Pretoria, refused to come home or to see me. He told me, through lawyers, that he wanted a formal separation, not a divorce. I was to have the house, furniture, car, money, anything I wanted . . . except him.

Those first few months there were plenty of friends and well-wishers who buzzed round and tried to get us back together again. They couldn't understand why we'd broken up, and how was I to give reasons when I didn't know them myself? If I'd told them I knew it wasn't final, that one day Morry would come back to me, wouldn't they have thought, 'Poor thing, they all believe that?'

When I spent all those weeks delving into the old records and talking to people who'd known Morry in his youth, it was not, as some of my friends hinted, a nostalgic trip. Whatever had driven him away concerned his life—the part I didn't know. Close as we'd been, I'd failed to know him well enough, and that ignorance I had to repair.

A year after the break, I left Jo'burg and came to Durban. I wanted to work with the African woodcarvers there, and I wanted a change of scene. I had friends in Natal, among them Mark and Bianca Ramsay.

It was Bianca who told me that Mark had agreed to stand in the Parkhaven election, and that Morry would be in Durban for three months, working as his election manager.

XXV

MORRY ARRIVED AT the coast early in January, as I knew from Bianca. Though from pride I kept away from the Ramsay's house, I picked up news of him all round town. He'd been seen by friends, he'd talked to the Parkhaven committee, his photograph appeared in the *Gazette*; but he never tried to get in touch with me.

I found this time very hard. During the past few years I'd built up a sort of discipline, no fantasizing allowed. But it was difficult, with him so close, not to imagine a meeting, not to sit at home in case he called.

20 January was my birthday. I made up my mind that if he didn't phone me then, he never would. No call came, so I went into a travel agency the next morning, and booked to fly to Europe at the end of February. To cement my resolve, I wrote to my overseas agents and told them I'd be bringing over stuff to sell.

At that time I was working on a marble for the Terblanche exhibition, and, as my departure date for London was 28 February, I had to work overtime to finish the polishing and mounting of the piece. It was done at last, and that night I fell into bed dead-tired. About midnight I was awakened by someone ringing my doorbell. I looked out of the window and saw Morry standing on the front steps; and I let him in.

It was so typical of him, to appear that way. There he stood, at an ungodly hour, unannounced, giving my living-room that quick button-eyed stare of his, like a second-hand dealer who means to beat down the price; and instead of feeling insulted, I was just witless with joy. I wanted to talk all night, and find out everything that had happened in three long years, I wanted to go to bed with him and make love all night.

Then he turned to face me, and I realized that whatever this meeting might turn out to be, it wasn't our big reconciliation scene.

Morry looked terribly tired, and somehow distrait. I offered him coffee, and he sat down at my kitchen table, and after a little while, asked me about Amyas Mochudi.

I told him what I knew. It was a long time ago, all that, and I'd buried it deep, not wanting to remember it. As I talked about Amyas and Ben and the days when the Spear of the Nation was at its zenith, the emotions of that time revived in me. I felt the exhilaration, the closeness to great issues, and the fear.

Morry listened, mostly in silence. He never explained why he was interested in Amyas, nor did I ask him. I had just enough sense to realize I must play this one cool, and when he finally got up to leave, I gave no sign I hoped to see him again.

All that night, I told myself to stay out of trouble. I would go ahead with my plans to fly to Europe. I would not sit around to be a sort of political enquiries counter. Wednesday morning, Morry 'phoned to ask me if I would try and trace Mochudi for him. An hour later, I'd cancelled my flight bookings.

Over the next few days I played detective, without much success. I 'phoned old friends, but they could tell me very little about Amyas. Most of them were ex-Liberal, ex-Congress, ex-ANC, with the emphasis on the ex. Politics is like the Arts, you can't dabble, you have to be right in, or right out. When the Government, by its bannings and detentions, cut the balls off the black political groups, my friends were driven out, or quit. Often they didn't know the leaders of the new black movements. Those few who'd stayed active weren't anxious to discuss it, and I couldn't blame them. My credentials were ten years out of date.

Despite this, I did learn one thing, and that was that a Mochudi cult was developing in the townships. People were painting his name on walls and bridges. I was told the witch doctors were busy, spreading the tale that he would come to lead the people.

I thought Morry should know about this, so on Sunday night I 'phoned him. He was round at my flat in ten minutes, and though he still looked tired and tense, there was an exuberance about him that made me feel he was glad to be with me.

For a while we talked about Amyas. Then Morry mentioned a man named Don Hobeni, Amyas' half brother. Apparently this man had a big following among the younger factory workers, and Morry felt that he and Mochudi might be making a bid for power among urban blacks. He asked me whether I'd heard any talk of that, and I told him I'd heard none. I pointed out that I wasn't involved in politics, any longer, and didn't really want to be.

He seemed to accept that, and began to talk about the campaign. He told me how the Vigilantes were beating up canvassers, that they'd broken up a public meeting the previous Wednesday; and he said that warnings of trouble were coming in from every side, from people like Charlie Cameron, as well as from the black politicians. "I'm scared, Jess," he said. "There's a lousy mood in this city. Disaffection. It's got to everyone, blacks as well as whites. The people I talk to, the well-informed, active, sane people who should be able to tell what's going on, don't seem to know. The authorities seem to be suffering from paralysis, the white opposition's impotent, and the blacks bicker like pariah dogs. And all the time, something big is moving in on us."

"Are you talking about an uprising?"

"I don't know."

Suddenly I began to panic. I was remembering the violence of the past; people torn down from peaceable platforms and beaten unconscious, thugs waiting on street corners as we marched, batons and dogs and the stink of tear gas. I remembered the violence of minds intent on crushing out all ideas, all thoughts, that did not conform with their own; it had killed Ben, and now it seemed to threaten Morry. I put out my hand and took hold of his wrist.

"It's too late," I said, "can't you see? You're wasting your time. It's all been tried before, and it's all been useless."

I could feel the familiar warmth of his skin, the soft hairs on it, and the pulse beating under my fingers. I wanted to lean down my head, and say "Stay here with me".

For a moment he sat absolutely still; then he pulled his wrist away, quite gently, but it was a refusal, none the less. Soon after that, he left.

Sleep being far from me, I went out onto the porch and drew an old cane chair forward to the rail so that I could look down across the city. It was one of those starry, torpid nights, the sky and sea a uniform milky blue. Impossible to believe that anything so lovely and so indolent could suckle violence. Yet I knew Morry was right. It was here.

I sat on, going over things in my mind. I really had only two

141

choices. One was to say goodbye to Morry, go abroad and stop away long enough to forget him; the other was to stay and help him with his wild-goose chase.

After a while I fell asleep and woke at dawn, stiff with cramp, and the decision ready to my mind. I even had the name I needed, Ram Khoosal, and I went to my desk to see if I still had his address.

XXVI

IT TOOK ME three days to find out where Ram was. I achieved
it through his publisher. Some years ago, Ram and his wife Sita
wrote a book on yoga disciplines, and I'd seen that a follow-up
was being printed, so I telephoned the firm in Johannesburg.
They were able to tell me that Ram was in Zambia, but expected
back fairly soon.

On the strength of that, I flew to Johannesburg. Ram was
always jetting about the world, and if he hit town for an hour
or two, I wanted to be able to get to him.

The Khoosals have a rag-to-riches history. There was an old
grandfather who lived to be nearly a hundred; came from India
as a stripling, worked as a wash-dhobi, and spoke nothing but
Tamil from a mouth stained scarlet with betel-chewing. This old
stallion married three wives and sired fourteen children. One of
his sons was a friend of Mahatma Gandhi when he lived in Natal,
and shared in the Passive Resistance campaigns. Another, Ram's
father, built up a huge fortune in property deals and trading
stores throughout the province, so Ram was born into great
wealth. He carried on his father's interests and added others
in Zambia, Botswana and Rhodesia, often using white front-men
to beat the racial laws.

When I first met him he was about 35 years old; slim, elegant,
abstemious, with wonderful good looks. When I see pictures of
the Indian gods, with their large shining eyes and straight noses
and delicate expressive hands, I think of Ram.

He always maintained he was a-political. But, of course, being
Indian, he knew South African politics by bitter experience. His
family owned a house in one of the best Durban suburbs until
the Group Areas Act forced them to move. With all his great
fortune, Ram couldn't own premises in Durban's main street. He
sent his children to school in England to dodge the discrimi-
natory Indian Education laws.

Though he was not politically active, he allowed us to use his
home when we needed a refuge, he gave a great deal of money to

143

causes he thought misguided, and he was always an invaluable source of information about the affairs of southern Africa.

When I reached Johannesburg, I booked into a hotel and sat down to await a message. Ram 'phoned late on Wednesday afternoon. It had been a blistering hot day, with a dry wind blowing, and I had a headache. I was lying on my bed when the call came through, and Ram's quiet voice said, as if I'd seen him yesterday, "Hullo, Jess. You wanted me?"

"I'd almost given you up," I said. "Are you in Jo'burg?" His voice sounded far away.

"Pilgrim's Rest. Sita and I are having a little holiday. Could you come?"

A whole lot of questions went tumbling through my mind. As I hesitated, he said, "Do come, Jess. I will send a car to fetch you. It's very beautiful here."

"It's problems, Ram. I'd disturb your peace."

"Come and we'll talk. Sita says she will give you some real food. I'll send the car at once, won't you agree?"

"Thank you. Yes."

Ram's nephew Monan collected me an hour later. He was a silent young man with bad skin and a shock of silky, blue-black hair. He was driving an Alfa and broke the 90 km limit whenever he thought we could get away with it, so by ten o'clock we were near the edge of the great plateau of Africa that overlooks Mozambique and the sea.

Once through Pilgrim's Rest village, we left the main road and turned north-west. We bumped along badly-graded tracks, between ranks of pine trees. Up and up we climbed, the air cold and fresh and the stars seeming to explode like pop-corn in a vast blue-steel pan. After about an hour we came to a little house with a tiled roof, and Sita came out to greet us.

On the way out, I'd been nervous, reflecting it would be quite a deal, to ask favours of the Khoosals. Though ten years ago they'd been close and trusted friends, since that time we'd seldom seen one another. Some of these fears were dissipated by the way they welcomed me.

Sita must have gone straight into the kitchen when she heard I was coming. There was a delicious supper waiting for me, chicken pilau, and freshly-grated coconut in its own milk; popadums and chili-bites, sliced tomatoes and cucumbers and little sweet-potato cakes. Finally, to "sweeten the guest's mouth", a ground-rice dessert.

Sita trained in the Bharata Natyam as a young girl—that's the Indian dance form which is looked on as a special way of invoking the divine. Later she took up the discipline of yoga. Never a beautiful woman, she had incredible grace of body and of spirit; she had the healer's power to create a reserve of energy within herself, and to allow anyone who wished to draw upon it. Watching her, I began to feel calm and relaxed.

We ate, and Ram chatted, and afterwards Monan vanished to his own room and the rest of us went to the sitting-room on the far side of the house. This had a wide window, and through it I could see the moonlit land rise to the west in a jumble of hills, and on the east, drop sheer away into darkness. Far off there was the glint of a waterfall, close by, the tops of pine trees, and the sparkling sky over all.

I asked Ram how he'd found such a jewel of a place.

"I don't own it," he said, and his smile was quizzical. "It was lent to me by someone I know. A Government official, as a matter of fact."

"Times have changed."

"Indeed they have. I'm like old Satan, you know, I travel up and down in the earth. I bring in foreign exchange, and information that some people value. But don't worry, Jess. I'm not a Quisling, yet."

"Nor a Boss agent?"

"Not yet." He talked for some time about the countries he visited, their men of influence, the economic and political pressures that shaped their dealings with South Africa. His manner was urbane as ever, but there was a nerviness in him that was new.

"All this beautiful country," he said, taking in with a sweep of his arm the landscape before us, "you realize, if Rhodesia collapses then this territory becomes our soft underbelly? Northern Transvaal, right round to Northern Natal. The Communists could strike through here, as well as Namibia. The arms are already being smuggled in."

"Are they? What sort?"

"Light, at the moment. Grenades, machine-pistols, the material for terror weapons, like detonators and solanoids."

"Is that hearsay, or fact?"

"My dear, I don't have affidavits; but let's call it information from usually reliable sources."

I glanced round the room. He had said it was owned by a Government man. Did Ram confide these stories to him? What was the Khoosals' attitude to a war of liberation, what was mine? Ram watched me with a slightly wry smile.

"It is a dilemma, isn't it?" he said. "I ask myself, what would I do if I encountered a group of men crossing the border at some illegal point? Going out, perhaps, to train in the techniques of urban terrorism? Coming back with a shipment of arms?"

I wanted to answer, "I'm out of politics, now," but it was no answer. I got up and went over to the window, leaning my hands on the glass. In it I could see the dim reflection of Ram and Sita, superimposed on the dark view of Africa.

"We never fought our cause," I said, "in order to let an outside power come in and take over. I hate the present régime, but I don't confuse the régime with the country."

"A generalization," Ram sounded impatient, "it's too late for that. Be specific. A terrorist comes to this house, tonight, what do you do? Do you welcome him as a freedom fighter, do you report his presence to the authorities, do you look the other way?"

"It's a hypothetical question."

"Is it?"

I turned to face him. He was sitting with legs elegantly crossed, as if we were enjoying an academic discussion, but his gaze never wavered from my face.

"I'd report him," I said, "but that's only my personal decision. I can't lay down principles for other people. They may have had more to bear than I have, they may have passed the point of no return."

"And what if the terrorist proves to be someone you knew, someone you cared about?"

"Then I don't know what I'd do."

He appeared to brood about that for a moment, and then abruptly changed the subject. "Well Jess, now tell us, what brings you to the Transvaal?"

"I came to see you."

"Particularly? That is very flattering."

"To ask a favour. I'm looking for someone we knew a long time ago."

"Who is that?"

"Amyas Mochudi."

He looked taken aback. "Amyas? I thought he was on the Island."

"No. He's out, but nobody seems to know where he's got to."

"I certainly don't. I haven't seen Amyas for years." Ram slowly rubbed a finger down his jaw-line. "One could try. . . ."

"Will you?"

"Not tonight, it's late. Tomorrow we can think, hmm?"

My bedroom did not overlook the valley, but faced the pine woods and a little dam surrounded by arum lilies. There were frogs in the dam, and their croaking merged with the soughing of the wind in the trees. I slept deeply.

When I woke up, just after six o'clock, the weather had changed. It was colder, and a thin mist hung motionless outside my window. The house was quiet. I got up and bathed and dressed and went through to the living-room. Sita was there, dressed in a gold sari with a brown cardigan over it. She had been straightening the room, but put her duster aside when she saw me.

"You're much too early, you were supposed to have breakfast in bed. Did you sleep well?"

"Marvellously."

"Come through to the kitchen. Ram won't eat yet, he's meditating. Do you like cooked things, or not?"

I chose home-made bread and honey, a boiled egg and fruit. Sita made coffee, and while we were drinking it, she suddenly said, "Jess, have you seen Maurice?"

The question made me jump. Sita's ability to read minds was always a bit spooky. She didn't look at me, now, but took some grapes from a bowl and held them up to the light so that they were almost transparent. "I heard he'd gone to Durban," she said, "and I wondered."

"Yes, I've seen him."

"You want him back?"

"Yes."

"Is that why you're here, to see if Ram can help you?"

"Yes, in a way it is."

147

She nodded calmly. "I told him. He was very nervous, last night. They send people to spy on him, you know. I told him you're not one of them, he can trust you."

I nodded. Somewhere along the line, you have to stop asking for guarantees, and rely on your own judgement. There was no reason Ram should trust me, or I him, other than past experience. That would have to do us.

Ram appeared at noon, carrying a bundle of raincoats. "Come on out, we'll work up an appetite."

"It's misty," Sita said, "we'll get lost."

"Not if we stick to the road. If we're not home by lunch time, Monan can arrange a search party."

He walked us briskly up hill, the cold damp air swirling about us; and after a mile or two, said: "You want me to trace Mochudi. Why?"

"Maurice asked me to do so. I want to please him."

"I see. But why does he want Amyas, do you know?"

"No. I don't think Morry himself could give a precise answer. I think he believes—like a lot of people—that Mochudi is somehow a key figure in what's happening in Durban."

"The strikes?"

"More than that. A general pattern of unrest."

Ram walked for some distance without speaking, then said, "But Natal has been very free of trouble, hasn't it? Last year, when the other provinces had riots and burning, the Zulus remained very peaceful."

"Because of people like Buthelezi, and the Inkatha movement. But I have the feeling that just because Natal has remained free of trouble up to now, she may become a target. They'll try and foment trouble."

"Who is 'they'?" Ram broke off a twig of eucalyptus pine, and held it under his nose. "The Commies?"

"Possibly."

"You think Mochudi knows something about it?"

"Perhaps. People in the townships are talking about him. I told Morry that in the old days Amyas supported strike action, but not subversion. . . ."

"But after five years on Robben Island, he might have changed?"

148

"I don't know, Ram. I'm in the dark."

"What does Maurice think? About the unrest?"

"That it's planned, that it's operating through several different groups of people."

"And you agree?"

"There's something on. You can feel it. Have you been in Durban recently?"

"Yes. I know what you mean. Like drums on a hot summer night, you can't tell quite where they are, what they are, but they make you afraid." He threw the leafy switch away. "And Amyas has vanished?"

"Off the face of the earth." I hesitated. "He had a brother."

"Half brother," amended Ram. "Don Hobeni. I knew him. He went out of the country for a time."

"Where?"

Perhaps I sounded too eager. Ram looked at me evasively. "I'm not sure. The States, I think."

I didn't press him. He went on asking questions until I'd told him all I could, and at last said, "I'll have some enquiries made. Monan and I go back to Johannesburg tomorrow morning, and we'll set the thing going. In the mean time, why not stay here with Sita, it will be company for her?"

"I would love to."

"Good. Relax, rest, enjoy yourself."

For the next 48 hours I did as Ram suggested. There was no use chafing about time. Sita and I went for walks or sat out in the sun. I even did a few gentle yoga exercises, sitting on the floor, stretching, breathing, saying "The fire of my life is rising to my heart, healing me in every way...."

On Friday evening there was a big storm. We watched it drumming up from the south, the earth blackening under the clouds, the long runnels of lightning followed by vast pillars of rain. After it cleared, we walked to the edge of the escarpment and saw the brown flood water begin to move down the river, far below, down to the broad plain and the fever-green thornveld.

I had forgotten how much I loved my country.

Ram returned on Saturday afternoon.

That night it was cold enough for us to light a fire of pine cones and wood. We sat round it, after supper, and Ram told us what little he'd been able to ferret out.

"Mochudi is certainly a mystery man," he said. "He was released—as we already knew—from the Island. Transkei apparently put pressure on the Minister, asked for the release you see as a gesture of goodwill to a newly-independent State. It so happens that Mochudi has been in poor health for some time. He was allowed his freedom on condition he returned to Transkei, and the people there undertook to be responsible for his good behaviour. Seems they bit off more than they could chew, eh? Because on 23 December last year, he vanished. Clean as a whistle. I am told the police in Transkei and here have been—ah —greatly exercised in their minds about this." Ram put out a sleek little hand and chose a lump of coconut ice from the dish in front of him. "I am also told—in strict confidence—that Mochudi has been urged to attend the Black Summit in two weeks' time. It is to take place at my hotel in Durban, had you heard? Did Morry tell you Mochudi is to attend?"

"He never mentioned it. But if it was a secret, he wouldn't."

"Sea green incorruptible." Ram licked his fingers. "How lucky I have no such scruples, I tell all. Well, the invitation has gone out, it seems. We don't know whether M has accepted, or not."

"Would he be allowed to attend a conference in Durban?"

"Ah, that is a tricky one. Mochudi was not placed under any restraints when he left prison. No banning order, no house arrest, since that would hardly be conducive to goodwill. But one does not know whether this latitude would extend to letting him come to a major city, to attend a highly emotive black gathering. That I rather doubt. And yet—when you think of it—how to restrict him, without stirring up trouble in Transkei, and among his followers here in Natal? So much better that he should remain— umh—incommunicado."

"You think he's dead, don't you?"

Ram shrugged. "It's possible. Let me say I would not rate his chances very high if he went to Durban. Too many long knives are sharpened for him. The best he might receive would be preventive detention."

"So we're not much further, are we?"

"Not much. I have put out some feelers. I can't rush about

asking, 'Where's Amyas?' But I must say I find the silence very interesting. There are so many people who are ready to sell information, these days, that I'm surprised no one will even give us a hint where to look for Amyas. I'm inclined to think the reason that nobody tells is, nobody knows."

"And Hobeni?"

"Ah, now there I was more successful. Hobeni is 26 years old, a great deal younger than Amyas. Their mother married twice. The first husband, Amyas' father, was a tribal dignitary, the second, Don's father, was a lecturer in one of the big universities. Hobeni was brought up in the city and given a good education. He has a degree in Commerce. From June '70 to August '72 he was in Europe, furthering his studies."

"Which side of the Iron Curtain?"

"The West. He returned to South Africa late in '73, having worked his way down Africa. He found himself a job in Industria, something at the semi-skilled level. Now that is a fact to ponder, Jess."

"Looks as if he wanted to be on the factory floor."

"Yes, doesn't it? But the odd thing is, he took no part in the strikes of '73 to '74. The description one gets of him is a fly-by-night, a heavy drinker, runs up debts round town, and so on. But one person—this is interesting—swore that Hobeni helped to prevent rioting among the school children last year. The school kids are radical to the point of anarchy. They wouldn't cross the road for a man who was just a bar-lizard."

"Is Hobeni Marxist?"

"Nobody said so. Radical at university, very anti-white. In Germany, took a course in trades unionism. But then, this black-power man comes home with nothing but a taste for whisky. Labour trouble blows up, and he is not involved. The things don't match up, you see." Ram felt in his pocket. "I have a picture of him. Here. Taken when he was a student."

The smudged print showed three young men in tracksuits.

"This one." Ram indicated a shock-headed youth who stared at the camera with lowered chin. There was aggression in the stance, and power. It was not the body of a man who enjoyed the back seat.

"Well?" said Ram.

"Perhaps he changed as he grew older."

151

"Perhaps. Perhaps he's nothing but an alky. Perhaps he's yellow. Perhaps he's a sleeper, biding his time."

"A what?"

"An agent planted for long-term purposes. Remains inactive for a long period, until everyone has forgotten he's there. Well, now he's vanished, like his brother. It's difficult to avoid the conclusion that they've got together, somewhere."

"What do we do?"

"Persevere, persevere. Monan is going into Johannesburg on Monday morning, he'll keep us informed. Meanwhile, let us enjoy our holiday. If it's a good day tomorrow, we can take a picnic in the forest. Somewhere where there is running water, to carry away our cares."

Sunday we had our picnic. At eight o'clock on Monday we waved Monan off to Jo'burg. At eleven-thirty there was a news-flash on the radio, and we learned that Mark Ramsay had been shot dead.

XXVII

THAT FIRST announcement just gave us the bare facts. Mark was dead, and a clerk, and Walter Brock was badly hurt. I went into a black spiral of panic about Morry.

"He must be all right," Ram said, "his name wasn't mentioned."

"I have to know, I want to hear his voice!"

"Of course. We'll 'phone the party office."

But getting through to Durban from a branch line in the backveld, was something else again. It took time for the operator to make the Durban connection, and then we found that the Party lines were jammed solid. I tried calling Charlie Cameron at the *Gazette*. He was out, but another reporter told me that Morry was unharmed. "One of our chaps was in the courtroom," he said. "Mr Faber's okay, that's for sure."

All I could think of was getting back to Durban. I had a wild idea I could hire a car from the local garage and drive myself down, but Ram vetoed that.

"Better we take you into Jo'burg straight away. If we can fix you on a 'plane, good, if not you can go by road in one of my company cars. But Jess, isn't it more important for you to finish what you came up here to do? Find out about Mochudi?"

"I don't give a damn about that, now."

"I think you should. It could be that Mark was killed because of his interest in Mochudi. If so, then anyone close to Mark could be in some danger. Morry, you, Mark's family. So it becomes very urgent to know where Mochudi is, and what he is doing."

"Better to cut and run."

"Where will you run to, Jess?"

"I want to be near Morry."

"You want to protect Morry, don't you? Well, the best way might be to stay up here. Listen, my dear, if you go back to Durban today, do you think Morry will be able to see you? Will he not be up to his eyes in problems, police enquiries, dismantling the campaign . . . my goodness, Jess, the candidate is murdered, can't you imagine what that must mean for his manager?"

"I can't think at all, my head's spinning."

"So, let me decide for you. We'll take you to the International Hotel. It's close to the airport. We can fix your flight. In the mean time, Monan will keep in touch with us and tell us if he's got anything about Mochudi. Now you go and pack your things. We'll leave as soon as you're ready."

The International is a brand new hotel, in the style best described as Boer Baronial. We arrived there late in the afternoon, and found it packed with delegates to a housing conference. The Khoosals booked us into a suite on the tenth floor. While Ram was signing the register, I went over to the kiosk and bought all the evening papers. The murder was headlined everywhere.

The early editions carried a short statement that a man named David Tindall had been nominated as a surprise candidate, independent of any party. Later editions gave more details. A blurred photograph in the *Evening Post* showed an undistinguished face, the mouth secretive and the eyes obscured by thick-lensed glasses.

Looking at the picture, I realized suddenly that I was never going to see Mark again, and I began to cry.

That time was like the time when we heard about Kennedy's assassination. There was the feeling that everyone was thinking about the same thing.

Ram and Sita and I sat in the living-room of our suite, with the radio and the television turned on. Every now and again the pips would sound and there'd be a fresh bulletin.

I kept trying to get through to Morry, without success. The Party office lines were constantly busy—I found out later they were being kept for outgoing calls—and I didn't know the unlisted number. Calls to his flat got no answer. I told myself Ram was right; Morry must be snowed under and there'd be no chance of seeing him if I did hurry back to the coast.

My thoughts, that first night, were entirely with the people I loved : Morry and Bianca and little Nick. I didn't worry about Tindall's nomination, or see anything sinister in it. I accepted the facts as they were handed to me.

The police were plugging the line that there was no conspiracy to kill Mark, and that it was the act of a criminal lunatic by the name of Calgut. He'd been shot by a policeman as he tried to make his escape. It was a comforting idea, because if the guilty man was dead, then Morry was safe.

But there was a lot of speculation in the press that this was a political killing. The white Vigilantes, some said, and others, black terrorists. The hotel was full of rumours, everyone had a theory.

About seven o'clock on that Monday evening, we had a visit from a black reporter who worked on *The Sphere*. He'd been tipped off by a waiter that Ram Khoosal was in the hotel. He came in and drank a whisky with us.

"Man," he said, "that conference downstairs is washed up, nobody can talk about anything but this Durban shooting. My God, and Soweto is buzzing, I can tell you." He glanced at me. "I'm told you knew this Ramsay?"

"Yes. My ex-husband was his election agent."

"Truly? You spoken to him since?"

"No."

"To anyone else down there?"

"No." I was curt, and he let it slide.

"Know what they're saying? Saying the pigs did it. Ramsay was going to win this election, right? That wouldn't suit them. These days, the pigs don't like you, you're dead."

"Do you really believe that?" said Ram. The reporter shrugged.

"I'd say, this killing is more like kind of a Reichstag Fire. Know what I mean? Now the Security boys can have a good time, pulling in the BPC and SASO boys, and maybe some more newsmen like me. You can forget about the Summit talks, too. Man, those are the dodo."

Ram shook his head. "I don't see how the SB can arrest the black élite because a white politician gets murdered by a white maniac."

"Listen, they'll see Cubans in the cupboard and Frelimo in the fridge. Three o'clock tomorrow morning, they start knocking on our doors."

After he'd left, the hotel desk rang me to say they'd been

155

unable to get me on a 'plane that night or next day, because of people returning from a pilgrimage to Mecca, but they had me wait-listed.

At eight, supper was brought, but none of us could eat much. The TV news was mostly about what they were now calling the Ramsay assassination. There were stills of Mark and Bianca, and then movie film of the building where it happened. A Colonel Buddler, standing beside the broken fourth-floor windows. A stretch of blood-stained pavement, presumably where Calgut was shot. There was a photo of him, too, a wicked triangular face with malformed bones.

"He looks a killer," Ram said.

"Perhaps," Sita answered, "the other one does, too."

"Which other one?"

"The one who shot Calgut."

"That was a policeman."

"So? He shot a man dead, he is also a killer, why don't they show us his picture?"

"The circumstances are rather different."

"We have not been told all the circumstances."

I thought at the time Sita was merely expressing her hatred of all violence. Later, I understood her meaning. The character and motives of that policeman were vitally important; the silence surrounding his actions, highly significant.

Monan Khoosal 'phoned about nine-thirty. He had no fresh information about Mochudi, but said he had "initiated certain lines of enquiry which might prove fruitful". He promised to ring again, next day.

That night I couldn't sleep. I've always been bad at waiting for news. All Tuesday, I tried to stay calm and reasonable, but I could feel my courage evaporating like water from a salt pan. At five in the afternoon, I suddenly reached a decision; went to Ram and Sita and told them I was going back to Durban.

"I have to see Morry."

Ram's eyes searched my face for a moment, and then he stood up. "Okay. Go and send him a telegram. I'll see what I can do about getting you a flight. All these holy pilgrims, maybe one of

156

them is my mother's second cousin."

He went out and I sat down on the sofa next to Sita.

"Have you changed your mind, then, about going back into politics?"

"I'm not going back in, I'm going to fetch Morry out."

"Can you?"

"I have to try." I found I was shaking violently. "Sita, I'm terrified. For him, for myself."

"You have suffered a terrible shock, Jess."

"Enough to warn me. I've been remembering. I had ten years of being scared. I don't want any more."

"You're thinking of Ben?"

"I'm thinking of fear. Fear itself. Nobody can understand what it's like, being under constant threat. Knowing you're never safe, that there's no lock strong enough to keep you safe, that there's hardly a friend you can be sure of, that your job may go, your freedom, perhaps your life. You become paranoid. I can't live that way, and I won't allow Morry to. You need armour against that sort of fear. You have to believe in something so strongly that the fear doesn't count. I don't believe that way."

She watched me, her eyes pitying. "You made a good pretence of it, once."

"When you're young, you can fool even yourself. I was seventeen when I married Ben. I got drawn into politics without understanding them. I liked Ben's friends . . . they were like artists, committed and passionate. I thought I was one of them. But I wasn't. I can't love theories, I can't worship a philosophy and set it higher than flesh-and-blood people.

"Even when Ben was alive, I let him down. I used to tell him, 'Why don't you stop, you'll be banned, you'll be put in prison'. He'd look at me as if I was talking a foreign language. I'd say, 'What use are you to anyone if you're banned? Don't print that pamphlet, don't make that speech, it will destroy you and what good will that do?' He'd say, 'It has to be done'.

"So he was banned. I thought 'Now he'll understand that he must bend a little, he can't beat the system alone'. That shows you how little I understood. I know I helped to kill Ben. I left him alone. He was under such a strict banning order that I was all he had to rely on, he needed my total support and belief. All

157

I did was say, 'Become someone else'. He couldn't, so he took poison."

Sita put a hand on my arm. "You shouldn't blame yourself for that. I knew Ben, remember. He was not an ordinary man. He was a fanatic. If he had been more balanced in his mind, he would not have committed suicide. Morry is not like that. Not so intense."

"Don't kid yourself! Morry is as deep into politics as ever Ben was." I could hear my voice rising hysterically. "Deeper, because Ben went in for intellectual reasons; but Morry goes in because of what he is. Morry goes in because he identifies with people. He sees himself as a coloured man."

I wanted to turn away from Sita's wide gaze, I wanted to stop talking, but I couldn't. It all came boiling out of my heart.

"That's why he left me," I said. "He thinks he has coloured blood. He's believed that since he was fifteen. He only married me because he thought I could never have children. Then I fell pregnant and he realized we might have a dark child. His mother did, you see."

"Wait," said Sita. "Take it slowly." She went and poured me a glass of iced water. I took a few sips, held the frosted tumbler against my forehead.

"It was after Morry's father died," I said. "His mother shacked up with a Swede. She had a baby and it suffocated. The story was she was drunk and overlaid it. There had to be an inquest. I read all about it after Morry left me. I spoke to the probation officer who was on the case, and he said, no doubt about it, the baby was coloured. So Morry took it that he must also be coloured, through his mother."

"But that is ridiculous. It could be on the Swede's side."

"He denied paternity."

"Naturally he would, to save himself trouble. Morry should check up on him."

"He'll never do that. If the Swede was speaking the truth, then how does it help Morry? No, he'll let sleeping dogs lie. But in his mind, he thinks of himself as coloured."

"Do you care?"

"No."

"Surely Morry understands that?"

158

"He understands I love him. But we live in South Africa. If we have a child who is dark, then that will mean the whole of life will change. Race classification, hassles about where the child goes to school, who he might marry when he grows up. That is what Morry can't face. Not for us, but for the child."

"You could avoid having children."

"He would see that as the worst defeat of all, to deny one's own humanity in order to fit this system." I set down the glass. "In my book, we have to take our chances. I want to live with Morry and have his children. Surely, in return, he can pull out of Party politics?"

"You want to strike a deal with him?"

"I mean to try."

She thought that over, and at last said, "Jess, you hope to take Morry away from the violence of politics; but it is everywhere in the world, today". She put her hand on my head. "I hope you get your wish."

A few minutes later, Ram came in, very pleased with himself, having booked a passage for me on a plane next afternoon.

Monan Khoosal came to dinner and told us all he'd done to trace Mochudi. It was an amazingly thorough search he'd set up, extending all over the country through business links, political sources, and, I suspected, some near-criminal contacts. It had produced nothing, in the way of facts; plenty in the way of surmise.

"I can tell you this much," said Monan. "Black opinion does not link Mochudi with this murder. Blacks say, One : Mark Ramsay was not killed by a loner, but by a conspiracy. Two : the murder will finish the Black Summit. Three : Mochudi and Hobeni had no part in it."

Ram frowned. "All these fables about them, but no proof they are even alive."

"We can only keep asking."

Sita, who had been silent most of the time, now said, "Why don't you consult the witch doctors?" Then, as Ram started to chuckle, she said, "I mean it. Amyas Mochudi was a sick man when he was released from prison. It could be he decided to consult one of his own doctors. Why don't you try and find if he's been treated by the sangomas?"

159

"You could throw the bones," Ram said, but Monan did not smile.

"It could be worth a try."

Next afternoon, I flew to Durban. I went straight from the airport to Morry's flat, but he was out. Thereafter I sat at home and phoned him every half hour, with no success.

It was about ten o'clock when he arrived on my doorstep, looking on the point of collapse.

XXVIII

IN ALL THE time I'd known Morry I'd never seen him ill, so his appearance that night really frightened me. He lay on the bed shaking with rigors like a malaria victim. He refused to let me call a doctor. I covered him with blankets and put a hot drink and Aspirin beside him. Every now and again I'd go and look at him. He seemed, after a while, to have fallen asleep.

About one o'clock in the morning, as I was getting ready to go to bed, I heard him shouting my name, loudly, like a child waking from a nightmare. I ran through to him. He was sitting on the edge of the bed, fumbling for the switch of the bedside lamp. The light came on, and he turned towards me. The tears were pouring down his cheeks. I went and put my arms round him and he began talking and crying, tumbling out words that hardly made sense. After a little while I made him lie down and I lay beside him, just holding him in my arms, and he fell into the really deep sleep of total exhaustion.

I didn't dare move, but stayed where I was, my arm slowly going numb under his weight, and the lights burning overhead and beside the bed. Towards dawn I eased myself free, and went back to the living-room.

I lit a cigarette and sat and smoked it through. I thought about Morry, how he'd been the last time I was in Durban, tough and stroppy as hell; and the way he looked tonight, defeated. He'd never before asked me for help.

At half-past five I looked into the bedroom. He was lying on his back, still dead asleep. I went over to his jacket, which he'd dropped on the floor, and found his key-case. I slipped out of the house and drove to the crummy holiday flat he'd rented, found his suitcases and packed all his things. Then I scrawled a note to the caretaker: "Mr Faber has gone to 93 Garrick Street. Mail can be sent there."

I drove home, put the suitcases in the upper hallway, and went and ran myself a bath.

I was still in the tub when I heard Morry moving about in

the living-room. He called out, "Jess?" in a panicky sort of voice.

"Here, in the bathroom."

He came slowly to the door and stood there uncertainly, like a buffalo that's arrived at the wrong wallow. Then he moved to the chair and sat down.

"I'm sorry about last night, making all that scene."

"Ach, so what? I fetched your things. They're in the hall."

"I can't stay here."

"You can, until you decide what you want to do next."

"I'm through with the campaign. I told them. I'll have to get back to Jo'burg." But he was picking at the palm of his hand when he said that.

"Don't rush it," I said.

He stared at me sombrely. His mouth pulled back in a kind of grimace.

"Hand me my towel, Morry," I said. "We can talk after breakfast."

The next three days had the quality of a Pierneef landscape—reality blurred by an intensity of light.

There was a heat wave over the city. From dawn to dusk it shimmered across land and sea, deadening contour and sound, adding to the sense we had of being isolated from the everyday world. We stayed in the flat, the door closed and the 'phone off the hook.

It was not as lovers that we cut ourselves adrift. Sometimes, as I watched Morry pace about my rooms, or listened to him talk, I felt I was cooped up with an enemy rather than someone I loved. His need was to talk. He was like a diver who has come up too fast from the deeps, and talk was the decompression chamber to save him from the boiling of his own blood.

Over and over again he returned to the subject of Mark's death, recalling the details as if in that way he might expel the horror from his mind. Time and again he came back to the same questions: Who had really been responsible for the planning of the murder? Why at that time? Why in that place?

Yet I began to realize that, terrible as these memories were, he was using them to veil something more. He seemed to be veering away from something, and as I listened, I became convinced

162

that it concerned Bianca Ramsay.

At last I asked him point blank if he'd seen her. Yes, he said, and immediately tried to change the subject.

I persisted. "How is she?"

"All right, I suppose."

"But you saw her? Spoke to her?"

He scowled at me, not answering.

"Morry?"

"Well, go and see her yourself if you want to know how she is. I'm not stopping you." He got up from his chair and poured himself a tot of brandy, then set the glass aside without drinking.

"Bugger the whole lot of them."

"I want to know about Bianca."

He came back and stood over me. "Bianca is a bitch who doesn't give a damn for you or anyone else."

"She loved Mark."

"Don't fool yourself. She doesn't even want to know why he was killed."

"How can you say such a thing, Morry?"

"She told me."

"Did you have a fight with her, is that it?"

"You could say so."

"And?"

"She blames me for his death."

"Nonsense!"

"I am telling you what she said. People like me are in politics because we're neurotics. In it for kicks. She said Mark died because I have a bad conscience."

"Well, there's an element of truth in that. Whites go into politics because of conscience; that's no bad thing."

"Bianca didn't use the word 'white'." Morry's half-muttered words hardly reached me. He started to turn away and I caught hold of his arm.

"I want to know exactly what Bianca said to you."

"Nothing. . . ."

"Tell me!"

He stared down at me in anger and misery. "She said I was a failure, couldn't keep a wife, couldn't keep a home. She called me a bloody coloured man."

"So? Does a coloured man have a special sort of conscience?

Government issue or something, for use in his own group area?"

"He has a special sort of guilt, perhaps. The guilt of the try-for-white who got away with it, and has that much more going for him than his black half-brother."

I let go his arm carefully, because I felt that even an awkward movement might send him out through my front door for good.

"Morry," I said, "why the hell are you allowing Bianca to con you? You know who you are. Mark's friend, a good man, solid. So who gives a damn if your great-grandmother was white, black or yellow?"

His face went blank.

"Isn't that why you left me?" I said. "All that old grot about your mother and the baby that died?"

"Who told you about that?"

"The probation officer in Fordsburg."

"That was a breach of confidence."

This time it was my turn to say nothing, and after a moment he sighed. "I suppose you had a right to know."

"It would have saved us a lot of pain if you'd talked to me about it."

He sat down facing me and said slowly, "I thought . . . if we didn't have kids . . . I wanted to marry you so much, and if you couldn't have kids, then there'd be no harm."

"There was no harm, there is no harm, there can never be any harm."

He shook his head, and the tension in him warned me that I hadn't convinced him. I wasn't going to untangle the knots in him with one sure touch of my calloused palm. I said, "Leave all that, for the moment. Tell me what your immediate plans are. Do you want to go back to Jo'burg? What's in your mind?"

"I want to get back to work, Jess. I need to be busy."

"But not in the campaign."

"I'm out of that."

"Is the Party out?"

"Not completely. I think they'll give Tindall some support. I can't talk them out of that."

"Why should you?"

"Tindall's a crook."

"Why?"

"He has to be a crook, or a nut, to stand in Mark's place. I don't believe he's a nut, I think he's sharp."

"What does he hope to gain by standing?"

"A seat in Parliament."

"I shouldn't think he has a snowball's chance of winning."

"He just might. Sympathy vote."

"But . . . why does he want a seat at all? To commit murder, to win a seat in that three-ring circus? That makes him the nut of all nuts."

Morry was giving me the stubborn look of a man who talks nonsense and believes every word of it. "Mark's murder was planned, I'm convinced of it. I don't accept that psycho theory. I think there was a conspiracy. Mark could have been killed to make way for Tindall. And it's a certainty Mark's killer was wiped out so no one had a chance to question him."

"By a police officer?"

"By a police officer who happened to be standing in just the right place, at just the right time. He shot Calgut three times, you know. The third shot was close-range, right through the brain. He made sure."

"You're saying the police are in this conspiracy?"

"One policeman. That particular policeman." Morry reached into his hip pocket and pulled out a tattered newspaper cutting, which he flicked into my lap. "You remember I told you our meeting got broken up? Calgut was ringleader of that mob. Kray happened to be passing in a prowl car, stopped, dispersed the mob. Then Calgut shoots Mark; and again, it's Kray who happens along, just as Calgut is trying to escape, and puts three bullets in him."

"It could be coincidence."

"Yeah. Or it could be that Kray was detailed to silence Calgut, whenever or wherever he made his hit at Mark." Morry made a weary gesture. "Anyway, it's no good speculating. The official story's laid down. It's none of my business, I'm shot of it, now."

I didn't argue with him. I wanted him out of politics. For that reason I didn't go out and buy newspapers, thinking they'd give too clear a picture of what was building in the city. The radio reports were bad enough. The strikes had engulfed 40 firms, and the latest to be hit was a big containerization company on the

165

docks. If the unrest spread to the harbour, then it became a national crisis and they'd bring in the troops.

On the Friday morning I found a letter in my postbox. It was unstamped, and must have been dropped before dawn. I opened it standing in the garden.

The envelope held a single sheet of paper, pale green, with smudged black print. It was a price-list of herbal medicines, the sort of thing that is handed out at the African market in town. On the top, right-hand corner, rubber-stamped in mauve ink, were the words "B. Cele. Brakvlei."

I stood in the sun for some time, studying the list, and thinking. I was pretty sure that one of Ram Khoosal's minions must have dropped the thing in my box, and that B. Cele was the sangoma in Brakvlei.

It was a lead, perhaps, to Amyas Mochudi.

The problem was, what to do about it.

If I showed it to Morry, it could take him back into the search again. I didn't want that. I wanted him safe, with me, a long way from trouble.

I went quietly to the kitchen, found matches, and burned list and envelope together.

When I returned to the living-room, Morry asked if there'd been anything in the post.

"Only bills."

By late afternoon, the heat was intolerable. Morry said, "Let's get out of this hellish town for a couple of hours. We could take the car and drive down the coast, have dinner somewhere?"

We went to a new beach restaurant about 40 kilometres away. They had good seafood, and salad and cheese and coffee, and we took our own wine.

By common consent we left our problems behind. We talked a lot about my work, Morry always having been interested in it. I think he looked on artists with the same fascination he felt for sword-swallowers and fire-walkers.

From my work to his work, to what we'd done in the years we'd spent apart . . . we talked until the candles were discs of wax, and the proprietor yawned us to the door. Then we walked along the beach. It was utterly deserted, the tide far out, expos-

166

ing the green dripping skeletons of the reefs.

A long way from anywhere we turned from the damp sand and climbed up the dunes to a little hollow lined with coarse grass, and there we made love.

It was so quiet, out there. As he turned me in the crook of his arm, came over me, began slowly to enter me, I felt no doubt or fear any more. The surge of his body lifted me into safety.

XXIX

We had another 24 hours of peace, at my flat, and spent a good part of them in bed.

But at ten o'clock on Sunday morning, Morry made me put the telephone back on the hook. It rang almost at once and a male voice demanded to speak to Mr Maurice Faber.

"Who is it calling?"

"My name is Buddler, Mrs Faber."

"Of the police?"

"That's right. Is Mr Faber with you? I've been trying to reach him since last night. . . ."

"He's here."

"He should have notified me of his change of address."

"The caretaker at his flat has it."

"I can't spare men to chase about, and I can't guarantee the safety of people who don't tell me where they are."

I handed the receiver to Morry. After listening to some angry quacking, Morry apologized and said he'd give proper notice of any further moves.

"Is that all he wanted?" I said. "To tick you off? The man's in a rage."

"He's scared." Something in Morry's tone made me look at him.

"Of what?"

"Being steam-rollered. Nobody enjoys that."

"How do you know, you've never tried it?"

He grinned at me, but, after that, our seclusion was over.

Lisa Page 'phoned during the morning then Dick Tuttle, and at noon I answered the 'phone and it was Wally Brock, home from hospital.

Wally spoke to Maurice for a long time. I knew he was pressing Morry to rejoin the campaign. Morry listened, didn't say much, watched me from the corner of his eye; and I sat on my hands, so as not to snatch the receiver and tell Wally to leave us alone. But Morry made a promise to go to the Brock's house within the next few days.

"You're a fool," I told him. "Now they'll twist your arm to get back in."

"I must hand over in the proper way, Jess."

"Why? Why can't we just cut and run?"

"For one thing, the police wouldn't allow it. I'll be needed at the inquest."

So the thin little threads wrapped about us. On Sunday night we felt the web tremble to the weight of the spider.

I live in the top half of a double-storey building in a cul-de-sac. There's a big garden all round, with tall trees, and, since the downstairs tenants were overseas at that time, the property was pretty well isolated. The front door could be seen from the road, but the kitchen stairway was enclosed, and the back yard screened on all sides by high hedges.

About half-past eight on Sunday night, there was a knock at the back door.

I said, "Don't go". But Morry was already heading down the passage. I followed, trying to grab his arm.

The kitchen was in darkness. The upper part of the back door is glazed, and burglar-guarded.

Morry leaned towards me, muttering, "Where's the switch for the outside light?"

"Don't. They'll shoot through the glass. . . ."

"Where's the bloody switch?"

I reached round into the kitchen, felt for the knob and pressed it. Light flooded the area beyond the kitchen door, and at once a voice spoke urgently in Zulu. "Nkosi, help me."

"Who is it?"

"Pitso, Nkosi. From the factory."

We could see the figure of a man against the glass, leaning with his head drooped forward.

Morry called out, "Raise your hands over your head". Slowly the hands went up, empty, palms towards us.

"Don't let him in! He may have a gun!"

There was a bumping, slithering noise as the man sagged and fell; then silence. Morry started forward.

"No!" I yelled.

"It's all right, love. I know him. He's from Filey, Lofts. He worked with Hobeni."

"He's no business of ours."

"He's bleeding."

"Then call an ambulance."

I was wasting my breath. Morry was already at the door. I ran to the dresser and grabbed the carving knife. Morry jerked the door open and the man fell over the threshold. We lifted him inside and I slammed the door shut again. There was no one on the outer stairway.

Morry snapped on the kitchen light. The man at our feet was about 25, slight, nattily dressed in tan pants and a loose gold Hawaiian shirt, the latter blotched with blood. His tan and white shoes were mud-stained. He lay on his back, breathing stertorously. His face was so swollen that the eyes looked like razor cuts, the nose almost level with the cheeks, the lips protruding.

Morry fetched a towel and dipped it in cold water and held it against the man's skin. After a while the slitted eyes opened enough to show the glint of the pupils.

Morry said in Zulu, "Who hit you, Pitso?"

A bright pink tongue flickered between the lips. "Give me some water."

I brought a glassful, lifted the man's head and let him drink. The water dribbled from the corners of his mouth at first, but, after he'd swallowed a few mouthfuls, he lay back quietly, reached out a slow hand, took the wet towel from Morry and pressed it to his face.

"Is this place bugged?" he said.

Morry went over to the table and switched on the portable radio that stood there. The music of Abba swelled through the kitchen, and across it Morry repeated his question.

"Who hit you?"

"I don't know. Many." Pitso eased himself into a sitting position, his back against the dresser.

"How did it happen?"

"They jumped me. I was near my house and they came for me. Four, five. I could see they were going to kill me. I ran."

"Not quite fast enough?"

"Two caught and held me. The others beat me."

"Robbery?"

"They took my money." Pitso switched suddenly into English.

170

"Coupla rand. I didn't have much."

"Could you recognize any of them?"

"No."

"Who did you think it was?"

"I thought, maybe the Nanchuka gang. They work that area."

"So why didn't you go to the police?"

Pitso closed his eyes. He seemed to be thinking. I studied his face. The bruising was certainly recent. And his hands were damaged, too, cut and puffy, though the skin over the knuckles was unbroken. It looked as if Pitso had used them to shield his head, rather than to throw punches at his attackers. He smelled of rancid sweat.

"Why did you come here?" I said.

He opened his eyes and I saw the greed in them, as well as the terror. "I must have money. I must get out of town."

"How much do you need?"

"Twenty rand is okay. I can get to Empangeni. I have friends there."

"Empangeni's north," said Morry. "Aren't you from the south, from Transkei? You spoke Xhosa at the factory."

"It's no good if I go home. They'll be waiting for me."

"Who will?"

A smile brushed the swollen lips. "Whoever did me over, boss."

Morry pulled a chair towards him and sat down. "You didn't go to the police. Are you afraid of them?"

A shrug.

"Why are you afraid?"

Silence.

"Was it the police who beat you?"

"No." The word was vehement.

"So who, then?"

"All I know, they asked me, 'Where's Hobeni?'"

"And did you tell them?"

"I don't know where he is!" The man ran the tip of his tongue round his mouth. "I told you that, when you came by the factory."

"So you did."

A sideways glance. "I thought, maybe you found him yourself?"

171

"No, I haven't found him." Morry leaned forward. "Pitso, I think you're a lucky man. Five tsotsis set on you, and you're still alive to ask questions."

"Only because the children came."

"What children?"

"Those who follow Hobeni."

I felt my heart begin to thud under my ribs. This man with his swollen face and desperate eyes was infinitely dangerous to us, that I knew. The kitchen was full of the smell of fear and blood.

"The children who follow Hobeni," said Morry softly. "Why should they help you?"

"They know me. They know I'm Hobeni's friend, too."

"And how did it happen they were able to save you? How did they get to you in time?"

"I can tell you." Pitso raised eager hands. "I was walking up the hill, to my house. I lodge, you understand, I have a room. The road is dark, no lights. I became wise to someone following behind me. I saw men coming, and I started to run. They caught me, held me. Then some started to punch me all over. I screamed out. There were two boys in the roadway, and they began to call and to whistle. Others came, young, all of them. They closed in like dogs about those who were hitting me, till they let me go. They took me down to the railway station, put me on the train. Aiee, ai! Without those children, I was dead."

Morry watched him thoughtfully. "Pitso, you want twenty rand from me. For that much money I want to know why you chose me out of all your Mlungu friends, to ante up?"

"The children told me to find you."

"How did they know my name?"

"I don't know. How do you expect me to say? I am half killed; they told me, go to the house of Mr Ramsay, talk to his friend, talk to Mr Faber, he will save you."

"And you went to Ramsay's house?"

"Yes. I went there, but not to go inside. I was stopped at the gate."

"Who by?"

"The man who came to the factory with you."

"Tindall?"

172

"I think maybe that's the name. Small, like a mouse, with spectacles. He met me at the gate. He told me the police were watching the house, they had someone in the garden there. He said I shouldn't go in there."

"Why are you afraid of the police?"

"Because of Hobeni. Everyone is looking for Hobeni. First you come to the factory. Then, yesterday morning, the police went there asking for Hobeni and for me, but I was off shift. How long can I keep my job if these people come there about me? Then tonight I'm beaten up, by people asking 'Where's Hobeni?' If I go to the police, they won't help me. They'll think I know something, they'll hold me, maybe a long time. And when I come out, if I come out . . . those others will still be waiting for me. I want to get out, boss. I must be out of here."

His eyes were glittering, and for the first time I felt he was speaking the truth.

"Pay him," I said, "and let him go."

Morry pulled out his wallet. "Listen, Pitso. I don't know anything about Hobeni, and I don't care. I don't care much about you, either, but I'll give you twenty rand, to get to a doctor and get yourself fixed up." He held out the notes.

Pitso scrambled to his feet, and took the money. His fingers trembled as he tucked it into a purse inside his belt. "Thanks." He flexed his shoulders a little, a scared animal preparing to make its last wild break for life.

"Wait," I said. I ran through to the bedroom and snatched up a shirt of Morry's, a sweater, a long knitted scarf of my own and a couple of white hankies. I added a bottle of disinfectant and some Aspirin, and took it all back to the kitchen.

"Change your shirt," I said, "and wrap your face up, as if you had toothache."

Pitso did as he was bid, tying a handkerchief round his lower jaw and mouth, as blacks do when they have a tooth drawn, and then winding the scarf round his head. It helped to hide the bruises. He took off his blood-stained shirt, put on the clean one. It sagged over his shoulders, making him look like just another shabby manual worker. The medicines and the stained shirt I put into a plastic carrier.

We took him down to the back yard. The gate there gives onto open ground, recently cleared for building. He slipped away into the darkness without a sound.

"What do you think?" said Morry.

We were back in the kitchen. The radio was still playing, and the air still smelled of Pitso's sweat.

"A liar," I answered. "The only time he convinced me was when he said he wants to leave town."

"Yes, he's terrified. He's been beaten up, he's terrified, he wants to get out—yet he comes here. Why?"

"To get money."

"Why should he expect a handout from me? No, there's something else." Morry leaned over and dimmed the music. "Pitso's a punk. I don't believe he was ever Hobeni's friend. But perhaps he thought he could turn a fast rand.

"Let's say he worked with Hobeni and knew something of his character. Knew he was involved with black power, knew he had a following among the township kids. Hobeni disappears, and, soon after, Mark Ramsay and I come calling at the factory. Pitso begins to think that Hobeni's whereabouts may have a market value. So on his free Sunday, he sets about trying to trace Hobeni.

"He goes to the youngsters in the area where Hobeni used to live. Asks questions. The kids see through him, and rough him up, as a warning to keep his nose out of Hobeni's affairs. But Pitso, scared as he is, is a very greedy man. He decides on one last throw to get money out of me. He goes to Mark's home, meaning to get my address, meets Tindall at the gate. He asks for my address and Tindall gives it. Goes to my flat, gets redirected here, tells us his story about being beaten by thugs. Asks about Hobeni, gets nothing."

"And leaves," I said. "So now we can forget him."

Morry stared through me. "I don't think that was the way of it," he said. "I don't think the kids beat him."

"Somebody did."

"Yes. And it was a pro job. Face battered, arms, hands. Ribs kicked, you could see the boot marks when he took off his shirt. But no damage to the vital organs. In the townships, a hiding like that is a warning, or an inducement. I think Pitso was gone

174

over, and then sent here, by some persons, some organization, that wants very much to lay hands on Hobeni. Doesn't it strike you how many people want Hobeni? Us, his creditors, the police, and others." Morry moved restlessly about the kitchen. "So what's our next move? My nose tells me the smart thing would be to 'phone the police at once."

Then the fear, which I'd been thrusting aside all these past days, began to close on me, like a huge hand squeezing my chest. I felt my skin go cold and clammy; and Morry, catching sight of me, came across in consternation.

"Jess, love, what is it?"

"Don't go to the police."

"Darling, if I speak to anyone, it will only be Colonel Buddler."

I shook my head. It was no good trying to explain, because Morry had never been arrested, or interrogated, or spent nights wondering whether anyone outside knew or cared what was happening to him.

"I'll get you some brandy," he said, and went and fetched it. But before I had time to drink it, we heard a car drive up to the front door.

Morry walked to a window and peered down.

"It's that tit, Tindall."

"If we don't answer, maybe he'll go away."

"Not him, he's the persistent type."

Sure enough, a steady hammering set up. Morry went down to deal with it.

XXX

MORRY HAD SPOKEN with such dislike of Tindall, that I'd been expecting a real durr. In fact, he wasn't bad looking. He was small and tidy, even dapper in his young executive gear. His hair had been shaped by a good barber, and his tan looked as if he worked at it. The eyes behind thick lenses were blue-grey and mild. He held a canvasser's pack under his right arm.

Smiling, I said, "Sure, Mr Tindall, I'll vote for you".

He blinked at me. "Oh, I didn't intend . . . I mean . . . are you one of my voters? You are Mrs Faber, are you not?"

"Yes, to both questions. D'you want to see me, or Morry?"

"Both, as a matter of fact."

He had a slow, almost stammering way of speech. It seemed incredible that this myopic mouse might occupy a seat in Parliament. He perched on the edge of a chair and looked at me.

"I expect you have guessed why I'm here?"

"Not really."

"I want Morry . . . Mr Faber . . . back in the campaign. As my manager. Of course I would g-guarantee all expenses."

Ten o'clock on Sunday night and he dropped in to ask favours. I began to see why Morry found him infuriating.

"It's quite impossible." Morry sounded dangerous, but Tindall ignored the signals.

"Would you mind explaining your reasons?"

"It's a matter of personal disinclination."

"You mean the fact I'm standing, upsets you?" Tindall fingered his spectacles. "I can understand that the circumstances of my nomination look like opportunism. I do assure you that I dislike the rôle. It's very distasteful to a man of my temperament to be in the public eye."

Morry shrugged. "So why did you stand?"

Tindall regarded him thoughtfully. "I committed my head to the block," he said, "because I was, for a time, clean out of my mind. Mark was my friend for twenty years. It just stuck in my throat that a chap like Colley Burman might get in unopposed."

I decided Tindall was smarter than he looked. No other argument could have got to Morry, at that time.

"Well, so you had your reasons. It still doesn't change my plans. I'm going back to Jo'burg as soon as the cops close the case."

"That means this week."

"If that's the way it goes."

"The case will be closed this week." Tindall moved back in his chair. Behind his glasses his eyes were bland, watching Morry.

"You sound very sure. Have you special knowledge, or are you guessing?"

"Knowledge. Colonel Buddler told Bianca she would be free to leave Durban after the end of this week."

"So you're still staying in the house?"

"Yes. She was nervous. Her sister's husband went home right after the funeral, you know, and for two women and a child to remain there alone, even with police protection. . . ."

"Is Buddler providing that?"

"Oh yes. And of course he has kept Bianca abreast of the main events. The inquest will be held this week, and he is confident that the verdict will be uncontroversial."

"Meaning?"

"The court will find that Calgut was the sole agent in the murder. He has a long record of anti-social behaviour. . . ."

"A psychopath, yes. That doesn't mean he acted alone." During Tindall's last speech, Morry's face had been growing bleaker and bleaker. I wanted to warn him not to let Tindall con him; because that was what was happening. Tindall was quietly, deliberately needling Morry into losing his temper; and for Morry, I knew, being angry was right next door to being concerned, and involved.

Now he said fiercely, "You don't have to swallow that tale that Calgut was a loner. It just happens to be the line that suits the police. God, you'd think people would have the sense at least to wait for a coroner's verdict. . . ."

"I don't think Buddler is pressing for an early closure." Tindall sounded meditative. "He just states there will be one. And really, I don't see what we can do about it. It's a *fait accompli.*

177

Suits your book, anyway, doesn't it? You'll be free to leave for Jo'burg . . . unless you change your mind, and join my campaign."

That 'my' did it. Morry swung round. "If you must know, Tindall, I think it was a bloody irresponsible thing to do, to stand, and I don't happen to feel an irresponsible action should be shored up by a lot of Party money, and Party work. Is that plain enough?"

"But—there are no Party funds in my campaign. I've raised private donations, and put in quite a large sum myself. . . ."

"What do you mean by 'private donations'? Did you approach Party members? Party sympathizers?"

"Well . . . some . . . yes."

"Then how in hell can you say you're not tapping Party sources?"

Tindall's expression didn't change, but colour began to burn under his tan. "No doubt you would rather have Colley Burman as MP for Parkhaven?"

"I'm afraid Parkhaven is going to get Burman, whether you oppose him or not."

"That is an offensive remark."

"It's factual."

"Dick Tuttle and others say I have a goodish chance of beating Burman. My canvass returns are very good, and I have a lot of Party support. Walter Brock will be helping me, soon as he's fit."

Both of them were shouting, now. I got up and moved between their chairs. "Mr Tindall, you may be right in all you say, but you're wasting your time. When Mark was killed, my husband suffered a great loss, as we all did. You've reacted in your way. I think you should allow us to react in ours."

"Are you asking me to leave?"

"Yes. I'm sorry."

He stood up, pulled off his glasses and rubbed his eyes. "Mrs Faber, surely you're not so naïve as to expect fair play, at this stage of our history? You won't get it. I want Morry in my campaign. I don't ask him to like me. Just to help me win."

He put his glasses on again and started for the door. He'd almost reached it when Morry shouted, "Tindall!"

"What?"

178

"Tell me, why did you send Pitso round here?"

"Pitso?" For a moment he looked blank. Then, "Oh, you mean the man from the factory?"

"I mean the black spiv with beat-up features. He said he'd spoken to you. Why did you send him here?"

"But I didn't. I merely warned him not to enter Mark's garden, because there were police there. I thought he was drunk."

"He'd been hammered half unconscious."

"Had he? It was dark, you know. . . ."

"But you recognized him?"

"Yes, I knew he was the man from the factory, Hobeni's friend. And he came here?"

"He did."

"That's very interesting." Tindall moved slowly back into the room. "What did he want?"

"Before we discuss that, there are a couple of things I'd like cleared up."

"Well?"

"You seem to have Colonel Buddler's confidence."

"I've talked to him, on several occasions. I witnessed a murder. I expect a certain amount of questioning."

"How do you like the colonel?"

"Like? He's been frank with me, even friendly."

"Doesn't that surprise you?"

"In a way, I suppose it does."

"In these cosy chats with Buddler, did you discuss political issues?"

"Only in a general way, in so far as they might form the background to Mark's death."

"You mean Buddler thinks there could be a political motive?"

"He didn't say that."

"Do you think he accepts the line that Calgut acted alone?"

Tindall shifted uneasily. "I must admit . . . I get the feeling he's unhappy."

"Why?"

"Well, naturally he wouldn't tell me that."

"Do you think he suspects a conspiracy?"

"It's possible."

"Political?"

"Possibly."

179

"If that was so, wouldn't you expect there to have been some poking around by the Security Police?"

"I . . . yes. I would."

"So would I. Instead, the case is going to be closed, if the colonel's right. And he should know."

Tindall said nothing.

"Well . . ." Morry shrugged. "Let's leave that, for the moment. Let's get back to Pitso. He called here about two hours ago. He said he visited Mark's place. As he was about to go inside, you stopped him and warned him there were police around. Why did you do that? And don't give me that 'thought he was drunk,' line. You could see he'd been beaten up. Couldn't you?"

"I suppose . . . I thought . . . I thought if he went in, he'd be arrested. It was a . . . spur of the moment reaction."

"Was Pitso going in by the main gate?"

"No, the back. I happened to be there, in the garden."

"Was Buddler in the house at the time?"

"Yes, as a matter of fact he was. Talking to Bianca."

"Did you want to prevent Pitso from meeting Buddler?"

Tindall chewed his lip a while. "Yes. I think I did."

"And you sent him to my flat. Why?"

"I . . . thought he might know something useful."

"What about?"

"Mark's death."

The words fell quietly. As Morry's expression sharpened, Tindall added almost casually, "Did he tell you anything?"

Morry shook his head. "He wanted money. We gave him enough to see him home."

"Oh. I see. Perhaps it's just as well."

"What does that mean?"

"Well, I didn't trust him, did you?"

"No."

"Who do you think he's working for?" The voice was still gentle, but I caught a note of tension in it.

"You tell me," said Morry. "Buddler. The Security Police. Subversive elements. Himself."

"If he's a police informer, then presumably he was on his way to report to Buddler when I warned him off. That's rather ironic."

"Very," said Morry drily.

"Do you think he was?"

"No." Morry's eyes were bright and hard and watchful. "I think Pitso was sent here by the people who killed Mark. I think they want to know how to reach Hobeni. I told Pitso we don't give a damn about Hobeni. I hope he believed me, because by now he will have reported back to his employers. If he believed me, we'll be left in peace."

"And if he didn't?"

"Then possibly, you and I and some others may be on the chop-list."

"Why is Hobeni so important?"

"I have no idea. I don't want to know. I am leaving town. I think I mentioned. Maybe you should do the same."

Tindall looked like a startled rabbit. "Me? How can I, I'm the candidate."

"Of course. I forgot. You could withdraw, though. It's possible to withdraw."

"Not in my view."

Morry said nothing for a moment, then leaned forward. "Tindall, I hope you feel strongly enough to risk your neck; because that's what you're doing."

"If you must know, I'm scared out of my mind."

"Then pull out. Nobody's going to hold it against you."

Tindall shook his head. A half smile touched his face. "Tell me one thing, Morry. Do you really suspect me of being a party to Mark's murder?"

"Well . . . I had considered it."

"Why? Just because I'm standing? That's supposed to be a motive? Jesus Christ." He broke into sudden, crackling laughter. "You're out of your skull, man."

"That could be. Another question for you. Why do you think Buddler is having the Ramsay house watched?"

"Obviously to protect Bianca and Nick."

"But Calgut is dead, so technically the danger is past."

Tindall frowned impatiently. "It merely confirms that Buddler doesn't believe Calgut acted alone."

"And nor do you?"

"I have thought from the outset that there was more than one person involved. That's why I'm staying on in the house.

181

I've tried to get Bianca to leave, but she can be very stubborn."

"Where would you have her go?"

"To her brother's home in Johannesburg." Tindall answered without hesitation. "He's a fat cat, owns a property with a ten-foot wall round it, guard dogs and burglar alarms. Bianca and the child would be safer there than here."

"So how do we persuade Bianca?"

"God knows. She's in a dreadful state, still. Wants to stay in the house because she was happy there with Mark. Well, you know. She's not rational."

"You can say that again."

Then Tindall said a surprising thing. "You're the only person she might listen to, Morry."

"Me? Boy, she threw me out on my ear. She hates my guts."

"No, she doesn't. Bianca's trouble is being a rich girl. She's spoiled, and can't get on with people. She's always been jealous of you. She resents the influence you had over Mark. But she respects your opinion."

Morry gave an odd little jerk of the head, as if he was refusing a gift he wanted to accept.

"Maybe we should get Buddler to persuade her."

"He's already tried, I think. She won't listen to him."

"Well, let it be. Last question. Did you mention Pitso's call to the gallant colonel?"

"No. Do you think I should?"

"I think someone should. Leave it to me, if you like. I'll 'phone him tomorrow morning, and tell him."

Tindall left soon after. and Morry and I went to bed. Neither of us slept much. The air over the city was turgid with heat, lying like a warm sponge on the skin. I stayed topside of the sheets and listened to Morry tossing about. When I did doze off, I dreamed of Pitso's swollen face, or Tindall's eyes shrewd behind the spectacles.

About four in the morning, I heard helicopters overhead.

I got out of bed and walked onto the porch and saw three of them, their port and starboard lights winking. As I watched, they arched apart, two heading northwards and one inland.

Morry came and joined me. "Trouble in the townships."

"Looks like it."

By four-thirty, the ambulances were coming past on their way from the north coast to Queen Elizabeth Hospital. We could hear the sirens wailing down the main trunk road.

At half-past five, Charlie Cameron appeared on our doorstep.

XXXI

I'D NEVER MUCH liked Charlie, but I'd always admired his nerve. I'd seen him grubbing after his stories under a hail of snubs, official warnings and gangland threats, and, each time, bringing in the facts. I'd seen him tired, evasive, abusive, and stone drunk, but never beaten—until that morning.

He came into our living-room and stood wrinkling his eyes as if the light hurt him. He was dirty and dishevelled. I waited for the usual snide, cocky greeting, but it didn't come and I realized that for once Charlie was out of words.

Morry mixed him a whisky and milk, which he drank in one tilt of the wrist. Setting down the empty glass he said.

"Hell broke loose. I've been out there all night."

"Kwa Mashu?"

"All round. All the townships."

"Police reports?"

"Been there myself."

Now it is strictly illegal for whites to go into the black ghettoes without a permit, and no white man in his right white mind would do so at night; but Charlie is not definably normal. Now he flopped down in one of our chairs.

"I didn't think I'd get out, I'll tell you."

Morry refilled his glass, which he held cupped in grimy hands.

"Yesterday afternoon," he said, "Sunday, my day off, I went to talk to a chap I know. Works in Bantu Admin. and gives me a tip off from time to time. That was . . . about half-past three. We chatted for an hour or so. His home is in Clairville. Other side of town from Kwa Mashu.

"Five o'clock or so, I climbed into my car and started home. I had to pass the big hostel for single men, up on Umdusi Road. As I got near it, I saw a crowd of men standing there, both sides of the track. They weren't armed or anything. Just standing. I dunno why, but I thought, 'Trouble. I'm gonna be stoned.' I'd locked the doors and windows of the car, of course. But I slowed right down. Kept going.

184

"Suddenly they swung round in two horns and began to close in on me. I didn't stop, just kept on, slow and straight. I knew if I so much as touched one of them, they'd let me have it. All I could see was faces leaning down to look in at me, and palms pressed against the glass. The car was rocking, you know. I thought, Christ, I'm gonna get killed, out of the blue I'm gonna get killed. Some of them were standing in the roadway. I'd have hit them if I'd gone on. I stopped the car.

"It was dead quiet. No shouting. I felt that if anyone shouted, they'd go berserk. As if they were waiting for a signal. Then I thought, Hell, so long as I'm in trouble, I may as well try to get out of it. I keep my press sticker in the shelf over the dashboard, and I picked it up and turned it so they could see. And I put up my other fist in the black power salute.

"There was a great big bugger beside the driving window, and he bent down and stared at my hands. Then he laughed. I could see these big teeth and the open mouth. Next minute he waved his arm. The men in front jumped back out of my way. I drove on, nice and steady until I'd passed them, and then I went like a bat out of hell for the main road." Charlie paused and took a swig of his drink.

"And then of course you went home," said Morry.

"Like hell! I 'phoned the paper and told them what happened, and then I drove round the boundaries of Clairville, taking a long, careful look. Several times, I saw big crowds. Just waiting, it looked like. And down by the police station I could see a whole lot of Hippo trucks lined up, waiting too.

"I decided to drive over to Umlazi. I'm on good terms with the black police there. I didn't get to talk to them, though. Things were really crazy there, I saw a stinking great cloud of smoke, and the fire engines were clanging up and down the main road like yo-yos with bells on. A man told me it was the Zambesi Road schoolhouse burning. Someone set it alight with petrol bombs. And they also got two beerhalls and another school, last night.

"So then I started my private tour. I drove right round the ring roads, visiting all the townships. In Lamontville there was faction-fighting between Xhosas and Zulus. Seven or eight guys got dead. The story there was, it was a straight tribal clash, settling old scores."

Charlie fumbled out a cigarette and lit it, sucking in the smoke

185

greedily. "I drove north. Clermont. Chesterville. Kwa Mashu. Took me all night. In each township, there was trouble. And each place gave a different reason. Some said it was tribal stuff, another lot said it was because of schools policy, another, the bus fares had gone up and they were going to start a boycott.

"But the worst of all was the shack-dwellers . . . up beyond Kwa Mashu, you know it. There's 100,000 of them up there, among those rotten pondokkies. And they were gathered at the top of the hill. While I watched, they started to move, slowly down the hillsides, like lava flowing. Not armed or anything. Just moving, flowing together, building up. I got out of there fast."

Charlie was sitting hunched in his chair like a small bird. He fixed his eyes on us with feverish intensity. "You know what scares me? I can't find the reason for all this. Oh, I got lots of answers, but they weren't the truth. It's as if someone has been walking round a great big pyre, lighting a twig here and there. Easily beaten out, see. But what if someone throws in the big torch? Then the whole lot goes up. . . ."

Morry said, "Was there no common factor to the troubles?"

"One. All over the township approaches, on the walls, alongside the bus ranks, the railway stations. Scrawled in the mud, in the dust, painted, daubed . . . just the letter M."

"For Mochudi?"

"I think so."

"Do you think he's behind this?"

"Don't know. Don't effing know. I can't even get a glimmer."

Morry moved to stand over Charlie's chair. "And the police reaction?"

"Confused. Uncertain. In a way, it's under-reaction."

"How d'you mean?"

"Well, last time I covered a riot situation was the Cape, in '77. The police were there in droves. Camouflage-dress, riot arms, tear gas, Hippo trucks. Bloody well organized. I'd have expected the same here, they've had enough warning. But the pattern of police activity is irregular. Umlazi is well policed, so is Kwa Mashu, but, at other points around the city, there seems to be very little protection. The technique in a riot is you try for quick, firm action to smother it before it takes hold. But I didn't see that. I got the feeling, God help us, that there's muddle in high places."

186

"Did you check the hospitals?"

"Yes. Casualties much higher than a routine weekend. Knife wounds, panga wounds, fractures."

"Gunshot?"

"Not yet. Not that I could discover."

There was a short silence. Then Morry said, "Why did you come to me?"

"Because . . . you remember, after your meeting was broken up, I told you we weren't being allowed to print half we wanted to?"

"Yes."

"Same thing now. I went into the office an hour ago. The place is lousy with police. Can you credit it? The assistant news editor intercepted me and told me to get the hell out, because I was in trouble, someone saw me round Kwa Mashu. As if it matters who broke the regulations, at a time like now. Listen Morry. I want to tell you what I think. In case anything happens to me, understand?"

"Yes?"

"Remember that night at the café, we talked about the Summit, the Black Summit?"

"Yes."

"Did you know Mochudi is to attend?"

"I heard he'd been invited . . . no thanks to you I heard."

"Well don't gripe about that now. He's asked to the Summit. And his name is on all the walls. He's the big cheese, to all those blacks out there. They're pinning their faith on the Summit. They're pinning their faith on Mochudi. They're keyed up to desperation point, dry powder, waiting to be lit. See?"

"So?"

"If Mochudi comes, boy, and anything happens to him? The way it happened to Mark Ramsay! Then God help Durban."

Morry shook his head slowly. "You think it all ties together? Mark . . . and this. . . ."

"Yes. I can't give you proof. Just the feeling in my gut. Did Mark know about Mochudi coming here?"

"Yes."

"Then perhaps he learned something he shouldn't." Charlie's teeth showed in something not a smile. "You think it over, Faber boy. If you know anything, if you have any ideas, anything true, pure, lovely, or any fucking use, you think on those things,

187

because we don't have much time." He pulled himself to his feet. "I'm going home to sleep."

As he started for the door, Morry went after him. "If I find anything, I'll call you."

"What for, man?" Charlie's voice hovered between weariness and anger. "What can I do? Don't you get the message? You'll need a bigger gun than me."

Morry saw him out. I stayed on the sofa and felt a despair so intense I wanted to throw back my head and howl like a hyena. Morry came and sat beside me, watched me, saying nothing.

"All right," I said. "I know. You have to go back."

He slid his hand inside my blouse and kissed me. "Listen, darling . . . you go to Jo'burg and wait for me there."

"Don't be a silly sod. I'm staying. But I'd like to know what you hope to achieve."

He didn't answer at once, but sat looking at me with an expression of great pleasure and tenderness. Then, leaning back in his corner of the sofa, he said : "Remember, a little while ago, you asked me what I'd do if there was trouble? And I said I'd have to play it by ear? I wasn't just evading the issue.

"Back at the start of the campaign, Mark and I spent a lot of time talking. He wanted to analyse the situation. He was looking at things, looking into himself, for his credo, if you like.

"He believed we're moving towards social anarchy. That the things people rely on—laws and institutions—will be eroded, but not at an even rate. Some parts of the apartheid structure will collapse before others. Some parts of the country will be affected before others. In those parts—particularly the black townships close to big cities—the established authority will just not be able to retain control. It's happening already, in Soweto.

"This breakdown of the established way of things will bring certain responses from whites. A small section will try to meet anarchy with anarchy. Call for dictatorial powers, set up groups like the Vigilantes, use violence.

"A second, much larger section, will fall into what Mark called the lethargy of crisis . . . paralysed and unable to take any constructive action.

"A third group will exploit the situation for their own gain. Into that group you can lump the criminals, gun-runners and currency sharks, and the political lice that suck on any sick animal. They'll be behind the demos, the street riots and the urban terrorism.

"In a short time—months rather than years—we will be into a spiral of growing unrest in the cities, wider strikes, greater violence. We could be headed for the death spin.

"But Mark also believed there can be a fourth response. That as the fabric of apartheid frays, as the confusion and the discord build up, people will be approachable. They'll be searching for something to replace the old, moribund system. They'll be looking for some sort of initiative. And, above all, they'll be looking for individual leadership . . . for the men and women, white or black, rich or poor, in or out of the establishment, who can lead them."

"As Mark could have done."

"As Mark could have done."

Morry had risen to his feet and was standing looking down at me. The sullen, lost expression of the past few days had gone, and his face was eager.

"That's what Mark would have told you. He'd have said this is a time for individual action. Each of us will have to act by his own light. A few people, scattered across the country, are going to make a life-or-death difference to the outcome of events."

Morry went over to the box where I kept cigarettes, talking as he went.

"Mark rode his hobby-horses hard," he said, "and he was looking for leaders, particularly among the blacks. That's why he was so anxious to trace Amyas Mochudi, a radical black who could lead young black activists. He was determined to find Mochudi. I told him to forget it, we had other things to attend to, but I'll lay any odds you like he didn't listen to me.

"I think he spent his last days secretly trying to reach Mochudi or his brother Don. I think somehow he got hold of information about them. I think that's why he was killed."

"You mean they fixed his murder?"

"Not necessarily." Morry came to stand in front of me. "Listen, Jess, either Mark was killed by a madman, in a motiveless, crazy act; or he was killed for sane and logical reasons. I'm arguing there was a motive for his death, and that that motive tied up with Mark himself; what he did, what he was, what he knew. If that's true, then it's no good looking at the murder in isolation, you have to hold it against Mark's life, and particularly his recent life. Umh?"

"The campaign?"

"The campaign was one part of it, the surface level. But deeper than that, far more crucial in Mark's mind, was the black power struggle. Look at recent events, look at the key issues around us now. The labour unrest, Hobeni was involved. The youth gangs. Hobeni was said to be a king pin. The Black Summit, Mochudi was being urged to attend. The unrest in the townships. Mochudi's name is on every wall. Those two men lie at the heart of whatever is going on in this city. I think that in trying to reach them, Mark cut across forbidden ground. He found something so explosive that someone decided to kill him.

"Forget the official version, for a moment. Forget the idea that Calgut was a lone agent, and consider him as a trigger man in a conspiracy. It provides an answer to one of the key questions, which is, 'Why shoot a man in a nomination court?' The answer could well be that Calgut was instructed to do so, because that was the first and only chance available.

"I've been turning that thought over, putting together what few facts I have. Colonel Buddler told me Calgut slept at his ma's house on the Sunday night. He worked as a shift man with the Cleansing Department, but apparently he was off duty that Monday morning because he was home at nine-thirty, when his mother went out to buy bread. She came back to find him gone. Now it would have taken Calgut at least twenty minutes to travel from his house to the Government buildings on the Esplanade. Say he got there by a quarter to ten. By that time, we'd been inside the building for some time."

"Why couldn't Calgut have waited until the hearing was over? If he'd done that, he could have shot Mark in the street, with a far better chance of getting away."

"He couldn't wait. What does a candidate do, straight after nomination . . . particularly if he's into publicity, as Mark was?"

"Talks to the press?"

"Right. He talks to the press and tries to give them a statement they can blow up big. Headline in the evening paper, follow-up next morning. Now, when Mark and I arrived at the court, Timmins of the *Standard* came up to us and asked Mark if he had anything good, and Mark said, 'Yes, front-page stuff'. I thought

190

he was just kidding, but now I think he meant exactly what he said. He had a really big story. He was excited that morning."

"If he knew something so vital, wouldn't he have told someone? The police? You, at least?"

"Perhaps he didn't have time to tell me. Remember, I was with Mark the Sunday before he died, right up until eleven o'clock that night. He didn't mention anything to me. His manner was quite normal, he seemed to be concentrating on the election. But when I went to collect him on Monday morning, he was quiet, and seemed to be puzzling something out.

"No doubt in time he'd have discussed it with me. But you know what Mark was, he liked to take the risks—and the kudos —himself.

"The way I see it, he picked up his information, whatever it was, late on Sunday night, or in the early hours of Monday morning. Someone—call him X—got in touch with him. It's unlikely they'd use the telephone for that sort of deal. I'd guess the informer called round at Mark's house, that he was seen to do so, and that set Mark up as a target for murder.

"Calgut was chosen to carry it out. He was a listed psychopath, with a record of violence. He'd been a mercenary in Angola and owned a rapid-fire machine-pistol. Most important, he was known to have a hatred of liberal politics. If he shot Mark, people would be likely to accept the killing as the work of a madman.

"But Calgut was also a loudmouth. He had a habit of boasting in the pubs. So if he was used as the murder agent, then he had to be silenced straight after. He had to be killed. That second killing was duly carried out, by the one sort of man nobody would question, a cop."

My skin crept, and I shivered, but Morry took no notice, rapt in the twists of his own argument. "I believe that Mark got his information very early on Monday morning. The informer was seen at his house. Someone was told. The murder was set up. That would take time. A gunman—Calgut—had to be selected, located, and briefed. Two gunmen, in fact, if you count in Calgut's killer. Arrangements like that couldn't be made on the telephone, there would have to be meetings, someone would have to talk to Calgut. That person must have called at his home while his mother was out, because he took the gun with him when he left, he didn't come back for it.

"Calgut didn't set out until nine-thirty. By the time he reached the Government buildings, we were in the anteroom of the court. Mark had to be silenced before the court rose at eleven, before he gave his story to the press. Calgut moved in just after ten o'clock, shot Mark, and tried to make his escape. He got as far as the main entrance, where his own killer was waiting for him."

"It's . . . so grotesque."

"Yes, it is. But so is our world. It's grotesque to hijack a plane-load of people, to spray bullets through a room full of school kids, to post a letter-bomb to someone you never saw in your life. We live in a diseased, grotesque world. The only difference this time was, we knew the victim."

"You're suggesting a conspiracy that included a police officer. That would be. . . ."

"Front-page news."

Another picture, at once simple and terrible, was forming in my mind.

"You think an informer visited Mark's home, and was seen there by this . . . gang. You mean the informer was followed to Mark's house."

"Possibly. Or perhaps the the witness was already there."

"Tindall?"

"It's possible. Tindall was staying there, he could have seen or heard the visitor, and passed the information on. He could have done that innocently, or deliberately. He could have been a party to Mark's death."

"Do you believe he was?"

"I thought so at first. Now I'm not sure."

"And Bianca, she's in great danger, we must warn her. . . ."

"Bianca will not listen to warnings."

"The police? If we went to them?"

"Calgut was shot by a policeman. A section of the police could be involved. We don't know which section."

"Then what do we do?"

Morry glanced at the doorway to the porch, where daylight was already beginning to glow. He said slowly, "This is point of no return for us, Jess. Either we talk to nobody, cut and run; or we take up where Mark left off."

"We? You'd come with me, if I left."

He met my eyes. "Yes."

"And if we stay, what will you do?"

"'Phone Buddler. Ask for an interview. Tell him that Pitso called on us. Watch his reaction. And after that, I think we should talk to Mark's black friends."

"All right," I said. "Go on and 'phone Buddler."

XXXII

MORRY PUT THROUGH a call to Colonel Buddler at seven o'clock. He 'phoned again at hourly intervals, and each time was told the colonel was not in his office.

It wasn't hard to guess why. The eight o'clock news carried a guarded story of the township rioting. At eleven o'clock we learned that the situation in Umlazi and Kwa Mashu was calm, and there was no cause for alarm . . . a sure sign that there was.

At noon, Buddler arrived.

He drove up to the house in an old Buick, evidently his own. There was no one with him. I knew from past experience that policemen ride in pairs when they hope to con you.

Buddler climbed slowly out of the car. I studied him from my window. He was wearing slacks and a camouflage jacket, both very dirty. His face was caked in dust and sweat. He stood looking about him until he saw the garden tap and then he walked over and turned it on and began to splash water on his face and throat. I went downstairs and opened the front door.

"Come inside, I'll lend you a towel."

He swung round, wiping his sleeve over his forehead. Came towards me.

"Mrs Faber?"

"Yes."

"My name is Buddler. Your husband 'phoned me."

"Yes. Come upstairs."

He followed me, quick and light on his feet. I left him in the bathroom and went and turned on the coffee percolator, then joined Morry in the living-room. Buddler appeared a couple of minutes later.

His face, clear of grime, was thin and sallow. Light-brown eyes surveyed us with the usual cop coldness, the long mouth, pouched at the corners, was set in the usual cop patience. But under this formal mask was a strangeness that I couldn't at once analyse. He sat down, accepted a cup of coffee, and asked briskly what was the purpose of Morry's 'phone-call.

"I could have come to your office, Colonel, you didn't have to come here."

"No, well, it's on my way. I'm going home for a bath and sleep."

"You've been in the townships?"

"Ja."

"Bad?"

"Contained. Your call, Mr Faber?"

"I had a visitor, last night. I thought perhaps you should hear about it."

"Does it relate to Mr Ramsay's death?"

"I don't know. It could."

Morry described Pitso's visit. Buddler listened with few comments, interrupting only when he wanted a point clarified. At the end he sat silent for a while. I felt he was matching what Morry had told him with some other picture.

"What did you feel about this man? This Pitso?"

"A chancer."

"Tsotsi?"

"No. More the sort of guy that holds down a job, but chisels on the side."

"Did he threaten you in any way?"

"No. He wanted money, but there were no threats. He didn't try to blackmail us."

"Yet you gave him money. Why?"

"Compassionate grounds. He'd been badly hammered, and he was scared rigid. I thought if he didn't get clear, someone might try and finish the job on him."

"And he asked, did you know where was Hobeni?"

"That's right."

"Mr Faber. Once before I asked you the same question. You said you didn't know where Hobeni was. Do you know now?"

"No."

"Pitso worked with Hobeni."

"Yes."

"Do you think he knows where Hobeni is?"

"No. I think someone tried to beat that information out of him. If he'd known, he'd have told, fast. He's not the heroic type."

"Who beat him?"

195

"He said, township thugs."

"You think that's it?"

"No."

"So?"

"I wondered, Colonel, if it might have been the police."

Buddler's eyes became sharp and yellow for a moment. He shook his head. "That's not so, Mr Faber."

"I thought," persisted Morry, "that when he called at Mark Ramsay's house, he was looking for you."

"Why would he do that?"

"I don't know. Protection, perhaps. Or to make a report."

Buddler and Morry were staring at each other like circling dogs. Buddler suddenly drew a half-sniffing, derisive breath.

"Pitso's not working for me."

"Well, you'd say that, wouldn't you?"

"He is not my informer, Mr Faber. I didn't send him here." The voice was soft. I realized with surprise that I believed it.

Morry leaned forward in his chair. "Colonel, do you still accept the theory that there was no conspiracy to kill Mark Ramsay?"

Buddler's shoulders moved slightly. "There is no proof otherwise."

"But if there were? If you found evidence of a conspiracy, what then?"

"It would be investigated."

"By you, or by the Special Branch?"

"That would be dependent on whether it was a security issue."

"Don't you think it is?"

Buddler hesitated. "I have no evidence of that."

"What do you think?"

"My thoughts are neither here nor there. I'm a policeman. I deal in facts."

"Have you asked for the security aspect to be investigated?"

"I don't propose to discuss that with you."

"But you think it should be discussed, don't you? You admit that a conspiracy is at least a possibility?" As Buddler made an impatient movement, Morry put out a hand. "No, wait. If you won't answer that one, here's another. The inquest. . . . !"

"Will be held very soon, I can guarantee that."

"I'm not talking about the inquest on Mark. I mean the inquest on Calgut."

"That will come."

"Also very soon?"

"It will come."

"And will there be a full enquiry, Colonel, into how Lieutenant Kray came to shoot Calgut? How he just happened to be on the spot at the precise moment? Whether he'd ever met Calgut before?"

"Naturally, if these questions arise, they will be answered."

"Will they arise? Why aren't they being asked now, publicly? Let me put it more bluntly. Is someone in the police force trying to protect Kray?"

"What are you trying to say?"

"Have you questioned Kray?"

"Of course."

"Are you satisfied with his answers?"

"Definitely. I am definitely satisfied."

"Good. I'd hate to feel that a member of the force might be tied into a murder conspiracy. Or that you could be pressurized into any cover-up job."

Buddler looked up slowly under his brows. He seemed to hang on the brink of some emotion—fear, was it, or a private despair? —but he pulled back from it, saying quietly, "You don't have to worry about that, Mr Faber."

"I suppose," said Morry, and his tone was insolent, "that if the worst comes to the worst, I can see that questions are asked in the House."

"Ja, you can do that." Buddler got to his feet. "But I'm warning you, don't try asking them outside of there. You don't have parliamentary privilege. You can run into big trouble."

We walked down to the car with him. He climbed into the driver's seat, sliding one arm along the wheel. Glanced up at us. "Thanks for telling me about Pitso. I'll see it's followed up."

As the Buick rolled away, I turned to my husband. "Why did you needle him like that?"

"To see his response." Morry squinted through spread fingers at a helicopter that was bumbling across the northern sky. "He didn't deny being under pressure, you notice? Just said he could deal with it."

"So he can. He's got the weight of the Government behind him."

"But what if he hasn't?" Morry lowered his hand and faced me. "If Buddler had a hundred per cent backing, do you think he'd have come here? A senior cop doesn't drop by for a chat. He doesn't exchange confidences with a layman. Buddler is acting way out of character. That's what scares me. My guess is he suspects a conspiracy, he's tried to conduct his enquiries along those lines, and he's been warned off."

"By whom?"

"That's the jackpot question. You can rule out bribery, or threats. Buddler's record is integrity and personal guts. He wouldn't tangle with racketeers or listen to threats. I don't think he would take orders from any living soul outside of the established authorities. So it must be that someone pretty high in those circles is putting the screws on him. You think about that, Jess. A conspiracy that includes people in power jobs : Government, police, people strong enough to muzzle the press and alter the course of a vital murder investigation. If that frightens you and me, imagine what it's doing to Buddler. He's living with a knife at his back. Doesn't know who to trust, any more. I think that's why he came here, he's desperate for quick leads, knows he hasn't got much time. I hoped that if I got under his skin he might open up a bit, but I suppose he couldn't bring himself to do that." Morry slid an arm round my shoulders. "Come inside, there's one more line I want to try."

What he did was 'phone Ocky Heubner, who once carried a lot of weight in National Party circles. I sat and listened.

"Ocky? Maurice Faber. Fine, thanks. Yes, I got your letter. I appreciated it. No, you don't replace men like him very easily. They're all right. I hope so. Ocky, that other matter I spoke to you about, did you make any enquiries? No, I know the difficulties. I understand. I see. Did you learn any names? I appreciate that. But Ocky, listen, the townships are like tinder right now, and these retrenchments . . . it's a matter for national concern, surely? Okay. I understand. Thanks. See you some time. 'Bye."

"No dice?"

"No dice."

"What did you ask him to do?"

"Check some facts for me. Just before Mark was killed, we

198

were picking up stories that the factory owners in Industria were being advised to fire all their Xhosa workers. There were hints the advice could have come from policemen. I wanted that checked. Ocky actually agreed to find out what he could. Now he's reneged. Refuses point blank even to try."

"Is he afraid to?"

"Not for himself. I think he's frightened of what he might find. Worms in his own little apple. He's decided to look the other way. Buddler, though . . . I don't know about him."

"If you're right, if there's a conspiracy involving part of the establishment . . . then it won't last long. The smelling-out will already have begun."

"True enough. But have you thought, my darling, that whoever is planning this may not need much time? They can pull their coup, dispose of any redundant agents, the way they disposed of Calgut. A short-term project. . . ."

"Like?"

"The destruction of the Black Summit."

"All this, to stop a conference?"

"A conference that can bring consolidation of black opinion, weld it into one force, with one leader and one common strategy . . . oh yes, there are people who'd commit murder to wreck it. The Summit's due to start on Friday evening. Gives us less than five days to find Mochudi and his brother."

XXXIII

"DUDU NDHLOVU's the most important contact," Morry said. "We'll try him first."

We were driving down towards the centre of town. The heat had raised glistening bubbles of tar along the side of the road, and the sky to the south was a drumhead stretched for thunder.

"Where do we find him?"

"Good question. Technically, he's retired. But he does a selling job for Chamonix Car Sales. Handles their black clients. They take messages for him."

We found the place, went inside and asked for Mr Ndhlovu. A little coloured girl rolled her eyes at us and asked us to wait in Mr Ndhlovu's office. This was a cubicle with a battered desk, a couple of chairs, a filing cabinet and a lifesize poster of Tap-Tap Makhathini. I tried the cabinet and found it locked.

After ten minutes, the girl came back and said she was sorry but Mr Ndhlovu was out. Something about her expression was wrong. The blankness was terror, not stupidity. Morry smiled at her and said, "We need to get hold of Dudu urgently. We're friends of Mark Ramsay."

"I don't know." A sticky little tongue came out and licked the pale mouth.

"Don't know what?"

"Him. Who you said."

"Mark Ramsay? Well, never mind. Has Mr Ndhlovu been in today?"

"Oah yes."

"And will he be coming back?"

"Oah yes I'm sure."

"Listen, love, I've told you, it's urgent. Can you see he gets a message?"

The girl looked over her shoulder at Tap-Tap. "You can leave it. Yes."

Morry found pen and paper, scrawled a note, added my telephone number. He gave the note to the girl, who promptly started twisting it into a spill. When he tried to thank her she turned and bolted down the corridor.

Back in the car, I said, "She'll take that message straight to the manager".

Morry didn't answer. He was frowning into the rear-view mirror. I glanced round, but couldn't tell whether or not we were being followed, the traffic being very heavy.

We took the route along the railway track, and then threaded among factories until we reached a stretch of sheds with the words "Merritt Metal" stamped on each. We found a place to leave the car and asked our way through workshops as hot and noisy as hell, to reach an open yard right on the Bayside. The wharf was breached at one point by a little repair dock, filled with oily water. A number of pieces of iron, vast as the parts of a giant's cistern, were scattered about the yard and, against one of these, on a long scaffold, two or three welders were at work. The one near us had his visor down over his eyes, and a torrent of sparks spun round his gloved hands, like rubies and sapphires.

Morry waited for him to extinguish the torch, and then called out, "Peck!"

The man swung round and raised his mask. He had a thin, hard face, scarred across one eyebrow. He said, "Hi, Morry," and glanced enquiringly at me.

"My wife," Morry said. The man nodded.

"Hi, Mrs Faber. Morry, I was sad to know about Mark. I saw you at the funeral, I wanted to talk but you ran away too fast."

"I freaked. Have you got a minute, now?"

"I can take ten." Peck Mkise dropped into a squat and then a sitting position on the platform. "So?"

"We're looking for Mochudi or Hobeni."

"Can't help you. I asked around. No one knows where they are. I 'phoned Mark and told him."

"When was that?"

"Oh . . . two, three days before he died. It was . . . Friday. Friday, after work." Peck's narrow eyes considered us. "You not the only ones want to know."

"Have you been approached?"

"Not me, but the informers have been offering big money round the townships for those two. No deal, yet."

"What do the people say about Mochudi?"

"Man, they say everything. He's coming, he's not coming, he's dead, he's alive, he's in Durban, he's on the moon. It's all talk."

"And what's your opinion?"

"I keep quiet. Look, if I go about and speak Mochudi, then people are going to say it's Mkise started all these troubles. I'm not guilty. I'm a trades unionist, I got work to do. I can't do it in the tronk, can I, so I better try and stay outside."

Morry said slowly, "I'm surprised you've stayed out as long as this, Peck".

"Yeah. I been thinkin' about that."

"And?"

"If they've left me outside, maybe I'm supposed to do something, umh? Like lead them to where Mochudi's hiding? Well, I don't know where that can be. So. I get on with my work."

"Well, watch your back."

"I do. I live in a good Zulu sector. If someone comes for me, I'll have help."

"Who's behind it all, Peck?"

Mkise lifted his shoulders in a graphic shrug, expressing contempt as well as ignorance. "I hear anything, I'll let you know."

"Here's the number." Again Morry wrote my name and address and handed it over. Mkise read it a couple of times before crumpling the paper and flicking it into the dock. He reached down a hand to brush my fingers. Across the yard a bell squealed. Mkise stood up and jerked the mask over his face.

Morry and I started to pick our way back across the quay.

"You're laying a wide trail," I told him, "giving our address to all and sundry."

"That's the idea. Peck's right, the reason we're still at large is because someone hopes we'll lead them to Mochudi."

"So you're staking us out as bait?"

"What else can we do?"

I glanced across the harbour, the blue-green dragon-water curled about cargo ships and tankers, rolling beyond T-jetty and the Island to its white-foamed mouth. How long before the strikes got a grip on dockland?

"Something I didn't tell you," I said. "I got a message from Ram Khoosal on Friday." I repeated the conversation I'd had with the Khoosals just before I'd left Johannesburg. "Sita believes Mochudi might have gone to the sangomas. Ram's message was merely the price-list of a B. Cele, of Brakvlei. Some sort of herbalist, I think."

"It's a wild shot. Brakvlei's miles from here. But in the last resort. . . ."

We emerged into the main road, clogged now with sluggish traffic.

"Ram spoke about sleepers," I said. "Agents who remain inactive for a long time, until they're needed for some particular deal."

"I've thought about that. That there could be a political organization that's managed to worm its way into key jobs— factories, essential services, even the security forces;—if Mark stumbled across their tracks, and they killed him to silence him? But it's a theory that doesn't get us any further, because we don't know who to trust. Any of the people Mark dealt with could be involved. If we talk to the police we might pick a sleeper, even there. What it comes down to, is we're on our own."

There was a public 'phone-box next to where we'd left our car. Morry went in and 'phoned Dudu Ndhlovu's office. When he came out his face was grim.

"I insisted on speaking to the manager, this time. He admits Dudu hasn't been in to work at all, today. Usually he arrives early on Monday morning, to pick up new orders. Not today. The manager says the police have been told and enquiries are in hand."

"Is it usual to call in the police so soon?"

"No. But Dudu's a king pin in the Black Summit."

"He could have been held up somewhere in the townships. There've been pickets at the bus ranks."

"He'd have 'phoned his firm. He had appointments booked."

"So what do we do now?"

"Go and see Dr Simeyane."

We climbed into the car and swung inland towards Queen Elizabeth Hospital. I kept watch through the rear window. It seemed to me that a small van was keeping us in sight, but perhaps my nerves were beginning to play tricks on me.

203

XXXIV

We reached the hospital about four o'clock. It's always overcrowded, serving as it does a black population of millions; but that day the activity round about it was phrenetic. Hundreds of patients were streaming down the hill from the outpatients' block, straggling into the street and clogging the bus stops. I saw police on patrol, black and white, some with dogs.

The tide swirled past us. These people, sick and poor, were intent on personal survival. How to beat disease, how to buy food, how to get home before dark fell and the tsotsi gangs gathered in the unlit township paths—that was what drove them. On they came, some of them brushing the flanks of our car, and it seemed to me that this was the true revolutionary force, this slow amassing of human suffering that banks up until it must move of its own weight, crushing everything in its way.

We parked inside the main gates, went to Enquiries and asked for Dr Simeyane. We were told he was on duty in Casualty. If we cared to walk through, he might be able to see us, but they were very busy down there.

We made our way through long corridors that sweltered in the afternoon heat; passed long queues of patients, many of them with fresh injuries; asked for Simeyane at another desk, and were sent to a waiting room where we sat for twenty minutes. At last the doctor came in.

He was youngish, with a long, narrow face, pinched nostrils, and a full, petulant mouth. He stood with his fingertips hooked in the pockets of his housecoat, elbows turned out. The expression on his face was naked, vindictive dislike.

Morry got up and moved forward. "Doctor, we met at Mark Ramsay's house."

"I recall."

"Could we talk somewhere private?"

I thought Simeyane would refuse, but after a moment he beckoned us to follow, and led us through a side door, across a small courtyard, and into what appeared to be a common-room. It was deserted save for ourselves. There were several battered armchairs, tables, a bookshelf. In a raised position on one wall I noticed what looked like closed-circuit television, though the screen was blank at that moment.

Simeyane did not invite us to sit down. Now that I was closer to him, I noticed deep fatigue lines round his mouth. His eyes were bloodshot.

Morry said, "Doctor, this is my wife".

I held out my hand. It was ignored, so I decided to let Morry do the talking. He was taking his time; at length he said : "I've come for guidance."

"About?"

"These riots."

"I can't help you."

"By the look of you, you've been handling casualties all night. Have any of them mentioned how the trouble started?"

"You should go into Casualty, Mr Faber. People don't come there to chat."

"I wonder—did you hear any mention of Mochudi's name?"

"No." Simeyane's eyes, under curling lashes, were watchful.

"Charlie Cameron of the *Gazette* came to see me," said Morry. "He's been around the townships. He says there are agitators, and they're using Mochudi's name."

"You whites, you always talk about agitators. They are only the matches. The fuel is the social injustice against our people!"

"That's more or less what Cameron said. He spoke about 'the big pyre', and said someone might pitch in a torch."

Silence. Morry tried again. "Doctor, do you think the unrest could be aimed at wrecking the Summit?"

That brought a small, impatient shrug. "With this rioting, the Minister is bound to prohibit gatherings. The Summit is already a dead duck."

"I don't believe the Minister wants to ban it. That would simply inflame emotions still further, as well as getting us a bad press all round the world."

"Whites don't want the Summit. I'm telling you, they'll find a way to cream it."

"You can't blame everything on the whites."

Simeyane laughed.

"All right," Morry said, "you tell me, what's your own attitude to the Summit? You're supposed to be on the steering committee. Do you want it to fail?"

"I don't give a fart, any more. The Summit's not for me. It's for whitey's blacks."

"That's not true. But let it pass. I'd like to remind you that you gave an undertaking to Mark Ramsay before he died. You said you would help him to find Mochudi."

"No." The answer was vehement. "I never said that."

"Well, you said you'd try and find out what was going on in the townships."

"Now listen, man! I never spoke about Mochudi! I don't give a damn about Mochudi!"

"Are you saying he's whitey's black?"

"I don't say anything. I don't talk to you. And you don't come here, asking questions, telling me what to do! I owed Ramsay. I don't owe you." And Simeyane began to swear in Xhosa, shouting at the top of his voice. He reached out and thrust his palm against Morry's chest. "You whites! You killers! There are dead men in the morgue here, all black. All the dead men are black."

He was hitting Morry, and Morry reached up and grabbed his wrist, and I thought, Oh God, now there's going to be a fight.

But then Simeyane said, in quite a soft voice, "Dudu Ndhlovu's dead". And leaning forward, he almost fell, so that Morry had to hold his shoulders to steady him into a chair.

XXXV

WHEN SIMEYANE SAID that about Dudu Ndhlovu, I accepted the full truth of our situation. Up till then I'd thought of it as a nightmare that would pass, but now I realized it was our lives that had been changed. We were going to live differently, from that time on.

I actually looked round the common-room, as if there might be some escape. I remember, the closed-circuit television was running, showing a picture of people in a lecture-theatre.

"How did it happen?" asked Morry.

Simeyane was wiping his face with a handkerchief. "Shot in the back. Two bullets."

"Do the police know?"

"Oh yes. They're notified of all violent deaths."

"Where was he found?"

"In the canal, alongside Seisson Road. Industria."

"How long had he been dead?"

"It's hard to say. Lying in water, like that. But they think he must have been shot early this morning. A truck driver stopped to take a leak, and saw the body."

"I'm sorry."

Simeyane said nothing. He was sitting with his head in his hands, and I don't think he was hearing much. Morry leaned down closer to him.

"Doctor, have you been questioned?"

"Yes."

"By the regular police, or Special Branch?"

"I don't know. They wore plain clothes. I know nothing about all this." His hands began to shake violently, and he folded his arms across his chest.

Morry said, "You need rest".

"I'm off duty now."

"Can you sleep at the hospital?"

"Yes."

"Then do. Don't try and go home. It's dangerous for you,

207

because of your link with Mark Ramsay. Understand? Stay here."

"All right." Simeyane's voice had the dullness of exhaustion.

Footsteps sounded in the corridor outside, and the common-room began to fill with men and women apparently on tea-break. We left Simeyane sitting in his chair, his hands dangling limp over the arm-rests, as if he were already asleep.

We made our way back through the labyrinth. The sun had dropped behind buildings, and the car was relatively cool. We drove up the slopes of the Berea with the rest of the rush-hour traffic. After a while, Morry said, "Seisson Road. Why is that familiar?"

"It cuts through Industria, alongside the canal."

"That's it. We took it the other day. That factory . . . Filey, Lofts . . . that's near Seisson Road."

"Is that where Hobeni worked?"

"Yes."

"So Dudu Ndhlovu could have been on Hobeni's old stamping-ground when he was shot?"

"Looks possible." Morry frowned at the road ahead. "Another thing. When Mark spoke with Simeyane and Mkise, there was no mention of Mochudi's name. When I brought it up, today, Mkise said straight out he'd made enquiries, and 'phoned Mark about Mochudi. Simeyane denied any such involvement."

"So?"

"I think it confirms my suspicion that Mark kept up the search for Hobeni, without telling me. I think he probably chased up all his black friends. The buzz got round. Mark set himself up, all right."

"Morry," I said, "we can't cope with this alone."

He shot me a quick glance. "So who do we go to for help?"

"We could go to the Summit organizers. At least we'd have some help."

He detached one hand from the wheel and pulled me closer to him. "Love, what can they do? They have no real powers."

"I know. Forget it."

We drove a little way in silence. The sun was dropping behind the Ridge, sending up great spokes of dusty light. We turned off the trunk road and began to weave through a series of little lanes, bordered by high hedges.

208

"Where are we going?"

"Esperanza Convalescent Home." Morry grinned at me. "I'm going to turn you in." Then, as I started to protest, he said, "It's okay. I 'phoned from the call box. We're meeting a friend here."

The Home lay over the crest of the Berea, behind a barrier of gnarled mango trees. A board across the driveway announced its name in faded letters. Morry did not follow the drive, but turned off it to let the car roll gently across uneven turf to come to rest under a big jacaranda tree. Someone had built a bench round its bole, and sitting on the bench was a small, gnomish man in a cassock. He got up as the car stopped and came to meet us.

"Mr Faber?" His voice was surprisingly deep and strong.

"Yes, Father. This is my wife Jess. Father Quinn."

I found myself under the surveillance of bright brown eyes. "The sculptress? I've seen some of your work. I'm no judge of art, however. Won't you sit down?"

I took my place on the bench, the priest beside me. Morry remained standing, facing us.

"We won't stay long. We don't want to embarrass you."

"I doubt if that is possible. What's your problem?"

"You know I was Mark Ramsay's election agent?"

"Yes. A tragedy, his death. One had such hopes of him."

Morry was hesitating, as if trying to decide his best approach; then typically, he plunged straight in.

"I think Mark was shot because he was trying to reach a man named Mochudi."

"Amyas Mochudi?"

"Yes. Do you know him?"

"Only by repute."

"But you do know Father Ignatius Tanda?"

"Of course."

"Father Quinn. Mark made an appointment with Father Tanda ten days before his death. Tanda reneged on it. We were told he'd gone out of town. Now I very much want to get in touch with him. Can you please help me?"

"I'm afraid I can't."

"It's a matter of life and death."

"Yes, possibly, but it's simply that I don't know where he is." Father Quinn spread apologetic hands.

"But . . . aren't you his boss?"

"His superior. And I have no idea where he is." As he spoke, the priest had been scanning Morry intently. Now he leaned back against the tree trunk and closed his eyes. "I had hoped that you folk might be able to tell me."

For a moment the silence in the garden was so complete that I could feel it on my skin. Then the small man sighed, and opened his eyes.

"How well do you know Father Tanda?"

"I've never met him."

"I've known him for many years. He is very intelligent, very devout, a man with a true desire to serve God. He is also a black man and politically aware. These qualities make him vulnerable to attack, at times. Seven months ago he was detained and kept in solitary confinement for some weeks. He was never charged with any crime. He suffered, naturally. He has had to grapple with a weight of bitterness, and he has done so. But how often can a man endure that sort of thing? When the recent unrest began, one could see it was affecting him. He was torn between two selves, that of the priest, that of the patriot. You see? I wanted him to have a break. I wanted him, this time, not to be tested too far. I sent him away."

"On leave?"

"No." Quinn smiled. "I sent him to a seminary we run inland. Different work, away from the trouble zone, that's what I pictured. I'm afraid he decided otherwise. He never reached the seminary at all."

"Where do you think he is?"

"I don't know. Perhaps here, in Durban. I just do not know. And I can't have him searched for. Can't set the dogs on him, can I, now? I am fairly sure he is not in police custody."

"Father. Have you thought . . . something could have happened to him?"

"Indeed, yes. I have nightmares. Since Ramsay was shot. . . ."

"Not only that. I was told today that Dudu Ndhlovu's been murdered. Shot in the back and his body dumped in the Industria canal."

There was a silence. Quinn stared in blank shock.

Morry said, "Did you know Dudu?"

"Of course. We . . . we worked together, often. Oh, dear Lord! You think these murders are linked?"

"Yes."

"Tanda would have no part in such a crime, of that I am convinced."

"Unless the patriot proved stronger than the priest?"

"No. I refuse to believe that." The small man stood up abruptly. "Quite apart from the matter of his religious faith, there is the matter of his secular calling. Father Ignatius is a radiographer, a good one. He's been trained to save life, not to destroy it."

"There were doctors at Dachau and Buchenwald."

I intervened. "Father, where was Tanda's home kraal?"

He looked at me, puzzled. "His tribal home? In the foothills of the Berg. Beautiful country, along the Brak River. But his people were moved out some years ago, under a government resettlement plan."

"It fits," I said, as we drove back towards the crest of the Ridge. "It fits with what Ram Khoosal told me. Ram thinks Mochudi could be in hiding because he's ill. The news reports said he was released from prison on health grounds. He had tuberculosis as a young man. Tanda is a radiographer, who's worked in a TB clinic. Tanda's old territory is the Brak River country. The herbalist on Ram's circular lives at Brakvlei."

"It's a very slender link, my love."

"What else do we have?"

It was nearly six o'clock. The sea breeze had dropped, the land breeze had not yet woken, it was the time between day and night, the time when luck turns.

In the Parkhaven streets, Mark's election posters had been replaced by new ones carrying David Tindall's name. A few hours back that would have jolted me. Now I hardly gave the things a glance.

Our route home took us past the Ramsays' house. As we came up to it, we saw Buddler's old Buick parked in the roadway, and Buddler himself coming through the gate.

There's a look you see in mortal injury, a grey silence like a burned-out fire. It was on Buddler's face as we approached him that evening. He let us come right up to him before he spoke.

"I've been in to tell Mrs Ramsay, she must take the boy and

211

get out of Durban. It's not safe for them here."

Morry said, "We heard about Dudu Ndhlovu".

"Yes. There's that. And with the trouble in the townships, I'm short of men, I can't guarantee protection." Buddler ran a hand along the top bar of the gate, back and forth. "Anyway, I'm off this case."

"You were taken off?"

"Ja."

"When?"

"This afternoon."

"Do you know why?"

"I was out all morning, talking to people who knew Calgut. When I came back to the station, I was told, I'm off the case."

"A reason must have been given?"

"I'm needed to direct operations in the trouble spots."

"Who'll take over the investigation?"

Buddler shrugged.

"But is that normal procedure, to switch a senior officer like you, without consultation?"

"It's not normal. But you can be sure, Mr Faber, I'm not leaving the matter there. I've been on the force 33 years. I also have some friends I can call on."

"But Christ, man, how long is it going to take, before your friends see you right? Mark's dead, and now Dudu. You're being muzzled, that's the truth of it. By the time you're back in circulation, it'll be too bloody late. Who had you taken off?" Who's responsible?"

"I can't . . . discuss that with you."

"Your system, right or wrong, no matter who dies for it?"

Buddler raised his head. I saw anger in his eyes, and fear. He stared at Morry for a moment, then thrust past him, and, climbing into his car, gunned it away towards the city.

We turned towards the house. When we were halfway there, the front door swung open, and Nick Ramsay shot out and ran to spring like a monkey into Morry's arms.

XXXVI

"Why didn't you come? I was waiting and waiting for you."

"I wanted to come, sport." Morry's voice was gentle, but over the boy's head I saw his eyes, hard and bright, scanning the front of the house. "Where's your mum and everyone?"

"Inside." Nick rolled his head to look at me, gave me a half smile, looked back at Morry.

"My daddy's gone away."

"Yes, I know."

"There was a lot of people. They came and asked me things."

"Did they? Were they cops?"

A nod.

"Cops do that, you don't have to mind about them."

"Mum says they've gone away, too. But it's not true. He came back again today. The big one."

"I saw him. He's all right, Nick."

The child leaned back in the crook of Morry's arm. There were shadows under his eyes and his face was too tense for his years, but he was very like his father. There was something fierce in him, something that would sink its teeth and never let go.

"I didn't tell them," he said.

"Tell them what?" Morry's voice was sharp, and Nick, sensing adult concern, fidgetted in his grasp.

"Nicko," said Morry, "if it's a secret, I won't ask."

"It's not a secret from you." Round grey eyes surveyed me doubtfully.

"Jess is my wife. You can trust her, same as me."

The child was unconvinced.

"They said not to tell."

"Who said?"

"Dad, and the other man."

"The Xhosa?"

"Yes. Do you know about him?"

213

"I know something."

There was a bench close to us, overgrown by spears of bougainvillaea and golden shower. Morry walked over to it and sat down, placing Nick beside him. "Listen, sport. There are times when a secret is too important. Then you have to share it with someone you can trust."

"Would you do that?"

"Yes. Tell me, when your dad spoke to this man, were you listening?"

"Yes. I was in my place, you know, on the stairs."

"What time was that?"

"It was still night-time. It was dark outside."

"Did you see the man?"

"Yes. He wasn't very big. But his hair was big." Nick's hands described an Afro cut.

"And he spoke Xhosa?"

"A little. But mostly English. I couldn't hear very well because Daddy switched on the music. But then they didn't listen to it. They were talking."

"Nicko, can you remember anything they said?"

The boy's mouth began to tremble. He shook his head. Morry stroked his hair.

"It doesn't matter, sport."

"But I remember when they were in the hall, before the man left. I heard what he said then."

"What was that?"

"He said, 'Abebelele sebevukile'." The boy sounded the syllables slowly, rocking his body for emphasis. "Then Daddy saw me, and he said I mustn't tell. And I haven't told, till now."

"Good, that's good. You were right not to tell anyone except us. Now you mustn't talk to anyone else, about it, see? A secret again?"

"Okay."

"Nick, how would you like to go in an aeroplane?"

"With you?"

"With your mother, and Aunt Elizabeth."

"Yes!" Nick scrambled to his feet, flung out his arms in the perennial flying attitude and went whirling away over the turf.

"What did those words mean?" I said.

Morry looked at me. " 'Abebelele sebevukile?' It means, 'The Sleepers are waking up'."

"Jess!"

I turned round to see Bianca Ramsay standing on the verandah steps. She glanced uncertainly at Morry, and then came towards us. She had on a pale dress with a pleated skirt, and the swing of it somehow expressed her agitation. She stopped a little way from us. "Morry. About that last time. . . ."

"It doesn't matter, Bianca."

"Those things I said. I didn't mean them. It was all too much for me."

"I know, forget it."

She came to stand in front of him, gazing up in great anxiety. "Colonel Buddler says I have to take Nick away."

"Yes, I think he's right."

"He didn't explain. I'm terrified. About Nick."

"You'll be all right. We'll send you to your family in Jo'burg. If necessary, you can go abroad."

"But what's happened?"

"Another man has been shot. Dudu Ndhlovu. He was a friend of Mark's. It seems likely there is a conspiracy."

"But why don't the police do something?"

"There's some reason to think the white ants have got to them, too." As Bianca's face closed in panic, Morry took her by the shoulders. "Don't worry. It won't last long, I'm sure. But while it does, it's best you and Nick should be away from here." His fingers tightened, steadying her. "There's one thing that's important. The night before Mark died, someone called at this house. A black. Did you know that?"

"No. But . . . that night . . . I was nervous about the nomination, and I took sleeping tablets. I didn't hear a thing." She caught the implication, then. "Are you telling me Nick knew about it?"

"Yes. He was on one of his prowls, it seems. He didn't hear a great deal, Bianca, but you mustn't let him talk about it. That means, keep him away from people as much as you can. I'd like to get you away tonight. Can you arrange to stay with your brother?"

"Of course. He's been begging me to go up there."

"Great." Morry released her. "Then let's get moving." He turned his head and whistled to Nick, who stopped his gyrations on the lawn, and came bounding across to us.

Bianca and the child went upstairs to pack. Morry and I moved into the study, where he set about 'phoning first Bianca's brother, and then a friend at the airport to secure reservations. While he was busy, I searched Mark's bookshelves for his set of large-scale maps, found the one I wanted, and spread it out.

When Morry came to stand beside me, I pointed. "Here's the Brak River. Not much more than a stream. And here's Brakvlei. From there, it's not impossible to reach Lesotho, to the west, or the Transkei."

"Yes. It's well placed."

"The man who came to see Mark . . . you don't think it was one of these Sleepers, do you? You don't think he was mixed up in it?"

"Oh, God, no. No, by Nick's description—which is very vague —it could have been Hobeni himself."

"What's that mean?"

"I don't know." He folded up the map and returned it to its shelf. As he did so, there was a knock at the door. It opened, and David Tindall stood in the doorway.

"Morry? Can I speak to you?"

"If you make it fast."

"I hear you're getting Bianca and the boy out?"

"Yes."

"Good." Tindall came slowly into the room. "Buddler was here, did you know?"

"Yes. I met him at the gate."

"Did he tell you anything?"

"Nothing new. Except, he's been taken off the case."

Tindall nodded. "That could only have been done by a very high authority, I would think." He perched on the arm of a chair. "I think this house is under surveillance. It could be bugged, too."

Morry reached out and flicked the switch of the Hi-fi. On the turntable, a record started to spin, the lever swung across, a Mozart symphony rolled to the corners of the room. I wondered if it was the last music Mark had played.

216

Tindall was speaking across it. . . . "Tonight's paper. Ndhlovu's been shot."

Morry nodded. "I was in his office this afternoon. I spoke to Peck Mkise, and Zondi Simeyane, too. They couldn't help."

Tindall dropped his head back, as if he were trying to get a better view of us; and Morry watched him thoughtfully. It struck me that they both wore the same expression; that neither liked the other, but that by some alchemy other than speech, they had come to an agreement.

"Were you followed?" said Tindall.

"Possibly. I'm not clever enough to know."

"I was followed today, but I evaded pursuit. It's not difficult, if you employ more than one car. I have company drivers. In any event, my calls were scarcely such as to arouse suspicion. I have been tattling."

"What about?"

"Character." Tindall fingered his spectacles. "In particular the character of the men whose firms we visited in Industria. You recall? Yes, well. Zeffery is, as one saw at a glance, an inefficient racist who will soon be out of business. Norman Camberley is well liked and well-thought of. But Alex Condor is the interesting one. I concentrated on him, rather, because Hobeni worked for him, and Pitso too."

"You didn't go out there?" said Morry quickly.

"No, no, merely chatted around. People regard me as . . . er . . . ineffectual." Tindall's smile was faintly malicious. "It's stood me in good stead in the past, in dealing with industrial espionage. I get told all sorts of interesting things that no one would dream of telling a tough character like you."

"And what did you learn about Condor?"

"He has a public image. No private one."

"But I've read about him in the press," I said. "Polo, isn't it, and two children?"

"That's right. Neat and bland, like pre-digested food. The sort of stuff any good PRO can draft. He has an identity, but everyone tells you exactly the same things about him. Government supporter, conservative views, charming manners, nice family, quiet home, plays polo. It's a stereotype, no more. Except, from one or two businessmen—the shrewd ones—I got a gentle hint that they might not . . . er . . . buy a second-hand polo pony from him. Nothing definite, you know. They just sniff a little."

Tindall slid a hand into his pocket and extracted a slip of paper. "I have a little list for you. Condor's business interests, directorships, firms owned, shares, etcetera. The subsidiary firms he might be able to influence. Finally, his personal points of contact, clubs, and so on. I thought it might be useful."

"Might indeed." Morry glanced at the sheet as he took it. "Is this the only copy?"

"No. Others are lodged about the place, with my lawyers and so forth. I'm a nervous man."

For the first time in my knowledge, Morry gave the little man a smile. "And are you due at the election office tonight?"

"No. After Buddler's visit, I 'phoned and told them I would not be in."

Morry looked at his watch. "Come to the airport with us."

"Will there be room in the car?"

"Plenty, Nick can sit on a knee."

A few minutes later Bianca, Liz and Nick came downstairs. Bianca handed Morry a box, which proved to contain a small automatic pistol and two clips of ammunition.

"It was Mark's," she said. "Please take it."

Morry slid the pistol and magazines into the pockets of his jacket. We carried the luggage out to the Valiant, and in a few minutes were on our way to the airport.

It was a still night, with milky-blue clouds in the sky, and we lost sight of the aircraft almost at once. Looking after it, I felt like a besieged city when the non-combatants have been sent to safety.

On the way back, while we were still on the outskirts of the city, Tindall said, "We're being followed".

"Yeah," agreed Morry. "Black Merc with three big sods in it." As he spoke he swung our car from the freeway to the link road that led north. "They can come with us, if they want to."

"Where are we going?"

"To see Wally Brock. We're going to set up a little game of Chase the Ace."

XXXVII

WALTER BROCK IS a very wealthy man who runs a firm that does heavy construction work on roads, bridges and the like. He owns a flat in Durban and a small farm at Doveton, which is a country halt about 50 kilometres from town, and nearly 2,000 feet above sea level.

Wally has put most of his acres under trees. In the midst of the plantations, is a comfortable old bungalow, and two big paddocks for his horses. He bought the property partly to provide a half-way house for the big tractors, trucks and earth-movers used in his enterprises. The machines are kept in lock-up sheds near the eastern boundary. An electrified fence surrounds the whole, and Wally keeps guards on all the gates. In its way it's a maximum-security farm.

The black car trailed us from the city. There seemed to be no attempt at concealment. On the steep climb through Kloof, where the road twists a good deal, the car closed its distance; on the straights, it dropped back.

Morry kept to a moderate speed and signalled with his indicator before the Doveton turn-off. The Mercedes turned off after us.

We bumped slowly along the untarred road for some fifteen minutes, to reach Wally's main gate. As the Valiant slowed, the other car went past, its occupants gazing straight ahead. Morry leaned out of his window to speak to the gateman.

"Hullo Jonas."

"Hullo, Mr Faber."

"Will you ring the house, say I'm here with my wife and Mr Tindall?"

The man went over to the nearest shed, and came back a short while later to say we could go up. We drove through the gates, stopped. Morry said, "If anyone asks about us, Jonas, we're having coffee with Mr Brock, okay?"

"Okay, baas."

Wally's wife and two sons greeted us with flattering warmth, and ushered us into the big, airy bedroom where he was convalescing. He was lying with his injured arm propped on a sort of wire cage, his bed was covered with papers and he looked bored.

Morry started to ask how he was, but Wally cut him short.

"You didn't come out here to visit the sick, you sod." Then, smiling at me: "What is this, a second honeymoon? And if so, why the hell are you taking the candidate for Parkhaven along?"

"No time to explain in detail," Morry said. "Briefly, we think Mark's death is linked with a man named Amyas Mochudi."

"The black-power man?"

"Yes. We think we may be able to reach him, but we're being tracked by bloodhounds. Three chased us from Durban, in a black Merc. If they've got radio, they could be calling up reinforcements right now. So we have to move fast."

"What do you want me to do?"

"Lend us trucks, and horses."

"Right."

"How many truck drivers can you raise?"

"Tomorrow's shift. That's fifteen."

"Can you get your drivers to rig tarpaulins over the bodies, so it looks as if people could be hiding underneath? Then I want the drivers to take them out of the front gate, down to the main road. From there, they must scatter. As many different directions as they can work."

"A wild-goose trail?"

"That's it."

"Do you plan to be in one of the trucks?"

"No. The three of us will walk down through the plantations as far as the stream. We'll wait by the pump-house. We're going across country for a goodish distance. Do you think that you could lend us three good strong hacks?"

"Can you all ride?"

"Jess and I can. Tindall?"

"Yes."

Wally was already easing himself higher on his pillows. "I can do better than that. You'll need a guide if you're going cross-country, it's only footpaths west of here. Rollo!" He raised his voice in a shout, and the older of his sons appeared in the doorway. He was about nineteen years old, and by the shortness of his hair, recently back from Border service.

220

"Rollo," said Walter, "I want you to act as pathfinder for Mr Faber. They're planning a little jaunt."

Rollo's eyes glinted. "Where to?"

"Brakvlei," said Morry.

"Easy. Is it connected with this?" He jerked a thumb at his father's bandages.

"Yes."

"Good. What about taking Ted as well?"

"No. He must stay here, see the grounds are patrolled and look after your parents." Morry glanced at me. "I'd like Jess to stay here, too."

I shook my head. "I know Mochudi. You don't. I'm coming."

Walter leaned sideways, grunting a little as his wound made itself felt. He pulled open a bedside drawer and lifted out a ring of keys, which he handed to Rollo.

"Arm your party, boy. You can take my rifle and the revolver. Leave us the shotguns. And see they have a rucksack each, with basic camping stuff. Do you want tents?"

"No, too heavy."

"You'll need warmer clothes." Walter looked at my sandals. "And something heavier than those things. Mary, scramble up some togs, quick as you can."

The house began to resound with action. Walter looked as wistful as a child. "I wish I could go with you."

"You've got things to do here," said Morry. "Give us half an hour's start, then send the trucks out. If you get any 'phone-calls, don't answer. Just let confusion reign for an hour or so. That'll give us enough start. Once we're into the hills, nobody is likely to catch us."

Mary brought the clothes, Rollo the rucksacks and guns. Walter was already issuing instructions to his boss-driver. As we said goodbye to him, he called us back.

"What do I say about Tindall? Going to be a hue and cry after him, if he doesn't turn up at the campaign office."

"Good point. Say he's been called to Cape Town for briefing. Fix it with the boys down there."

"Fine. Right. Good luck."

By ten o'clock, we were on our way. We slipped out of a side door that led straight into the trees, wattles in their full leaf. In seconds, we lost sight of the house, and the carpet of needle underfoot deadened all sound. We reached the pump-house and waited there for a very short time, until Rollo and a black groom Jabulani, appeared, each mounted. Rollo led two horses, th groom one.

We mounted as quietly as we could. Morry walked from th cover of the trees to the brink of the stream, and gazed abov him, but there was no sign of any living soul besides ourselve We forded the stream, entered the pine plantations on the fa side, and began the journey to Brakvlei.

XXXVIII

IT TOOK US five hours to reach the village. We had to move slowly, because of the unfamiliar ground, but luckily the ponies were sure-footed and used to country work.

We climbed steadily. For most of the time the moon was veiled in cloud. We were in territory still marked as African Reserve. There were no white farms, and we kept clear of the Zulu kraals as much as possible. Sometimes we passed close to a group of huts, and the kraal dogs set up a baying, and a man or woman appeared in a doorway to watch us. When that happened, Morry called a few words of greeting, and we moved quickly on, the watchers motionless till we were out of sight.

Once or twice we heard voices in the far-away dark, voices pitched in the long-drawn cadence that meant a message was being sent across the hills, warning of our approach.

It may seem strange to say it, but I enjoyed that night ride through the blue-black plantations and over the humped silvery grasslands that rose and fell, almost part of the misty sky.

Crazy we might be, trying to save our future by such a wild hazard, pinning all our hopes on one chance-heard name. But the journey had a rightness. And I, having no religious faith to speak of, still felt that my stars had wrapped their threads about me, and were leading me safely on.

At three in the morning, the hills steepened. The paths we took scrambled between rocks, or plunged headlong into valleys crossed by small streams, till we emerged at last onto a plateau, in the centre of which lay a sheet of reed-clogged water, the Brakvlei itself.

That was a strange sighting. Behind us lay the reddening sky, and before us, the reddening water, the black rushes tipped with scarlet. It was utterly still, no bird or insect made any sound. Ahead, hiding the far side of the vlei and the village, rolled a thick and sullen mist.

We went forward. The haze enveloped us. The marshy ground grew firmer, becoming a sandy road tufted with grass. There

223

loomed above us the cracked façade of a building that carried over its porch a faded signboard: "B. Cele. General Merchant."

We tethered our horses at the stoep-rail. The clammy mist rolled about us. I could discern little of the village except the dim outlines of some shanties on the far side of the road, and a solitary petrol pump to the right of the store.

Morry climbed the steps and knocked at the door. The windows each side of it were protected by ancient wire grilles, behind which I could see a clutter of goods, pots and pans, clothing. No light showed. Morry hammered again, and this time a voice answered, harsh and husky.

"Who is there?"

"My name is Faber. I want to buy from you."

"The store opens at seven o'clock."

"I have to talk to you. I've come a long way."

There was a pause. Then, "Who sent you?"

"Ramisand Khoosal."

"I don't know him." The accent was hard to place, guttural, with something of the Zulu cadence and something of the Afrikaans.

"He said you are a great sangoma."

"I am a trader. Why do you come to Brakvlei with guns?"

"Only to defend ourselves."

"Against what? Lay them down."

We did as we were bid, placing the rifle and other arms on the stoep. As I did so, I noticed that a number of people had emerged from the shacks, and now stood on the far side of the roadway: an old Indian man, two or three black women and several children. They stood watching us, talking softly among themselves.

Morry said to Tindall. "Stay with the guns, don't touch them yourself, but don't let anyone else do so."

At that point we heard the bolts being drawn on the far side of the door, and a moment later, it swung open.

The woman in the doorway was short and obese; about 60 years old, with the brown-tallow skin of the mulatto, and grey hair matted in greasy curls. She stood with her head tilted far back, and at first I thought she was blind, for her pupils seemed to turn upwards under the thick lids, without light in them.

Looking at her, I felt an atavistic dread, a prickling of the spine as old as witchcraft itself. I saw that she was holding a heavy revolver in the folds of her skirt.

She addressed Morry. "Who are these others?"

He told her, naming us one by one.

"Where did you come from?"

"Doveton."

"And the horses?"

"Also from Doveton."

Her thick, purplish lips moved in and out. She lifted the revolver, gesturing with it. "You can come inside. You and the woman."

Morry and I followed her into the gloom that smelled of paraffin and crushed mealies, soap and acrid native blankets. The woman shuffled round behind the counter, and leaned there, the gun in her hand.

"You can buy."

Morry began to move about the dimly lit shelves, selecting oats for the horses, a plastic bucket, tinned food, biscuits, dried fruit and milk powder.

I said, "Are you Mrs Cele?"

The woman nodded without taking her eyes off Morry. I noticed, on the racks behind her, a good stock of patent medicines, and sundry vials and boxes that evidently contained herbal remedies. Two doors, both closed, led off this main room, and I thought I heard someone moving beyond one of them.

Morry brought his purchases to the counter and paid the bill.

When she had handed him his change, the woman reached back and knocked on the wall behind her, and a young black girl in a soiled overall came through and piled the stuff into two large cartons.

"We need a place to eat," said Morry, "and rest the horses."

"There is a field behind, and a shed. You can use them. The horses can drink from the stream, not you, it will make your bowels run. Send and I will give you water from the borehole." Her strange gaze turned suddenly to me. "Don't worry. No one has followed you here."

I started, feeling the hair rise on my neck. She might have been reading my mind. I stumbled out of the stuffy atmosphere of the shop, into the street.

It was full light, now. Our guns lay where we'd left them, our companions and the watching villagers had not moved from their positions. It was if a spell bound them. I found myself shivering, and moved closer to Morry.

"Don't let her bug you," he said.

"She is a witch."

"Oh, yes. Great sangoma. Jabulani told me, on the way up, she's famous. But it was your face, she read, not your thoughts. Scaring the pants off people is part of her stock in trade, like that trick with the eyes. Come on, let's get this stuff moving."

The field at the back was little more than a slope of tussocky upland grass, bordered on two sides by a single rank of wind-bitten wattle trees, and on the third by a strand or two of rusted wire. Beyond the wire, though we could not see them, must lie the foothills and the straight mauve ramparts of the Drakens-berg.

Close to the back wall of the store was a lean-to shed, large and more or less empty. Next to the shed was a corrugated-iron latrine with a shaky wooden door. It smelled powerfully.

Chicken pecked and clucked in the dirt, but apart from that there was complete, muffling silence.

The men took the horses up to the stream that ran through the right-hand line of trees. I made gratefully for the john. As I crossed behind the shed, I could see Mrs Cele moving about in a back room of the store, but she took no notice of me.

When the horses had been watered and fed, I made breakfast for the party. The sun was now above the horizon, and the mist seemed a little thinner in patches.

"Do you think we'll find Mochudi here?" I asked Morry.

"Perhaps. We must wait a while."

"We haven't much time. It's Tuesday already. Why can't we just ask the old bag where he is, what she knows?"

"Wouldn't do us any good. See, there are two possibilities. One is, she's a simple trader, who never heard of Mochudi, in which case she can't help. Other is, she does know him, and knows how to reach him. If that's the case, she won't talk to us until she's checked us out."

"What's she expect, written references?"

He smiled. "References of a sort. My guess is she's in touch with the people all the way from here to Doveton. She wasn't surprised to see us, you know. She'd had warning."

"You heard the hill-calling, last night."

"Yes. She knew we were coming, and where from. Now, I think she'll wait to make sure we weren't followed. There could be a big search on, by now. Helicopters, even. So we'll keep in the shed, the horses too. Until Mrs Cele makes up her mind we might as well rest. David and I will keep guard outside, you others try and catch some sleep."

I spread the sheepskin the Brocks had lent me, and, to my surprise, slept soundly. When I woke, it was past one o'clock, and warmer. I woke Rollo, and Morry and the others in their turn stretched out in the shed, while we took watch. Once I heard an aircraft bumbling far to the south of us. Once a group of village women went past with long trusses of reeds balanced on their heads, dream figures against the mist. Some of them passed quite close to us but did not look our way, nor call any greeting.

Rollo and I talked in a desultory way; but the heat and the silence oppressed me. I felt that all the power of this valley was flowing in, to distil and concentrate in the shabby little store. When a bird lighted on its roof, it seemed a portent. I found myself watching with unbearable anxiety.

At four o'clock, the back door opened, and Mrs Cele leaned out, beckoning me.

"Come," she said, "the water is here."

I picked up my bucket and carried it into a large untidy room, fiendishly hot. It seemed to be a combination of kitchen and dispensary. Groceries stood on shelves near a huge coal-stove, while the scarred enamel table was covered with an amazing collection of roots and leaves, jars of powder and twists of what looked like dried meat.

Mrs Cele was seated in a wicker chair, grinding something to paste in a mortar.

"You can fill your bucket from the drum," she told me.

I did as I was bid. The water in the drum was still and brown, reflecting my image. I dipped the bucket and set it down on the floor. Behind was the bright oblong of daylight. Should I go back to the field? Morry had said we must wait. I glanced at Mrs Cele. She sat impassive, grinding her herbs. She was challenging me, by her silence, by the valley's silence. If I left, she would not stop me. What did she want? What must I do? Sweat

227

trickled down my back.

I reached for a wooden chair and sat down opposite her. "What is that you're making?"

"Is for fufinyama." She meant the hysterical illness that attacks some black women, making them yell like banshees.

"I'd rather have tranquillizers," I said.

A shrug. "If you can pay for them. . . ."

"Don't you charge for your medicines?"

"Of course. Or nobody thinks they any good."

"How do people pay?"

"How they can. I help them. They help me."

"This must be hard country in the winter."

"It's hard all year."

"Is there tuberculosis?"

"Some."

"Do you treat it?"

The hand wielding the pestel checked for an instant, the dull eyes flickered towards me. "That is for the town doctors."

"I had it once. In the womb."

She grunted. "So? And now, have you children?"

"Not yet."

She stared at me, through me. "Perhaps you will."

"Can you see the future?"

"I can see the present."

I shifted in my chair. I could feel my heart pounding. "I had a friend once," I said, "who had tuberculosis of the lungs. He had to have an operation. Amyas Mochudi was his name. And another man I know, trained to take X-rays. He was born near here I think. His family name was Tanda. Perhaps you've heard of him?"

"Everyone in these hills is called Tanda. But most have moved away. The Government moved them."

"This man became a priest. I would like to see him again. To talk to him."

The fat woman gave an indifferent shrug. "I don't know him." She rubbed a finger under her nose. "You want hot water tonight, I'll heat some for you on the stove."

I thanked her and went back to the shed. Morry was just waking up. I knelt beside him and he put an arm round me.

"Where've you been?"

"Talking to Mrs Cele. Morry, I think I may have blown it. I mentioned Amyas' name to her, and Tanda's."

"Any reaction?"

"None. But I'm sure they're here. I feel it."

"So do I. Well, if they are, no doubt some message is being passed to them." He reached up and stroked my hair. "From what you remember of him, is Mochudi likely to give one good goddam about us?"

"I don't know. It was so long ago. He's been on the Island since then; and we're tainted by our white political links."

"Well, we must wait tonight, at least. If nothing's happened by morning, we'll go back to town."

I got on with making supper, stew and potatoes and tea. Beside us the horses grazed, leaning through the fence for the sweet grass beyond. The sun went down and it became bitterly cold. Then, with the rising of the moon, the mist lifted. Swiftly and totally it vanished, and we saw above us the great barrier of the Berg, sharp and clear, and the innumerable stars pouring down their light.

I watched the scene for some time, huddled under my saddle-blanket, and eventually I dozed.

Morry's voice woke me, calling from outside. I scrambled up and followed the others out of the shed. A horseman was cutting down the nearest hill, making for the road. We could see him in the moonlight, bareheaded, wrapped in a blanket that trailed over his pony's rump. He vanished behind the store and a moment later swung round into the field, coming to a halt before us.

We moved slowly towards him. Morry snapped on his torch and shone it briefly on the rider's face. Then he said in Zulu, "We greet you, Father Tanda".

XXXIX

THE PRIEST DID not dismount. He returned our greetings in a perfunctory way and then, leaning forward in his saddle, said urgently, "Mr Faber, is it true that Dudu Ndhlovu is dead?"

"I'm afraid it is."

"Murdered?"

"Yes."

"Ai-ai!" Tanda's voice lifted in the soft mourning sound of his people. "I heard, but I couldn't believe. Ai ai-ai! And the others?"

"Mkise and Simeyane are all right, so far as I know."

"Thank God for that." He straightened up. "I am sorry you have had to wait all day. We had to see if you were followed."

"And were we?"

"Not yet, but there is a search. We must hurry."

"Where to?"

"We want to talk with you. There's little time. At dawn we'll have to move away. Will you come?"

"Three of us will." Morry turned to young Brock and the groom, Jabulani. "I want you two to go back," he said, and then as the young faces dulled in disappointment, "it's very important that you cover for us. I want you to circle round to the south. Take your time getting home, and, when you do, say that the rest of the party has stayed behind, camping, near Talbot Dam. Don't say any more than that, understand, and don't speak at all unless you're asked. Okay?"

We helped them load most of our gear into their packs, and waved them off. Then we saddled our own horses and mounted. All this time there had been neither sound nor movement from the village. No light showed, no dog barked. I felt the will of Mrs Cele binding all to silence.

For the second time, we rode along the edge of the swamp, and at its southern end, swung west towards the mountains. The path soon dwindled and was gone. The ponies picked their way over trackless veld, by the light of the moon.

230

It was close on midnight when we left Brakvlei, and for four hours we threaded our way up the valleys. Colder and thinner grew the air, and the earth more sparsely covered; until at last we skirted a huge buttress of rock and came out on a massive slope that soared beyond, grey and glittering.

Tanda dismounted, signing us to do the same. "Be very careful here. The rock is slippery and loose. Let the horses choose the way."

We started upwards. Sometimes there was scrawny grass underfoot, more often nothing but the crumbling rock which slid at a touch. The gusting wind bit to the bone. I was shivering with cold and fear. I feared death in that place. I clawed for handholds, I listened all the time for the sounds of pursuit, I imagined bullets tearing into my flesh. Most of all, I feared Africa herself, huge and indifferent, towering in cliffs and summits unseen. Morry kept close to me, sometimes reaching out a hand in reassurance. I heard sobbing, and realized it was my own lungs labouring for breath.

At last we reached the end of the scree, rounding a shoulder to see a plume of water, burning silver, burst from the rock face and arch out into space.

I think I cried out. Tanda came back to stand beside me, gripping my arm. "It is all right, we go under the water. There is a path, quite safe."

He led my horse and I followed, blind, gasping as the icy spray blew into my face. Out on the far side, we were onto grass, blessedly firm, sloping wide and gentle to the stars.

We had reached the upper sponge-lands, source of streams and mother of plenty. I fell face down and dug my fingers into the turf. Morry leaned over me. "It's okay, love. We can ride now."

I heaved myself back into the saddle. We rode forward up the valley, which grew steadily narrower. Sometimes I thought I heard, above the wind's keening, the sound of voices.

We reached the crest; picked our way down a rocky defile for a short distance; and emerged in a little amphitheatre. Suddenly there was no wind, no sound at all. About a hundred yards away I saw a redness, which I realized was light streaming from the door of a mud hut. Against the glare, the figure of a man, facing us, waiting.

MAURICE FABER

Metallurgist, aged 37 years
South African citizen

XL

FROM THE TIME we reached Brakvlei, we were on Mochudi's ground. The village was too quiet for innocence. That was why I sent Rollo and Jabulani back, not wanting to run them into an ambush with the rest of us.

Twice, on the final climb, I heard movement on the mountain above us, and once I caught the flash of metal under the moon. My guess was we were in somebody's sights all the way up, and I was bloody relieved when we reached the top alive.

The man guarding the hut was armed. As we came up to him I saw the snout of a gun, half-hidden by the loop of his shoulder blanket, swing back and forth in a malign arc. It looked like some kind of rapid-fire weapon, but I couldn't see what make.

He spoke to Tanda in Xhosa. "Which one is Faber?"

"I am," I said.

He took a step forward, so that his face was in moonlight. He was stocky, the features flat, the eyes wide-set and slanting. He had a way of leaning on the balls of his feet; a man looking for trouble.

"What do you want?"

"To talk with Mochudi."

"He's not here."

Tanda said sharply, "Hold your tongue!" And then to us, "Come inside. It's warmer."

We dismounted, tethered our horses, and one by one ducked through the low door of the hut. It was roomy, and dry. By the smell of old dung, it was a winter shelter for cattle, but the daub was crumbling from the walls, and the thatch was rotten. A good pile of fire-blocks burned on a flat stone in the middle of the floor, giving heat, light, and a lot of pungent smoke, which escaped through the holes in the roof.

We dumped our packs against the rear wall. Tanda said, "Wait here, please. You will be quite safe." As he went out again, the guard intercepted him, bursting into a spate of Xhosa so rapid and idiomatic that I couldn't follow all of it, but there

234

was no mistaking its belligerence. After a while Tanda interrupted him impatiently.

"You know it was agreed to bring them."

"Not by me. Those other fools. What do they know?"

"There was nothing else to be done. . . ."

"Kill them now."

"Don't be such a child. . . ."

"Fools, letting this white manure come up here."

"You're so strong on that, why did you work with whites all those years?"

"That was planned. . . ."

"And take good pay for it, eh? Listen, while I was in detention, in solitary, you were taking girls to the shebeen every night. So don't tell me what I should do !"

Their voices faded as they moved away. Tindall looked at me. "What now?"

"We wait, as directed."

"And if that guy's speaking the truth? If Mochudi's not here?"

Jess, who had been kneeling close to the fire, lifted her head. "He's here somewhere." With her tangled hair, and the blue shadows of exhaustion round her mouth, she looked fey. "That young one," she said, "is it Hobeni?"

"I think so." I was pouring her a tot of brandy from the flask in my pack. "I've only seen a poor snapshot, I can't be sure. Here, drink this."

She sipped it slowly, shivering. "I couldn't understand what they were saying."

"A policy difference." Tindall eased down close to the wall. "Tanda and some others apparently voted for bringing us here. Hobeni—if it is Hobeni—didn't want that."

"He'd like to kill us, wouldn't he?"

"He used the word. I think—I hope—the decision doesn't rest with him."

"Are they terrorists?"

"I don't know." Tindall looked at me. "They had lookouts posted on the mountain."

"Yes, I think so."

"So what are our chances of getting out again?"

"That probably depends on what we say and do."

I settled down next to Jess, who turned so she could lean

235

against me. I thought that the one good thing that had come out of all this was having her back with me.

I sat trying to order my thoughts. No doubt we'd come to an armed camp, but what sort? The Lesotho border wasn't far away, and cattle-thieves worked across it regularly. A herdsman had been shot, only a month ago. But cattle-raiders would not own the sort of gun Hobeni was carrying.

So were these guerrillas, and, if so, were they foreigners or local men? Were they simply a gang drawn together to protect Mochudi, or were they part of something much bigger and more lethal? How did they tie in with Mark's death, Dudu's death? After a while I gave up puzzling. No doubt I'd get the answers soon enough.

We waited for almost an hour. None of us said much. The fire sank lower, sending up a single spiral of smoke. At last we heard horses approaching. They checked at the hut. A voice murmured something, and another answered. Then, with a quick, stooping stride, Amyas Mochudi came through the door.

I recognized him at once, though he was a helluva lot thinner than in the old pictures I'd seen of him, and his face was seamed with weariness. He was tall. Shabbily dressed in faded slacks, a sheepskin jacket, heavy boots. A knitted cap was pulled down over his ears. He might have been an upland peasant but for the force of his presence. The moment he entered the hut, he dominated it.

He looked round quickly, then walked over to Jess and helped her to her feet.

"Jess, it is good to see you. How are you?"

"Fine. But you. . . ?"

"All right. And tell me, why are you looking for trouble again, after all these years in retirement?"

"I could ask you the same thing."

"Mine was not of my own choosing." He glanced enquiringly at Tindall and me, and Jess introduced us. Mochudi studied us for a moment, chin lowered.

"I would very much like to know how you found out where I was." Although his voice was calm, I was aware of a tension in it; tired he might be, but not too tired to know if I lied to him.

"Guesswork," I said.

"You must be a good guesser, Maurice Faber."

"We strung a few facts together. The fact you'd been ill, Tanda's disappearance . . . a man who drops out of sight often goes back to his old haunts."

"But someone must have mentioned Mrs Cele's name?"

"My wife was told about her, by a friend."

"Who is the friend?"

I hesitated. Mochudi's gaze sharpened.

"A man named Ramisand Khoosal."

"The one who owns the hotel where the Summit is to be held?"

"That's right."

"Do you know how he got the information?"

"No. He has a lot of sources."

He nodded, but abstractedly, as if he was already considering something else. "Well, we may as well sit down." He did so, beckoning us toward the fire once more. I saw that Tanda and the young man had slipped into the hut and now stood one each side of the door.

"We'll have to be out of here by morning," said Mochudi, "so we'll have to talk fast. Tell me how it is in Durban."

"Bad. Worse than they're letting on."

"Riots?"

"General unrest. Your name is on the walls."

"Yes, I heard that."

"You're not responsible?"

"No. And Dudu Ndhlovu? What do they say about him?"

"I left before his death was made public." I paused, and Mochudi watched me with narrowing eyes. "He was shot in Seisson Road, near the strike area. Near Filey, Lofts, where your brother worked." I glanced at the young man by the door.

"Don is not involved in that. He was up here, with me."

"He still has some questions to answer."

"Maybe. What are they?"

I took my time. "A lot of people are anxious to find him. They think he can help them in their enquiries."

"The police?"

"And a man named Pitso, your brother's friend."

Behind me, Hobeni muttered something. Mochudi motioned him to silence.

"Tell us about Pitso."

"He called at my wife's home, late on Sunday night. He'd

237

been badly beaten. He was anxious for news of his old friend Hobeni."

"No friend of mine!" Hobeni moved to glare down at me.

"Your word against his," I said.

"I'm telling you! He tried to spy on me. He tried to sell me out. I'd be six feet under, if I hadn't got clear of him!"

"Mark Ramsay wasn't so lucky, was he?"

"What do you mean?"

"I mean that you led Pitso to Mark. He followed you to Mark's house."

"I never went there!"

"You went there on the Sunday night before Mark was murdered. You called at the house. You were seen there."

"Who saw me? Him?" Hobeni jerked his jaw at Tindall.

"It doesn't matter who," I said. "You were seen, and you were followed by Pitso. Not being able to sell you, he sold the fact of your visit. As a result, Mark died. That leaves you with some questions to answer."

He began to shout at me, but Mochudi's voice cut him short.

"That's enough. Sit down, sit down, man." As Hobeni slowly complied, Mochudi looked at me. "Ask the questions."

"I want to know why your brother visited Mark."

Mochudi shifted his eyes to Hobeni, who stared sullenly at the ground. I leaned towards him. "To quote your own words, 'Abebelele sebevukile'. The Sleepers are waking up. Tell me, who are the Sleepers?"

XLI

WHEN I SAID that, there was one of those silences that make
you feel everything is moving in closer. It was so quiet I could
hear a horse tugging at a tuft of grass, outside. Then Mochudi
spoke.

"The Sleepers are criminals. Specifically, the criminals of our
time and place."

"You mean urban terrorists?"

"No. They are not political. They are not part of any free-
dom movement. The organization they belong to has no cause
and no principles, except to make money. In some places it deals
in heroin, in others it ships the funk money away to secret
deposits. Here it is concerned with illegal arms.

"You see, my friends, crime is now part of big business, and
uses sophisticated methods. It owns computers. It sends its young
executives to the best training schools. It employs experts to do
market research. These people I am speaking about knew fifteen
years ago that southern Africa had a high potential for violence.
All the ingredients were here. Racial passions, political divisions,
great wealth next door to great poverty. It was a natural market
for guns.

"But a top-flight business organization does not merely use
the ready-made market. It develops new ones. It creates demand
by long-term programmes. It picks its personnel and deploys
them. That is what the Sleepers have done, here."

Mochudi's voice, soft though it was, carried a bitter conviction.
"The guns are coming in all the time, bigger and bigger quan-
tities. People blame the Communists. That suits the Sleepers.
Maybe they buy from the Communists now, but they aren't fussy.
They will buy from the West, too, if the price is right, and often
it is. The Sleepers are the agents of a world enterprise. They
have been working for years, burrowing into the flesh of the
nation : into the common life of the people . . . in the townships,
the white trades unions, communications, the media, the police
and the civil service.

"Their first task was to collect information and pass it to their international suppliers. Their second, to build the administration they need, to bring in the arms, distribute them and stockpile them. Their third, to create a seller's market.

"To make a big financial killing—and it will be hundreds of millions of rands—the Sleepers need certain conditions. They need racial conflict, on the widest possible scale. People must be desperate for weapons and ready to pay whatever price is asked.

"So the Sleepers, who have no politics and no cause, favour whatever may help to create the conditions they need. Once you understand what they are, it is easy to see that they favour corruption and stupidity in Government circles. They favour ignorance and misery for the masses. They favour violent and reactionary laws, to which people will react with more violence. Blessed are they that hunger and thirst after blood, for they shall be filled. Cursed are the peacemakers, for they are the destroyers of profits."

Mochudi raised his head to give us a steady look. "Believe me when I tell you. They are here. They have achieved all they planned. The time for the big kill is very close. That is why they cannot tolerate the idea of a successful Black Summit. It must not be allowed to succeed, because it might abort their programme.

"From the time the Summit was first suggested, two years ago, the Sleepers have done everything, everything they can, to block it. They have used their agents throughout society, including those they pay inside the Establishment.

"When I was released from the Island a few months ago, Dudu Ndhlovu came to see me. He told me how the Summit was going, and urged me to take part. I told him I must have time to think it over. I was ill, tired. Out of touch. I had to pick up the threads of my life. In politics, I had to learn the Who's Who, all over again.

"I stayed in Transkei. I lived very quietly. I kept in touch with Dudu, but I made no promises. I felt—how can I say?—like a chicken under the hawk's shadow. I knew I was being watched, and I asked myself, 'Why am I free? Why was I released? How are they trying to use me?'

"I decided to leave Transkei and go away, alone, where I could think. I told no one. I just got out one night, and headed north.

Came to Brakvlei. I knew Mrs Cele, because she looked after me when I was ill, as a young man. She arranged for me to hide up here, and sent me food. She brought Tanda, to be my liaison with Dudu and the others in town. After a while, some of my friends came to join me.

"It seemed safe. In fact, it seemed too safe. I know how strong the security police are. I was puzzled that they weren't making a real search for me.

"I knew about the strikes on the coast. Dudu kept sending me messages, I must attend the Summit. Black solidarity . . . I thought about it, was it possible, was it to be desired? The reports started to reach me, the people wanted Mochudi. In the townships, Mochudi was the name. Mochudi would lead. And I began to believe them. I began to be proud . . . what does the Bible say? Puffed up. I was puffed up. Lucky for me, I had my brother to bring me back to the ground."

Mochudi paused, and Hobeni, who had been staring moodily at the embers of the fire, raised his head. As their eyes met, I was sharply aware of the bond between them, and, also, of the clash of their wills.

"My brother came here last Monday," continued Mochudi. "He told me about the Sleepers. He said they had helped to get me out of prison. I refused to believe him. He said, 'Yes, they helped to get you out, and now they are building up your name in town. They are building a nice trap, down there, and you, Amyas Mochudi, are going to be the bait in it.' "

I looked at Hobeni. "Have you proof of that?"

He shrugged. "It is true."

"How can you know?"

"It is true."

There was only one way he could be that sure.

"You were one of them?" I said.

He nodded. "In a way, I was."

XLII

"CONDOR!" TINDALL'S voice was eager. "I told you, Morry.
A trip each year to the Mediterranean; shipping and trucking
facilities, and distribution points all round the country. Does he
operate from Filey, Lofts?"

Hobeni shook his head. The name "Condor" seemed to release
a spring in him and he started to talk rapidly.

"I didn't understand," he said. "I didn't know, at first, what
he was doing. . . ."

"How did you get into it?"

"When I went to Germany. I had a bursary to train in indus-
trial relations. While I was working there a group came from
South Africa on business. One of them—his name is not impor-
tant—came to me and he said, 'Why don't you make a specializ-
ation in trades unions? Germany has a lot of experiments, why
don't you learn them and take them back there?' We became
friendly, this guy and me. Go out for a couple of beers, you
know, and talk. I took his advice about the TUs. I was in Ger-
many two years. Just before I left there, this friend came back,
on holiday. We decided to make a holiday to Greece, drove
down. In Thessaloniki, he introduced me to Alex Condor. Con-
dor had this big boat, you know, a yacht. Big industrialist, they
told me, interests all round, Africa too. We had drinks on board
one night, and he talked to me. He said, 'If you come back to
Durban, look me up, I'll see if I can find you something'. And I
asked him, 'Do you know I am the brother of Amyas Mochudi,
who is on Robben Island?' He laughed and said, politics don't
matter to him, only profits.

"When I came home, I didn't go to him right off. I wanted
something on the Rand. But I couldn't find anything good. So
then I went down to the coast, and after a while I went to Filey,
Lofts. I thought Condor wouldn't remember me, but he did. He
asked me what I wanted to do. I said, 'Get trades-union rights
for my people'. People said Condor was a Government supporter,
I didn't want to start with him, and then get thrown out.

"He said, 'The trades unions will come later, not yet. I will give you a job that will allow you to train my workers in negotiation processes. You can liaise with management. There will be sufficient funds.'

"I said, 'And in exchange?' Because I was suspicious.

"He said, 'I will not have agitation. I want no trouble with the security police. I want you to see that I have a contented work force, here, and in my other concerns. I want the conditions I offer to be so good, that not one man will want to leave, or go on strike. You fix that and I'll be satisfied.'

"I couldn't believe my luck. I told him I would do as he asked, and I would like to start on the factory floor, not as an administrator. That is what I did. All the time I was with him, I stayed with the workers. After the first year, he sent me round to other towns, to his subsidiary companies, to set up the same systems. He kept his bargain, and I kept mine.

"In this time, I was also working with the young people in Clairville. Since so many of the schools closed, there were a lot idle on the streets. I was Mochudi's brother and they came to me. I began to have power with them, you understand?

"Condor knew about this. He did not object. Often, he would call me in to talk about our projects. He was very quick. He always knew the direction I was going, and he would make suggestions to help. I had to wonder, 'What sort of man is he?' I knew he had many friends in the Government. Yet he would talk about the labour laws as if he disagreed with them. I wondered, 'Could he be a Communist'. But I did not believe that. I believed he spoke the truth when he told me, the first time I met him, he was not interested in politics, only profits. And why should I worry, when I had things so good?

"So it went for two . . . two and a half years. Other factories had strikes. Not one of ours was affected. I felt very proud, for that."

"What made you change your mind?" I said.

"July last year, Condor spoke to me about Amyas. He wanted to know, how is Amyas with the young radicals, will they follow him? I said, 'Most will follow. But how can he lead, from the Island?' Then Condor said, 'If he is released, do you think he will agree to work here, for me?' I just laughed. I knew that no way will they release Mochudi, no way will they let him work on a factory floor.

"Condor smiled, as if he could see into my heart. He said, 'I got you, didn't I? Although you're Mochudi's brother, you work here, nobody interferes with you?'

"What he said worried me very much. I went to Dudu Ndhlovu and told him everything, about my job, how I met Condor, everything. Ndhlovu listened. At the end he said, 'Have the SP ever pulled you in for questioning?' When I said not he was surprised, he said, 'You're Mochudi's brother, yet they leave you alone? Why?' I told him, maybe I was watched, there was a man Pitso at the factory, I thought he was informing against me. But I was careful. I kept my nose clean.

"Ndhlovu said, 'You're a fool. Condor is using you. Now he's asking about Amyas. You must find out why.'

"I didn't want to believe him. I said, 'Condor is my friend. He has helped me and I can trust him.'

"Ndhlovu said, 'Hobeni, I will give you a warning. If Mochudi is released from the Island, you can know that Condor made it happen. And you must find out why. You are the only man who has contacts in all of Condor's works. You can find out the truth.'

"Two months after that, Amyas came off the Island. I went to Ndhlovu and said, 'I will do what you asked me to do.' "

"Did Ndhlovu help you?"

"No. I thought that would make suspicion. But I think, after I came up here, maybe he went to Filey, Lofts. I think, then, they killed him."

"How much did you find out about Condor?"

For answer, Hobeni reached into the folds of the blanket beside him and lifted out a gun, bringing it close to the embers of the fire so that its dull metal was blotched with red.

"I found this."

I bent to examine it. It was like nothing I'd ever seen; a little more than twenty centimetres long without the stock extended. Light, incredibly so. Fitted with a silencer.

"What's its firing speed?"

"1,200 a minute."

"My Christ!" I turned it over in my hands. "Where's it come from?"

"It's a Mac 11," Hobeni said. "An improved model of the

244

Mac 10 that the Green Berets used in Vietnam. The States banned their export. But Condor must have found a way."

"But this is a terror gun. With a dozen of these. . . ."

"Condor has already brought in nearly 50," Hobeni said.

XLIII

So many questions were exploding in my mind that I didn't know where to start. When I found my tongue, I saw that Hobeni had moved away from the fire and was sitting alone, knees drawn up, head sunk on his folded arms. I turned to find Mochudi watching me silently.

"Where did he get it?" I said.

"Bought it, to prove his point."

"Just like that?"

"No, not just like that. It took five months, and all the money he could raise."

I remembered the tales of Hobeni's debts. Cash, all he had. And he'd put his skin on the line as well, would continue to do so for the rest of his life. I handed the gun back to Mochudi.

"He showed it to Mark?"

"Yes." Mochudi looked regretful. "If Ramsay had gone straight to the authorities, as he promised. . . ."

"Mark liked to stage things to his advantage. He must have thought he had time. . . ."

"Not with these people."

"Why didn't your brother go to the police himself?"

"It would have been a little difficult for him, wouldn't it? Do you think he could take the gun into a police station, and say, 'Look what I bought'? Do you think they'd just take a statement and let him walk out and go home? The very best he could expect would be months of detention. And if he picked the wrong person—in fact, if it leaked out that he'd bought a Mac 11— then he would soon be as dead as your friend Ramsay, and Dudu Ndhlovu."

"Did he tell you where he bought it?"

"No. He won't discuss that, even with me. He won't put his contacts at risk."

"Weapons like that will be used against innocent people, black and white."

"Don is past those considerations."

246

"So how much did he tell you?"

"That Condor is the top man in the Natal division of an organization that covers the whole of southern Africa. That the organization is controlled and financed on a world scale. That it is running arms into the country: Scorpions, grenades, the sort of pistol you see there. The main receiving point is Condor's factory in Zululand—near Richard's Bay. We know some of the distributing agents. One is in the black security police. Another is a senior Government man. But most of the Sleepers are unknown. They will stay unknown until it is too late, for us."

"Why did Hobeni decide to speak to Mark Ramsay?"

"Ramsay was trusted by blacks. He also had the ear of important people. He had press contacts. Credibility."

There was something that didn't fit. It concerned Hobeni, withdrawn in his corner of the hut. According to Mochudi he wouldn't divulge how he'd got the gun, he didn't care how it was used. That was another way of saying he was committed to armed force, with the extreme radicals. So why had be gone to Mark at all? Why hadn't he left the Condor operation to achieve its ends? Second point. Having made contact with Mark, why was he so much against talking to us? Why had he opposed our coming up into these mountains?

What made Don Hobeni tick? What was he? Revolutionary? Playboy? Social reformer? Thinking about it, the eager way he's described his work at Filey, Lofts, it seemed to me that that was his real identity. Bright enough to win an industrial bursary to Germany. Dedicated enough to work on a factory floor, so he could get his ideas across. Condor had blown all that, conning Hobeni. Conning. Yes, that was closer to it. Why had Condor tricked this guy, why had he employed him at all? A labour activist was nothing but a bellyache to an industrialist, yet Condor had deliberately invited Hobeni into his circle, and nursed his interests. The answer to that must be, had to be, that Condor wanted Hobeni because through him he could reach Amyas Mochudi.

Mochudi was the key to it. He'd always been the key.

Condor wanted Mochudi. And with the Sleepers . . . if you knew what they were, then you knew what they wanted. They wanted to sell guns. They wanted a sellers' market for guns: unrest and corruption, stupidity and racial hatred. That they already had, the product to some extent of their own workings.

They wanted Mochudi now, not just free from the Island, not in seclusion in Transkei or lost in these mountains, but in the city. They had built a legend round him and they wanted him to accept the challenge implicit in that legend.

Mochudi must come down to lead his people. The Sleepers wanted it. There could be only one reason for that.

"Amyas, you can't go down there!" Involuntarily I spoke aloud. "They've set you up, man. If you attend the Summit, they'll blow you to Kingdom Come, and this whole country will go up in flames."

XLIV

THE NIGHT HAD ended while we talked. A deep red light was pouring through the doorway and the tears in the thatch. I saw that Hobeni had lifted his head and was staring at me intently.

"They will kill my brother," he said. "I warned Ramsay. He did nothing."

"What did you expect him to do?"

"Stop the Summit."

"He didn't have that power. He wouldn't have stopped it if he could, he considered it too important. That doesn't mean Amyas must commit suicide."

"You tell him that, he won't listen to me."

"Believe me, Mochudi," I said, "you have to pull out."

"I am in a dilemma."

"No bloody dilemma about it. You cut and run."

"A dilemma." His voice over-ruled me. "It is not a question of living or dying. It is a question of what I am worth. If I am killed, someone will replace me, in time. What I am . . . what I have always been . . . will remain. But if I do as you say, run away, then you know as well as I do what the results will be. The radicals will not attend the Summit. Many of the best young leaders will opt out. They're waiting for my word right now. And without them, the Summit is nothing. Black solidarity is finished. That is the first thing. The second is that if I run now, then I am finished. It is my time, now, Morry, and I must take it."

"Can't you get it through your head," I said, "that this goes way beyond the question of your own death or survival? There is going to be an attempt to assassinate you. Whether it succeeds or fails, that attempt can set the townships alight all round the country, and that violence will spill over into the industrial areas, the harbours, the mines. You're being used, man, can't you see that?"

I saw I was wasting my breath.

Mochudi wasn't listening.

I wondered what in hell he thought he could do against an organization like the Sleepers. Did he imagine that we were going to help him? It was the moment for sane people to split, and that was what I would do, I would take Tindall and Jess and get the hell out. And the blacks, what did he expect from them? Hobeni was a sullen bastard who could freak any time. Tanda didn't know whether to pick up a gun or a rosary.

I looked at Mochudi's face, ash-weary in the icy dawn light, and I knew something else. Hooked on his own legend, stoned on his own charisma, he would go down to the city alone, if he had to. I heard myself saying,

"What do you want us to do?"

Mochudi answered me at a tangent. "What do you think we have to do?"

"Expose the Sleepers . . . try and keep the Summit alive . . . try and keep ourselves alive. Amyas, you must see you can't handle this, with or without our help. There's only one way to deal with professional crime on this scale. You must go to the police."

"That is quite impossible." He shook his head with finality. "For one thing, we know the Sleepers have a line to the police. If we alert the police, we also alert the Sleepers. They will dismantle their operations, and Condor and his friends will be out of Africa before we can even reach them. There is a second consideration. Once the police know about the gun-running, they'll clamp down on all gatherings. The Summit will be banned."

"You can't suppress what you know. It would be totally irresponsible."

"I agree. The only card we hold is knowing about the Sleepers. We must play it, but at the right time. I shall release the information on Friday night, at the Summit. I want you to make a simultaneous announcement to your party leaders. They will inform the proper quarters, and they will be believed, even if I am not. Will you arrange that?"

A feeling of desperation was filling my gut. "Look, Amyas. You are doing precisely what Mark Ramsay did. Hanging onto lethal evidence, in order to gain a little personal glory. . . ."

"I?"

"Yes, my friend. Maybe you like the idea of going in there,

making your come-back into the big time with a big fanfare. Well, I don't give a bugger if you get yourself killed, but I do care about the hundreds of others who are going to get the chop to feed your vanity."

"I don't want glory." There was real hurt in his eyes. "I don't want you to be involved, more than to see that your people take the matter on, if I can't."

"I'm sorry. I accept your motives are pure. But there has to be a better way, something this side of martyrdom."

"I have tried to think of one," he said simply. "I don't know how we can spring the news early, without aborting the Summit."

It was true enough. Spring it too early, the Summit is banned. Hold on too long, Mochudi is killed and the balloon goes up. And yet. . . .

"There might be a way," I said, "at long odds . . . very long odds. If we could get police intervention on a limited scale. Something that would lead to action against Condor, and the Sleepers, and provide some sort of protection for you."

"You are still thinking of an approach to the police?"

Before I could answer, Hobeni exploded to his feet, shouting furiously in Xhosa. Mochudi silenced him with a raised hand.

"Morry?"

"One particular policeman."

"Who will go straight to the Security Police. You don't know the system as I do, Morry. As soon as it's a question of gun-running. . . ."

"We needn't mention guns. I will go to this man and tell him that he can be provided with evidence that will wrap up the Ramsay killing."

"And?"

"I'll need that evidence. The name of the factory in Zululand, for one thing. Hobeni must give me the details."

Hobeni laughed. "You think you'll find anything there, now? Man, they will have cleaned it up the same hour they killed Ramsay."

"Maybe," I said. "But we have one Mac 11, don't we? Can you have it planted at the factory?"

He stared down at me with narrowed eyes. "Perhaps."

"Perhaps won't be good enough."

"The factory has guards, security fence, dogs."

251

"If you had money? I have about 200. Tindall?"

"About 150."

I looked at Hobeni. "Would that help?"

He shrugged, and muttered something.

Mochudi had picked up the Mac 11, and was weighing it in his hands.

"What is the name of this policeman?"

"Buddler. Colonel Buddler."

"And you imagine he will trust you?"

"Not trust. Believe."

"Why?"

"Because he already believes in the Sleepers. He was working on the murder case, he got too close to the truth, and he was taken off it."

"You spoke of 'limited action'. What makes you think this Buddler will accept limits? Why shouldn't he do the normal thing and go to the SP?"

"He might. But I think not. I think he will want to get his hands on concrete evidence. He will play along until he has it. But I told you, it's long odds. I could be wrong."

Mochudi was silent a long time. Then he handed the gun to his brother.

"You will take it north, tomorrow. As soon as you have planted it, let me know. We'll arrange a safe place for you to leave messages." Then to me, "And you will speak to Buddler".

I nodded. "I'll have to know exactly where it's hidden. Buddler will have to fix a raid, but he must know where to look, we can't waste time with searches."

"And the timing?"

"Not later than noon on Friday. I may have to lay ground bait earlier than that."

"Well, we can discuss the details. As to myself, I plan to make a public statement about the Sleepers at the Summit dinner. There'll be black pressmen present. Can you communicate with the white press?"

"I have some contacts." I was thinking of what Charlie Cameron had told me. "There's a lot of pressure on them, right now. I don't know how much will get into print."

"But you agree, we must try and publicize?"

"Oh yes. The more people we tell, once we're ready, the

better for us. The papers will use it if they possibly can, it's a big story. The timing isn't too good. If you release it on Friday night, then nothing can appear until the Saturday dailies." I fell silent, unwilling to add the obvious corollary to all this.

Amyas said calmly, "So, Friday night is the danger point. That's when they're most likely to make their move. First, they are looking for dramatic effect. It will be best for them to choose Friday night, at the dinner. All the black leaders will be present, and in the townships, on Friday night, the liquor is flowing and people are ripe for trouble. Friday night, at the start of the dinner. After I have joined the gathering, but before I have time to speak. They'll try then."

"Yes," I said. "I think so."

Tindall reached across me, to hand Mochudi a bundle of bank-notes. "Here's the tom. What sort of security measures are being taken at this conference?"

"Routine police surveillance." Mochudi's mouth curved in a faint smile. "For once, we may be grateful."

"That means they'll check the streets round the Southern Cross Hotel, I take it?"

"I expect so."

"And inside?"

"They'll search it for possible bombs. Station men at key points, during the talks."

"Do you know the hotel?"

Mochudi shook his head. Jess said, "I do. The conference rooms are on the first floor, with the main dining-room. Then there's a roof garden with a restaurant and pool. Which are they using?"

"The roof garden," said Amyas.

"I don't like that much. There are two sets of lifts, but once you're up there, you'll be kind of trapped."

"Eleven floors up could be safer than one."

"If they attack from the street, yes. But they may have people inside : among the delegates, the pressmen, the hotel staff."

"I'll have to talk about the internal security with the Summit chiefs."

"You're going to tell them about the Sleepers?"

"Why yes. I must. I can't just turn up on Friday, and I can't put them at risk without any warning. I'll have to tell the chiefs."

"Then they might call off the whole thing." Jess sounded eager and Mochudi gave her his slow smile.

"I wouldn't count on it, my dear."

"Jess," I said, "could you get Ram to supply us with plans of the building?"

"I expect so."

"Good. We can study those, and try and work out our defences. Amyas, it's time we moved from here, isn't it? Where do we go?"

"Not to Brakvlei. You may have been traced that far, by now. We'll go north east, to the Witberg Mission. It's safe. We can rest there for a couple of hours, and move down to the coast after dark."

I was wondering where in Durban we would go. We needed some sort of hideout, but I didn't know the city well enough to name one. Jess answered the question for me.

"Ram will find us a good place," she said.

I hoped she was right.

We reached the Witberg Mission around noon. It was no more than a clutch of shacks round a corrugated-iron church and a cement-block hospital. But it was run by Tanda's order, and the people there made us welcome, gave us food and drink and water to wash in.

As soon as we got there, Jess asked permission to use the hospital 'phone, and put through a call to Ram Khoosal. Luckily she found him in his office.

Coming back, she told us we must stay put until nightfall. "He'll send transport for us. He has a place we can stay, wouldn't mention it on the 'phone, but the driver will take us straight there. He'll be in Durban himself, tomorrow. He'll book in at the Southern Cross and liaise with us from there."

Hobeni left us about three o'clock, cadging a lift on the milk truck that went 30 kilometres into the nearest town. From there, he said he could travel with friends, to Richard's Bay. The Mac 11, dismantled, was stowed under his jacket.

It was in all our minds that the two brothers might not see each other again. But, typically, Hobeni wasted no words, except to say, as he hoisted himself between the milk cans, "Go well, Amyas. I'll send news as soon as I can."

254

It would be another five or six hours before our transport arrived. Jess slept, sprawled in a cane chair on the stoep. The rest of us sat in the scrawny shade of some wattle trees that flanked the church, and tried to build some sort of plan of action for the next few days.

At six, a child came down from the mission to tell us supper was ready. As we walked up the slope towards the mess-room, Tindall signalled me to lag behind, and fell into step beside me.

"Have you given any thought to the form that an attack on Mochudi might take?"

"Not very much. It's difficult, without having seen a plan of the hotel. But I think Jess is right. They won't attempt an armed rush from outside. Too many police about. They probably wouldn't get past the downstairs foyer."

"I agree. The danger is likely to lie right inside. These are sophisticated operators. I think we should be prepared for some sort of explosive device."

"A bomb, you mean?"

"Yes. If they can bring Mac 11s into the country, you may be sure they have access to the material to build a bomb. Something small in size, but powerful enough to kill a man over a radius of several feet. They might even use radio to activate it."

"How?"

"Well, they would have to build the explosive device. That's not all that difficult. One would need plastic explosive, a solenoid battery which is about the size of a small coin, fine fuse wire, gunpowder to form the detonator."

"And the radio bit?"

"It's possible to use radio signals to trigger such a device. One would probably need three separate radio stimuli. A spring is released, that sets up contact, the battery is activated and the fuse wire heats, detonating the gunpowder and so, the plastic explosive."

"Three signals. You mean three people would be needed?"

"Not necessarily. One radio, sending three signals, could do it."

"From what distance?"

"Oh . . . a couple of hundred metres."

I began to feel sick.

"So one man, with quite a simple sender, could set off the

255

bomb any time he chose?"

"Yes."

"What can we possibly do to counter that?"

"Well, it's really a question of finding the device." Tindall gave me his owlish stare. "The police will doubtless make a search of the conference and dining areas. If that is done by an expert, who knows what to look for, and where to look. . . ."

"There's another 'if'," I said grimly. "If we can be sure that the man who does the search is not a Sleeper."

"Yes, there's that. I was wondering . . . what chance would there be of getting me in, before the crowd goes in to dinner? I could do a private check."

"We could probably arrange it, if Mochudi pressures the Summit to ask for it to be done. You could be billed as an electronics fundi—which you are—even if you have to go round in company with a policeman. Better than nothing. I'll speak to Amyas. Meanwhile, Dave, keep working at it, will you?"

He nodded. As we went up the slope once more, I saw his lips moving. No doubt he was thinking about all the things in the dirty-tricks locker. I was in too much of a muck sweat to think at all.

XLV

THE TRANSPORT provided by Ram Khoosal arrived at the Mission about nine o'clock, in the form of a battered goods van. The driver was a young Indian with acne, ringlets and sharp little eyes. Jess introduced him as Khoosal's nephew Monan. Talk wasn't his thing, but he was a good driver, and by midnight we were through the outskirts of Durban and heading for the city centre. I could see enough through the grating at the back to recognize the mosques and narrow shop-fronts of the Indian business district.

The van slowed, swung off the road, stopped. After a pause the rear doors swung open and Monan stood outside, holding up a hand to help Jess alight.

We were in a parking garage. Several other vans were already parked along the rear wall. Monan led us past these to a heavy wooden door; unlocked this and signalled us through; relocked the door.

The stairway was steep and narrow, but it smelled clean. At the third landing, Monan unlocked another door. What lay beyond was a welcome surprise : an apartment, close-carpeted, discreetly luxurious.

"Whose is this?" I asked.

Monan grinned like the genie of the lamp.

"My uncle's, now. It was made for my grandmother. She was, you know . . . purdah, old fashioned. She didn't go out but she ran things from here, the shops and the warehouse. It's a good place, because there are three stairways, and the lane at the back takes you right into the market, if you want to get lost. Please make yourselves at home."

There was food and coffee on a table. We ate, though we were too tired to taste. Monan showed us our rooms. Ours had a bathroom of its own, and Jess went straight in and turned on the taps. I lay down on a bed as big and white as a cloud, and fell instantly asleep.

I woke because someone was tapping on the bedroom door. It

was still dark, and I started to swear, and then remembered where I was, and got on my feet.

Father Tanda was standing in the passageway, fully dressed "Mochudi said I should tell you I am going to talk with the Summit chiefs. I'll tell them everything we've agreed, but it you have other messages. . . ?"

"Yes, I have. Tindall wants access to the hotel, particularly the roof-garden area, before the delegates go in. He wants to check for explosives. Do you think the chiefs could arrange to square it with the police?"

"Perhaps. We can try."

"How are you going?"

"Monan will take me in the van, and bring me back."

"Fine. Go well." As he was turning away, I remembered some thing else. "Tanda, could you get a message to Mr Walter Brock at his home? Just tell him, 'Morry says everyone's okay. Don' worry.' "

He asked for the address, and I told him. He went quietly away down the stairs. I waited on the landing until I heard the van move out of the garage.

When I went back to bed, Jess was still asleep, one arm thrown across her eyes. She half woke as I lay down, and mut-tered restlessly, turning into my arms.

XLVI

JESS MADE BREAKFAST for us. There seemed to be enough food in the place to see us through a siege.

About ten o'clock, Monan came up the stairs, followed by Ram Khoosal and his wife, Sita.

Khoosal was a strange little guy : smooth, quick, clever, but somehow detached. He listened to the history of the past few days with his head politely bent. One would have said he was being given an account of a seaside holiday. Certainly he didn't seem to give a bugger about the political nuances in the situation. Yet he'd been the one to track down Mrs Cele, and the Summit meetings were being staged in his hotel. I found myself wondering if we could trust him. Enigmas always worry me.

At about eleven he got up, saying he must get back to work. "Use Sita as your messenger. She can come and go in these environs without exciting attention." He gave me a bunch of keys. "Keep them, Maurice. The ignition key is for the green Datsun in the garage. Use it if you have need. The rest are for the doors in this building."

"You control a lot of doors," I said.

He gave me a bland look of the diamond-shaped eyes. "I am very rich," he said. "I can buy a lot of things."

"Like the services of Mrs Cele?"

"I didn't buy her services. I think one could not. But . . . information as to her whereabouts, yes."

"We're indebted to you. It puzzles me, your involvement."

"Does it? Well, I am an old friend of Jess. And perhaps, I have grown a little tired of passive-resistance campaigns."

After he'd gone, I spoke privately to Jess.

"You trust the Khoosals?"

"Absolutely." She looked astonished. "They've helped us find Mochudi."

"The Sleepers wanted Mochudi to be found. I'm more and more convinced of it. They wanted him found, and they've left us free to find him. Steadily moving us on, setting up the board

259

for their end-play."

"Not Ram and Sita. I trust them completely." Her voice sharpened. "We allow you to trust Buddler because you know him a little better than we do. I know the Khoosals."

I had to leave it at that.

At noon, I 'phoned Buddler. I had to wait a short while before he answered.

"It's Faber," I told him, "and I'm not wasting time. I can offer you information about the Ramsay murder. I would like to meet you this evening. You come alone, or it's no deal. Agreed?"

He hesitated only a moment. "Where?"

"I'll 'phone you later."

"Not this number." He gave me another, which I memorized. " 'Phone at seven-thirty sharp."

"Don't try and get a fix on me," I repeated, "or it's no deal."

He put down the receiver without answering.

Sita Khoosal went out shopping in the early afternoon, and returned with clothes for all of us, badly needed after the past few days' junketting. She also brought a large wooden box, which she set down carefully on the dining-room table.

From the box she took a number of bottles, pots and sticks of grease-paint, which she set out with the rapid neatness of a theatre sister arranging her instruments. Next she fetched a kitchen bowl, and filled it with strong bleach; and into this, dropped a frizzy Afro wig. We watched the thing turn colour, first to a virulent orange, then to a dirty greyish yellow.

"It will be all right when it's washed," she said.

Mochudi eyed it. "Who's it for?"

"You. We have to get you into the hotel. Ram thinks it will be best if we can get you right up to the conference floor without anyone recognizing you. At least we must get you past the crowds outside, or you'll be mobbed. I have thought of a . . . you know . . . a disguise. But I will have to practise it."

She took a photograph from her bag and handed it to me. It was a mug-shot a couple of inches square, the sort of thing you have done for a licence or passport.

The subject was hideously ugly.

He was an albino African—what kids used to call a white kaffir—with the short nose and full lips of the Nguni people, but a skin that, instead of being dark brown, was waxy-pink and blotched with huge yellow freckles. The hair was cropped in tallowy peppercorns, the eyes, staring straight ahead, seemed to have no iris at all.

Looking at it, Mochudi hissed between his teeth. "You can do that?"

"I can try," answered Sita. She picked up a pot of base paint and considered its contents. "The man is named Breen. Albert Breen. People like him don't find it easy to get work. Ram gave him a job twenty years ago and he's been with us ever since. He'll do anything we ask."

"What's his job?" said Mochudi.

"He does the electrical work at the hotel. Comes in at eight every morning and leaves at five; but he's often kept on overtime if we have a big function. He looks after the mikes and so on. Sit here, please, Amyas."

She looped a towel over Mochudi's shoulders, and went to work with the base-paint. Her fingers were deft. I remembered that Jess had told me Sita was a dancer before she married, trained in the special schools of India. To her the dance would have a religious significance, and to use her skill to deceive other people would be alien to her. To help us, she'd stepped outside of her true nature.

Then suddenly I saw that we had all done just that : Mochudi and Hobeni had left their black isolation to come to grips with whites like Ramsay; Tindall had dropped his prim respectability; Jess was back in a political dogfight she'd made up her mind to avoid; Tanda and I were way beyond the limits of our own sworn creeds. And I understood that this was all we had going for us, our ability to do the unexpected and to fight back with resources we never even knew we had.

Sita continued to work, referring constantly to the little snapshot. She mapped out the albino freckles, the lines at the corner of mouth and eye. When she was done, she sprayed on some sort of fixative from an aerosol can; stood back, and studied the effect.

"No," she said. "No good. Too obvious. And the skin is too shiny, I must find some way of dulling it. Amyas, I will swab it all off and we start again. I must have it good enough to stand an examination in the half-light, at least."

She began to clean Amyas' face with some sort of spirit. The "skin" peeled off in strips, horribly real.

"How do we make the switch?" said Tindall.

"Breen will be working all day at the hotel," she said. "We will see to it that when the security police move in, tomorrow afternoon, Breen encounters them a number of times. They can check his identity papers and get used to seeing him about the place. People tend not to look too closely at an albino. They stare for a moment, then they get embarrassed and look away.

"I think I can achieve a close resemblance to Breen. Amyas is much the same height and build, and Breen has a very distinctive walk—flatfooted, you know? I'll teach you, Amyas.

"About six o'clock, we'll send Breen over here to fetch something. Amyas will return in his place." She frowned. "The eyes are the problem, of course, but luckily Breen wears blue-tinted spectacles. He'll wear them at work tomorrow, and hand them over to Amyas."

Mochudi leaned back in his chair. "So tell me about this Breen. What does he speak, Zulu, English? What are his habits, his mannerisms? If I'm to be the star, I must rehearse."

We were hoping all day to hear from Hobeni that he'd planted the Mac 11; but no word came.

During the afternoon, I borrowed a typewriter from Sita and sat down and typed letters to Walter Brock, to my attorney, and to an eminent judge I know quite well. In the letters I made a resumé of what had happened, gave the facts we had about the Sleepers, and the few names we knew. I put the letters into envelopes and addressed them and marked them "To be opened in the event of my death or serious disablement".

Monan and I had already picked the place I would meet Buddler.

At six I dressed in my own clothes, which were dirty enough to make me look like a vagrant. I slid the letters, and the little automatic given me by Bianca Ramsay, into the pocket of my jacket.

On my way downstairs to meet Monan, I realized that Jess was following me.

"You're not coming," I said.

"Please, Morry. I need to be with you." Her eyes had a feverish look. Maybe mine did too. Anyway, I didn't argue.

Monan had the van ticking over in the garage. Jess and I climbed into the back, and we set off, north past the race-course. When we stopped at a traffic-light, I put my eye to the grating at the back, and saw a newspaper hoarding, "Mochudi Snubs Summit?"

Some reporter flying a kite, I thought; but it pleased me. The more people who thought Mochudi was back in Transkei, the better for us.

We crossed the river near Sea Cow Lake, and there Monan stopped at an Indian café so that I could make my call to Buddler, and tell him where to come.

From there, we doubled back across the river and turned inland, past the quarry to the flats where the railways were build-ing a small extension line.

We parked the van and followed a footpath that brought us to a wooden fence. Monan leaned down and pressed the base of a couple of the boards. They swung inwards, leaving a space just wide enough for passage.

"Take the path straight across," he said. "I'll keep watch here. I'll hoot three times if there's trouble."

Jess and I ducked through the fence, and the boards, with a soft final sound, fell to behind us.

XLVII

WE WERE AT the head of a slight rise, from which the ground sloped down for about a mile to the river. There were a lot of lights on the far bank, but on this side nothing more than the safety lamps on the storage sheds far to our left. Those would be guarded, but we weren't going near them.

Straight ahead the land had been cleared for workshops, and was still unfenced. For two acres there was not a blade of grass to cast a shadow, no place a man could hide. Beyond the clearing was a small halt, also deserted.

We set out for this, picking our way along a sand track. Roughcast steps brought us onto the concrete platform. Opposite was a signal box, its windows not yet glazed. To the right, a temporary bridge gave access to another expanse of open ground.

Buddler arrived at about a quarter past eight. He came from the far side of the track, on foot and alone; crossed the bridge without checking, and headed towards us.

A couple of paces off he stopped and stood looking about him, his hands on his hips. He wore dark slacks and jacket. There was a stiffness in the set of his neck and shoulders, the stiffness you see in the bar-room tough who'll shove a broken bottle in your face if you say the wrong word.

I said, "Were you followed?"

"No."

"Does anyone else know where you are?"

"My son knows, that's all." His voice was soft and flat, almost indifferent, but I could see runnels of sweat each side of his forehead. He turned to face me.

"Well? Come on, what have you got?"

"First tell me, what guarantees can the police give to informers?"

He smiled sourly. "No guarantees. Protection, sometimes."

"I want guarantees. I have information that can help you solve the Ramsay killing. It's not for free."

Buddler reached into a pocket, found a pack of cigarettes, shook one loose, lit it, blew smoke. The way he blew, you could tell he wanted to blow Jess and me and all humanity into the sea.

"Mr Faber, if you have such information, it's your duty to tell the police. If you don't, you're guilty of an offence."

"We're way past duty and correct procedure, Colonel. You're here because a subversive organization has infiltrated your little castle and tried to blow you out. I'm here, frankly, because I very much want to stay alive. What I know can serve both our purposes. But I want a deal, not crap about what's the proper procedure."

"What exactly are you offering me?"

"Names," I said. "Names and places that can lead you to the people who shot Mark Ramsay, Calgut and Dudu Ndhlovu. I can tell you some of the people in a conspiracy."

"On the force?" Buddler's eyes had a reddish glint.

"No. Except for the man who shot Calgut, I can't even guess at those. But there's one name on the SP strength. A black."

He was silent a bit. Then, "On what terms?"

"First, any information I give you stays buttoned."

"I can't guarantee that."

"And I can't put my life, and the lives of my wife and my friends, at risk so you can file reports in triplicate. As long as any member of the police force is suspect, or in a position to pick up what I tell you, I must demand the protection of secrecy."

"Lieutenant Kray has been transferred," he said.

"Where to?"

"The Transvaal."

"There could be other . . . risks, let's call it."

Buddler considered. "You can take it, at the moment I'm not sharing this with anyone. The only person who knows where I am tonight is my son—that's in case you're not such a good risk yourself. The people I talk to, I can trust."

"Okay, I'll have to accept that. Secondly, I want some sort of reassurance that you won't have me and my friends arrested or detained or restricted or any other of your fancy phrases for gaol without trial, as a result of having given you the information."

"If you've kept your nose clean, Mr Faber, I don't want to

put you in gaol. If you're involved in criminal activity, I can't protect you. What is more, I can't even guarantee action on what you say you can tell me. Subversion is a matter for the security police."

"I know it. That's why I want your word that my identity and the identity of my wife and friends is not revealed to anyone else for the next four days."

"Why do you say four days?"

I made no reply. After a while, Buddler said impatiently, "I told you, I can't give guarantees."

"And I told you, forget protocol, forget you're a good little copper."

Buddler stepped up close to me. "Listen, jong. I can have you detained indefinitely, and nobody is going to see you or hear from you until we say so. You can sit in the chookie for as long as it takes you to tell us what we want to know."

"So detain me and Jess, by all means. You won't get the facts until it's too bloody late to use them, and the results will be so bad that you'll have nothing left to do but jump from one of your tenth-floor windows. On the other hand, if you meet my terms, I will give you something useful. Then, when the four days is up, you can report to your bosses and claim my scalp and whatever glory that brings you."

Buddler took a last draw on his cigarette, dropped it, stamped it out. He stood with head bent for some time. When he spoke, it was almost to himself.

"You want me to suppress information. Suspend the law. Give you a blank cheque for four days."

"Yes. I'm staking my freedom. I'm asking you to stake your career. And I'm telling you that if we don't pull something out of the hat, my freedom and your career won't exist, and a lot of people who matter more than either of us don't have any future on this earth."

Buddler raised his head. His eyes, curiously empty of expression, raked my face.

"How many names have you got?"

"Seven."

"And evidence?"

"I can tell you how and where to find that."

His head turned sideways a fraction, like a sighting dog's.

"First," I said, "give me my guarantees."

"I'll do what I can for you."

"Not good enough. I want your word on four days."

"All right."

"Buddler, one last thing. All the power is on your side. If you spill this story to the wrong people, if you curtail our freedom before the four days is up, then the people who killed Mark Ramsay will get to us before you can get to them. The consequences to this country could be so colossal that you'll be sorry for the rest of your life . . . which probably won't be very long."

"Give me the names."

"Not yet. Tomorrow."

He made an involuntary movement of anger.

"Tomorrow," I repeated, "when I have the details. I'll 'phone you. Do I use the same number?"

"What time will you 'phone?"

"Not later than noon."

"Then you can use that number. I'll be there."

"One last thing. Can you set up a raiding party?"

"Yes."

"With a helicopter?"

"If I have to."

"I think you'll need one."

He stood chewing his lip. Finally he said, "Listen, Faber, why don't I just give you my uniform and you can do the job yourself?"

"Because you'll do it better."

He grunted, a sound of dislike and annoyance. But all he said was, "I'll see you in four days' time. You can count on it."

He turned away and walked back the way he'd come. We watched him as he crossed the stripped red ground, his figure dwindling until he seemed a puppet on a moon-waste.

"Will he do as he says?" Jess slipped her arm through mine.

"I think so."

"He frightened me. He looked as if he'd like us dead."

"We've made him break his rules. Come on now, let's get moving."

Back at the fence, Monan was waiting, the van's engine running. By nine-thirty we were back at Khoosal's. Soon after ten, Mochudi called us all together for a conference.

XLVIII

"HAVE YOU HEARD from Hobeni?"

The anxiety in Tindall's voice was reflected in every face round the table. Hobeni's rôle was crucial to the whole operation. If he failed to plant the gun, then I'd have nothing to give Buddler, there'd be no police action against the Sleepers, and they could move in on us any time they chose.

At the head of the table Mochudi nodded: "Sita brought a message an hour ago. My brother is in touch with a coloured electrician at the factory. It cost him the money you gave, and he must still find another 700; but that is to be paid only if the police find the gun."

"Where will they hide it?"

"In the roof of the office block. That is where they've kept any top-secret stuff when there was a delay in shipments. The entrance is behind a lighting panel in the manager's office. Our contact will go in to check the wiring, and hide the gun."

"Can we rely on him?"

"As much as on any bought man. He's scared. They are all scared up there, since Ramsay was shot, and the workers have got the idea it's a good place to be out of. So this one wants to feather his nest first. What arrangements did you make with Buddler?"

I told them what had been agreed. When I came to the bit about our getting four days' grace, long enough to cover the Summit, Tanda shook his head.

"Morry, you won't get four hours, or four minutes. Same with Amyas. If he gets up at that dinner and talks about the Sleepers, the SP will arrest him. Us too."

"You may be right. I'm hoping for some recognition of the fact we've exposed the racket. But if we don't get it . . . if we're detained . . . then that's the luck of the draw. I must tell you, I don't think any one of us has a great life expectancy. We've taken on an organization that's already killed three men. Do you think they'll let us run loose? So all we can do is make a play for our lives, not a very good one, perhaps, but better than sitting and waiting for a bullet in the back."

Mochudi said, "I agree. Tanda, tell us what the leaders said today?"

The priest leaned back in his chair. "I spoke to them about the Summit. They are adamant it must go ahead, it's the last chance we will have. They want Mochudi to attend, even though they know the dangers. They gave me full details of the conference arrangements. Lists of the delegates, observers, pressmen and staff. Names of the police personnel who will attend, where we know them." Tanda tossed some sheets of paper on the table. I glanced at them, without being much the wiser. Lieutenant Kray's name wasn't on the police list.

"And the security measures?" said Mochudi.

"Very good. The police are doing everything to avoid incidents. They will search the whole of the conference area, and the restaurants, tomorrow morning. After that, no one will be allowed in except under police supervision."

"How about Tindall?" I asked.

"I think we can fix it. But he won't have long." Tanda reached into a pocket and produced an envelope. "These are passes, signed by the leaders to take us into the hotel. Everyone must produce an identity document, as well. All the access roads round the hotel will be heavily policed from sundown tonight, and from tomorrow afternoon there'll be cordons checking traffic, and crowd-control squads. They're afraid of demos by the extremists. With all these measures, I don't think there is much chance of an attack from outside the hotel."

Tindall leaned forward. "You said I won't have long. How long?"

"An hour, hour and a half."

"My God, that's not enough! Do you realize how many places I must try to check? Restaurant, kitchens, storage cupboards, air vents, the mike system. Christ, it's impossible! Amyas, can't you call this deal off?"

Amyas shook his head without speaking.

"It's lunacy." Tindall sounded close to tears. "You don't appreciate how little I can do . . . how totally inadequate I feel. . . ."

"Nevertheless," said Amyas gently, "I shall be happier with

you at my side. Tell me, how do you think they will make their attempt?"

"I think . . . probably an explosive device. A bomb can be quite small, you know, small enough to tuck into a cigarette box, or a fountain pen." Tindall ran his fingers over his forehead. "Morry, do you stick by your theory that they'll go for Amyas in particular, rather than any of the other leaders?"

"I think they'll single out Amyas, for the reasons we've already discussed."

"Very well, then my view is this : we don't have the time or the manpower to cover every eventuality, so we must make up our minds what is the most likely line of attack, and defend that line. We should, I think, assume they will choose an explosive device, which they will detonate at a time when Mochudi will be the sole victim. It will be after he joins the conference crowd, but before he has the opportunity to speak to them. Working on those principles, I believe the moment of peak danger will be when Amyas gets up to speak. There'll be a standing mike, I understand. When he moves across to that, then they'll trigger the thing."

"How?" said Amyas.

"My guess is, by radio. They could use something like a walkie-talkie, in the restaurant itself, or the immediate surroundings."

"It sounds very technical," I said.

"It would be in character," Tindall answered. "These are gangsters with technical skills above the ordinary. They have access to Mac 11s, they can certainly obtain the material for anti-personnel bombs."

"So in a nutshell, we have to watch out for an explosive device in a small container; and also for some sort of sending radio?"

"That's about it."

Meeting Tindall's eyes, I thought of the number of places you can hide a cigarette packet in any good-sized restaurant; the number of people we could deploy to find it; and I was tempted, as he had been, to beg Amyas to pull out. But I held my trap. Amyas couldn't pull out, and asking him to do so would be nothing more than adding my fears to his shoulders.

"Ram," I said, "could we look at the floor plans, please?"

270

XLIX

KHOOSAL SPREAD A roll of papers flat on the table, signing to us to gather round him.

"This is the front elevation," he said, pointing to the topmost plan. "It faces an open plaza, about 100 metres deep and 300 wide. That is where the crowds will mass.

"The main entrance doors—here—will be closed to the general public from five o'clock. The leaders' party is due to arrive at six. People wanting to use the public bars tomorrow evening will have to use the side doors, and that whole sector will be cut off from the main part of the hotel. In other words, there will be no mingling of the public with the conference people.

"There will be police in the entrance hall, to check the guests arriving and to supervise the access to the lifts and stairways. Naturally, most of the people concerned in the Summit will be in the hotel, well before six. But again, they will not be allowed to enter the conference rooms on the first floor, nor the roof-garden area, without going through police check points. There are fire doors on every floor, which can be closed if need be."

"Who's in charge of security?"

"A Captain Erasmus."

"White?"

"Yes. But they're using a lot of black police. I think we can accept there will be a very heavy concentration of police in and around the Southern Cross."

I thought, a lot of them will have walkie-talkies. So who will watch the watchers?

Aloud, I said, "We have one thing going for us. The Sleepers can't be sure whether or not Mochudi will attend the Summit."

Tindall shook his head. "No matter. They will have a contingency plan. Perhaps more than one."

"Agreed. But we must keep them guessing as long as possible. We must move Amyas into the hotel at the last possible moment, and keep him under wraps until he's due to appear."

"The safest place," murmured Ram, "would be the penthouse. That has been set aside for the use of the leaders. But we'll come to that in a moment." He shuffled another sheet from the roll of plans, and pinned it flat on the table.

"This is the eleventh floor—the roof-garden level. As you see, it is divided roughly into five sectors, two on the left of the building, three on the right.

"This right-hand, central sector is the Moonshot lounge, with its bar and cloakrooms. It is served by the main passenger elevators.

"The back, right-hand area contains the kitchens, coldrooms, pantries and serveries for the restaurant. There are service lifts to the kitchens, so that one can reach them without being seen by the public.

"Over on the left half, you have the Stargazer restaurant, where the dinner will be held; and next to it, taking up the front, left-hand sector, the gardens, the open-air bar, and the swimming pool. You will see that the division between the pool-deck and the restaurant is mainly glass—even the five doors are entirely glass—and there are glazed panels in the dome of the Stargazer. The idea is that diners should be able to see the real Southern Cross.

"The main entrance to the Stargazer, however, is from the Moonshot.

"And finally, we have the remaining area, at the front, right-hand corner of the building. This is the penthouse. It is never let to the general customer. We reserve it for company fat-cats like myself, or important visitors. Sometimes we hold a board meeting there. And this weekend, as I've indicated, it will house the Summit leaders.

"Now, if you study the plan, you will see that the inner wall of the penthouse is curved; and right along this curve, there runs an enclosed balcony, extending from the pool-deck, across the Moonshot, to the kitchens. Here, here and here," Ram's finger pointed, "there are observation windows, made of one-way glass. One can stand on the balcony and observe this little eleventh-floor world, gaze upon the stargazers; a very useful asset for a hotel-owner, I can assure you.

"Two elevators serve the penthouse. One, as you see, is in the Moonshot sector, the other a service lift at the back of the building. I suggest we use the latter when we bring Amyas into the hotel."

"How do you propose we do that?" I said.

"We must make very careful arrangements; set the scene, as it were. I have already, at police insistence, had my staff at the hotel prepare schedules of all the duties they will perform during the entire congress. These schedules show that on the Friday night Breen will be on duty in the restaurant and penthouse zones. They also list certain taped music which is required to be played during the evening.

"At approximately five o'clock on Friday, those tapes will be found to be missing. Breen will raise something of a scene about this, I will appear and undertake to remedy the matter. I will send Breen out to fetch substitute tapes, I will obtain police permission for him to do so, and I will also try to get some sort of paper to help him through the police cordon.

"Breen will take one of the hotel cars and drive over here. He will be dressed in hotel overalls and cap. I will supply Amyas with a set of these, which he will wear over his own clothes.

"Breen parks the car in the garage downstairs. He comes up to this flat. Amyas leaves in his stead, making sure to take Breen's blue spectacles, and, of course, the cassettes. He drives back to the trades' entrance at the back of the hotel, where I am waiting, in my rôle of anxious patron, to push him upstairs. I bring him straight to the penthouse."

"What about the police inside the hotel?" said Tindall. "They're bound to station men in the penthouse, particularly if it's to be used by the leaders. What if they spot Amyas?"

"It's not a disaster," said Amyas. "After all, I am officially invited to the Summit. The police know it, and have raised no objection. If I choose to arrive in somewhat unconventional style, then it is merely that I wish to avoid being mobbed by my supporters in the streets."

"Nevertheless," insisted Tindall, "there could be delays. And with your split-second schedule. . . ."

"Very well. I will ask one of the leaders to be in the penthouse to meet me . . . and see me through Customs. Perhaps the president himself. Tanda, will you see to that?"

"Okay, so you get the red carpet." I glanced round the table. "For the rest of us . . . Ram, Sita and Monan can get into the place any time, by right of ownership. That leaves Tanda, all right because he's a Summit organizer . . . and Jess, Dave and me. What about it, Ram? Can you smuggle us in in a meat van? Have to be kosher of course."

"My dear Morry, the police will be checking every vehicle. Surely the best thing will be for you to walk in, as invited guests, through the front door."

"The objection to that is that the Sleepers know there's a connection between us and Mochudi. The moment we show our faces, they'll be on the alert for him."

Jess spoke suddenly. "We should go in with the leaders."

I stared at her.

"Well," she said, "you want it kosher. That's about as kosher as you can get."

"And as public."

"All to the good. I agree with Ram. We can't escape notice, so we might as well turn that to our advantage. We go in with the top brass. The attention of the Sleepers will be focused on us for a while, and while we're making our entrance by the front door, Amyas can slip in quietly at the back."

"What do you think, Amyas?"

"A good idea. We'll see to it."

"Right. Then, assuming we all make it into the hotel, where do we station ourselves? Tindall, you'll be doing your search of the restaurant and kitchen area, so that fixes you. Ram?"

"The same. Restaurant and kitchens. I can go places that the rest of you cannot."

"Tanda?"

"Let me take the Moonshot and the pool-deck. I know most of the delegates, I will be able to spot intruders."

"Good. And Sita, will you look after the downstairs reception desk? That way you can keep an eye on whoever comes in from the street, and you'll be close to the switchboard, so as to warn us if anything unexpected turns up. Monan, the same job at the tradesman's entrance? Okay? That leaves Jess and me."

"Take the penthouse," Mochudi said. His eyes were on Jess, and I knew he was thinking she'd be safer in the penthouse. Ram nodded agreement.

"The penthouse, Morry. There's an intercom there, with lines to all the main points in the hotel. It will allow us to keep in touch with one another, if you control that."

"Right. Now, how does Amyas make his big entrance?"

Ram returned to the plan. "This way. At seven o'clock, we start shepherding the delegates from the pool-deck and the Moon-shot, into the restaurant. The leaders' party will not go in, but will gather here, at this door, which connects the Moonshot with the penthouse balcony. At, say, seven-fifteen, when all the guests are seated in the Stargazer, Amyas comes out and joins the leaders. They move into the restaurant, using the main door, and walk up the centre aisle to take their places at the high table. And then. . . ." Ram spread his hands in a gesture of deprecation.

I finished it for him. "Then the game will be on."

There was a purdah balcony on the second floor of the building, with screens of fretted brickwork that let in the air but excluded the prying gaze of the world. I went out there, when we'd finished talking. I felt restless and scared, not so much for myself as for the other people I'd involved in this thing.

I could see the tower of the mosque, the dingy façades of the the market sheds, and away to the left, the pale greenish pinnacle of the Southern Cross Hotel. The sky had a leaden sheen. The sweat of the whole city seemed to be rolling down the slopes of the surrounding hills, to settle in this low saucer of ground, thick and heavy as mercury.

While I was sitting there, Mochudi came and joined me. He didn't speak but pulled out a pack of cigarettes, offered it to me and lit one for himself. The smoke was pungent and made him cough. He leaned back against the wall, relaxed, so quiet he seemed part of the dark.

I looked at him with envy and wonder. Didn't he understand how gimcrack our plans were? Didn't he understand this could well be his last night on earth?

Then I remembered how, in the hills above Brakvlei, I had seen the fixity of his purpose. He was like Mark Ramsay in that way—implacable, once he'd made up his mind.

I fell to thinking about Mark, and the long friendship we'd had. About Jess, loving her and losing her and getting her back. About dead Ndhlovu, and the Summit, and the people swelter-ing in the townships, and my friends in the Party, who would pick up the threads of my life if they had to, and finish the job for me.

Then I understood that it was all these things, the totality of my life, that had brought me to this time and place, as surely as the totality of Mochudi's life had brought him. There was no need to think any further than that.

I looked up to find that Amyas had risen and was watching me from the doorway. He smiled at me.

"Go and catch some sleep, Morry."

I went inside to Jess.

L

FRIDAY WAS HOT as hell.

Ram called in early, to say the Summit delegates were pouring into the hotel, the security checks already set up there, and the press buzzing around looking for interviews.

"The police have been raiding the red-light districts," he said. "They've pulled in every thug and junkie they can lay hands on. The town's very crowded. It'll be worse after five, when the workers hit the streets."

At noon, Monan took me out in the van. I found a call box that worked, and 'phoned Buddler. I gave him the location of the Zululand factory, and told him where to look for the evidence. I didn't say what it was. He pressed me, I told him to go look for himself, and he swore at me by way of thanks.

At three, Sita put the make-up on Mochudi. She did his face, neck, arms and chest. He put on the hotel's green overalls, pulled a cap down over the horrible wig, and faced us with the patient, sad stance of the man who is used to being shunned.

"Walk around," said Sita.

He shuffled off, flat-footed, and she nodded approvingly. "Good. You could be Breen. But your hands are too clean for a maintenance man. Let me put black under your nails."

Hobeni telephoned from Zululand at four-thirty, sounding exultant. The police, with Buddler in charge, had raided the factory and found the gun. They'd come by chopper and taken away three men when they left—the manager, a clerk and the induna of black labour. The place was an ant's nest now, the workers being questioned and a police cordon right round. Hobeni wanted to stay close and pick up more news, but I told him to get the hell out, find cover and stay hidden.

After that, I got Jess to 'phone Filey, Lofts, and ask for Alex Condor. The answer she got was that Mr Condor was not available as he was in conference. "I hope that means in custody," she said, "but I'm afraid it means, in full flight."

The first edition of the evening paper carried a lot of stuff about the Summit, with photos of all the big wheels, but there was no mention of Mochudi, nor of the Zululand raid.

At five, Sita, Tindall and Tanda went over to the hotel. A few minutes later, Breen came up to the flat. When he saw Mochudi he clapped his hand over his mouth like a startled child. The likeness Sita had achieved was incredible.

The two of them talked for a while, Mochudi asking what police checks Breen had had to come through; and Breen handed over a note scrawled by Ram and countersigned by Captain Erasmus, which he said had got him through without any trouble.

Then Amyas, wearing the blue spectacles and carrying the package of cassettes, went down to the garage. We heard his car drive off.

It remained only for Jess and me to climb into Monan's van for the last time. At a quarter to six, he dropped us in the Anchor Street Parkade, where the Summit leaders' entourage was gathered. We were allocated to a saloon Chev near the end of the procession, and at five minutes to six the whole parade swung out into the main street, with four black motorcycle police riding ahead of it, and four more bringing up the rear.

From Monan's closed van I hadn't been able to judge the size or the mood of the crowds along the route. Although the main street had been cleared of traffic and the access roads closed, the pavements were clogged with onlookers, and others were still pressing in from every point of the compass. A lot of the buses at the big rank in Craig Street were moving off almost empty. Everyone was staying to see the Summit chiefs go by.

I've seen plenty of big crowds in Africa, some of them riotous, but never one that scared me as much as this one. It wasn't that they were rowdy. Quite the reverse. Once or twice, from a group of church women, from some school kids on a corner, a voice called out, but mostly there was silence. While on both sides of us, the hands rose, some in the clenched-fist black-power salute, some with the joined palms of Indian salaam, all the way from the Parkade to the hotel these arms lifted and swayed like reeds along a river.

In the plaza, people were jammed shoulder to shoulder. A phalanx of policemen, arms linked, was struggling to keep a central lane clear for the procession. The cars inched forward. And as the first one, carrying the president of the Summit, reached the hotel portico, the singing began.

Nkosi Sikelel i' Africa—"God Bless Africa", the anthem of blacks from here to the Limpopo. It started with a single voice, somewhere up front, and then it gathered and rolled across the square, and down the roadways beyond, bass and soprano and tenor together, like the voice of the earth itself.

Our car reached the pool of light at the main doors. I scrambled out, pulling Jess after me, and the two of us ducked inside the building.

The entrance hall of the Southern Cross was large, brilliantly lit, and packed. Forty or so of the black élite were waiting to welcome the leaders' party. I picked out old Choma Ndebele's bull neck, and the thin sharp face of Linda Muragan. Professor September from the Cape was talking to a bearded trio I thought I'd met in the days before SASO was banned.

The leaders began to move along the reception line and I took the opportunity of looking about me.

There were a lot of Summit officials in the foyer, some in tribal uniform, some in western gear. I couldn't see many uniformed police, though I guessed there'd be plain-clothes men mingling with the guests. But in the small lounge opposite the main rank of elevators, three policemen and a policewoman had set up what looked like a checkpoint. They were stopping everyone who went through, and going over briefcases, handbags and pockets. It was like an airport in the hijack zone, but that night I was glad of it.

We were nearly at the barrier ourselves when someone grabbed my arm from behind. I looked round into the Siamese-cat gaze of Charlie Cameron.

"So what're you doing here?" he demanded. "Joined the ANC or something?"

I tried to keep my voice light. "I'm invited as Jess's husband. She's some kind of honorary Indian."

His grip tightened. "Come on, boy. What is it, what's going on?"

"Nothing, I trust."

"You saw that crowd out there?" He jerked a thumb over his shoulder. "You know what they're waiting for? Not you and me, buddy. They're waiting to see Mochudi. Is he here?"

279

"Not to my knowledge."

Charlie watched me narrowly. Then he said, so softly that I hardly caught the words, "Well, I tell you who is. Kray."

"What?"

"Kray. The bugger that shot Calgut. Shakes you, dunnit?"

"Are you sure? Have you seen him?"

"Own eyes. He walked in this door, went through to the lifts."

"Nobody stopped him?"

"Why should they, chum? He's a copper."

"He is also supposed to have been transferred to the Transvaal."

Charlie's squint became fiercer. "Who told you that?"

"Colonel Cherry Buddler."

"Liar, then."

"Charlie, can you remember, was Kray carrying a walkie-talkie?"

"Hell, I don't know. Why?"

"Do me a favour. If you see Kray again, anywhere, any time, tell Sita Khoosal. She'll be at the reception desk tonight."

He grinned. "Nothing for nothing, Morry."

"A good story," I promised. "In a very short while. Make your reputation."

"You better be right." He let go of my arm and Jess and I moved on.

"Why would Buddler lie about Kray?" she said.

"Maybe he didn't. Kray could have strings of his own to pull, to get back here."

We went through the checks without any difficulty, and found Sita Khoosal, gorgeous in a flame-coloured sari, waiting by the lifts for us. The hand she held out to me was cold as ice.

"Breen's not back yet."

"Don't worry. He's probably been delayed by the crowds. He'll make it."

I told her about Kray, and asked her to warn the others he was around.

"Should I ask the waiters to keep a look-out?"

"No. Better keep it to ourselves."

Jess and I took the elevator up, with a bunch of delegates. When the doors opened at the Moonshot I could see it was packed, a vortex of exuberant sound and colour. Ram was chatting to a thickset man over by the bar, but I couldn't see Tindall or Tanda.

At the penthouse level, we stepped out onto the balcony. Silver-grey carpeting swept away to left and right. Down three shallow steps lay a 40-foot living-room, dotted with armchairs upholstered in cherry-coloured suède. A prayer rug on one wall shone like a jewel, and the junk on the tables looked like solid silver and jade. The only jarring note in the whole pad was the wall-to-wall policemen. Five of them—three Zulus, one Indian, one white. The white was Colonel Buddler.

L I

CAT'S BEEN FED, I thought, as we advanced down the steps to the living-room. Buddler was near-purring, his yellow-brown eyes half-closed.

"Well, my friends?" He held out a hand for our special invitation cards, inspected them, and nodded to his companions to get back to their posts.

"You have influential friends, Mr Faber," he said. "There aren't many whites in this hotel tonight, I can tell you. But I 'spose when the president wants something. . . ."

He gave the words a slightly derisive emphasis. I said nothing, and he turned to Jess.

"Mrs Faber, wouldn't you like to go up on the gallery, there? You can watch the fun through the windows."

She glanced enquiringly at me, and when I nodded, she moved off.

Buddler switched back to me. "Influential friends," he repeated. "And knowledgeable."

"Who you know is what you know," I said. "I could ask, how did you know I'd be here tonight?"

"Well, it wasn't so difficult. You asked for four days. That would take you to Monday, cover the Summit."

"Was the tip I gave you any good?"

He chewed his lip, seeming to debate within himself. "Good enough," he said at last.

"What did you find?"

"A machine-pistol."

"What make?"

"Let's say, one that shouldn't be in this country, Mr Faber."

"Smuggled?"

He nodded and smiled. "I want to know who told you where to look."

"I don't know his name."

His head tilted in disbelief. For Hobeni's sake, I had to make it sound good. "I received an anonymous 'phone call," I said. "Two, in fact. Each time, I passed the information on to you."

"Ja, so you did."

"What happened at the factory?"

"Maybe one day, I'll tell you. Perhaps when we have our little talk." He wandered off a short distance, picked up a carved stone horse, weighed it in his palm. "You gave me seven names. . . ."

"Yes. What did you do about them?"

"Those people are being watched."

"Watched? What good is that? I want them nailed."

"For that we need evidence, meneer. Your Party has made enough fuss about that, in the past. Tell me, why do you think this verklikker . . . informer . . . chose to come to you with his story?"

"I suppose because I was Mark's close friend."

"And who else did you tell, besides me?"

"Jess knows. And for our own safety, I've lodged the facts with certain others."

"Of course." He was watching me sideways as he circled the room. Hungry cat? Uncertain cat, unsure whether to eat the mouse or play with it a little longer. Suddenly a claw lashed out.

"Last Monday night, Mr Faber, you broke your word to me. I asked you once before to let me know if you moved your address. You said you would do that. Yet on Monday night, you gave us the slip."

"Those were your men in the car?"

"Yes. I set them to look after you. To protect you. Don't you realize the danger you're in? And you just skip out, you use a lot of childish tricks. Where did you go, when you left Mr Brock's place?"

"Camping."

"Camping. In the clothes you stood in?"

"The Brocks lent us stuff."

"And you went off for a breath of country air, eh?"

"If you like, yes. I saw a good friend murdered, Colonel. I needed to get the hell out and have some time to myself, without a lot of heavies blowing down my neck."

"Grief for your friend. That's very nice. But I don't believe it,

283

Mr Faber. I think you wanted to find Mochudi. You went looking for him."

"Is there a law against that?"

"No. But suddenly, when you come back from this little camping trip, you're getting anonymous tips about an arms racket. That raises a lot of questions, for me."

"You promised me four days. Have you changed your mind?"

He wheeled to face me. "You think that promise holds if it's a question of the security of the State? It seems you are in possession of facts relevant to State security. If you withhold those facts, then it is my duty to see you are detained until you decide to share them with us."

"You're threatening me with arbitrary detention?"

"I'm telling you, if you withhold facts. . . ."

"I've told you everything I can! I come to you in good faith, as the man nominally in charge of the Ramsay case, and your answer is to threaten me with arrest. Why don't you go after the real criminals. Condor and the rest. . . ?"

He pounced, "How do you come to mention Condor?"

"Christ, I'm not a bloody moron! I took the trouble to find out, Condor owns the factory you raided this afternoon. So what are you doing about him?"

"I'm sorry to say he has not yet been apprehended." Buddler's voice was silky. "Now, if you'd played level with us, we might have had him safe inside already."

"I played straight. It's a mistake I won't repeat. Next time I get that sort of information, I'll stuff it in the nearest trash can."

He stared at me sharply, then shrugged. "Come now, Mr Faber. I don't want to be hard on you. You did right to come to me, the tip was a good one, don't think we're ungrateful. And Condor and that lot . . . don't worry, we'll wrap them up nicely enough."

He smiled, cat no longer hungry, allowing mouse to creep away and bleed somewhere private. Because I was scared, hatred surged up in me like bile.

"I don't want thanks. I want Mark's killers in the dock. It doesn't look as if I'll live to be that lucky. Why did you lie to me about Kray?"

"Kray?" Buddler was standing perfectly still.

"You assured me, last night, that he was in the Transvaal. So why is he here in this hotel, tonight?"

"Who told you this?"

"Cameron, of the *Gazette*."

He began to move round the room, fast, his face bright with concentration. At last he stopped in front of me, his bunched knuckles lightly tapped my lapel. "Listen, now, Mr Faber. You have to tell me the truth. Is Amyas Mochudi coming here tonight?"

I hesitated. What must I answer? None of us had bargained for having Kray around. It made rubble of our plans. And the only man with the official clout to stop Kray, was Buddler.

So reason said, 'Talk.' But something older than reason and far more potent, prickled the hairs at the back of my neck, and warned me to keep my mouth shut.

I was saved by the sound of voices along the gallery. Three black men came into view. Two of them were musclemen. The third was the Summit president : medium height, bland, shrewd, jovial. He leaned across the balustrade at the head of the steps, and called, "Good evening, gentlemen. Mr Faber, could I have a word with you, if you please?"

Buddler accepted dismissal with a dour smile and moved away, calling to one of his men. I approached the president.

"Hullo, Morry. Nice to see you again. Where is Breen?"

I started to say, "Not arrived, yet"; and to make a liar of me, the door at the far end of the balcony, the one leading to the kitchen and service area, swung open, and Ram Khoosal came briskly through it, with Breen shuffling at his heels.

LII

I T W A S A N historic meeting, I suppose, but none of us had time to appreciate it.

Ram scurried back to the Moonshot, the president swept Amyas away to his own room so he could get cleaned up. I followed, with the black bodyguards.

Buddler was waiting for us further down the gallery. He let the entourage pass, but as I drew level with him, he reached out and grabbed my arm, forcing me to stop.

"That's Mochudi?"

"Yes." There was no point in denying it, now.

Buddler began to swear under his breath.

I said, "Have you found Kray yet?"

"I put out a call for him. He'll be up."

"I hope you're right."

I could hear a steady flow of exchanges in the bedroom behind us, Zulu and Xhosa. Buddler uttered one final expletive, then turned to a sergeant with a walkie-talkie strapped to his chest.

"Tell the men, Amyas Mochudi has accepted the Summit invite, and he'll be at the dinner. Nobody is to talk about it, clear? I want maximum vigilance. And anyone sees Lieutenant Kray, I need him right away, report to me at once."

The sergeant went off. Buddler, who still had hold of my arm, gave it a jerk.

"Come, Mr Clever, stand at the window. Maybe you going to witness another murder tonight."

The gallery was wide and gently curved. Buddler and I walked to a point where it broadened into a small bay, from which a short spiral stair led down to a lower hall. Near the stairhead was a table bearing a telephone and a large intercom box. Opposite this, in the outer wall, stretched a window some three metres long. Jess was standing there with her back to us, so absorbed she didn't turn at our approach. Piped music was flowing from an amplifier somewhere over her head.

I went and stood beside her.

It was a vantage point like the bridge of a ship.

Directly in front and to the right of us was the Moonshot lounge; less full than when I'd seen it from the lift, but still crowded. I could see the bar on the far side that masked the kitchen area.

Looking left, I could scan the whole of the pool-deck. The pool was lit from underwater so it sparkled like a pale sapphire. Beyond that was a blur of flowering shrubs and plants. Most of the younger delegates seemed to be out there. I saw Tanda talking to a group of them.

There were a lot of uniformed police on the pool-deck, some of them with walkie-talkies.

Straight ahead was the Stargazer restaurant. The wall facing us was almost all glass. The domed roof seemed to float on its thin steel pillars. I could look right through the dining-area, over the white tables and chairs and out through the far windows to a dark-blue sky studded with stars. It was a great piece of design. But all I could think of was what all that glass would do to the diners, if a bomb went off in there.

"That's the high table." Jess pointed to a crescent-shaped dais at the far end of the Stargazer. I counted twelve chairs. There was a table mike opposite the president's place at the centre, and a standing mike about six paces from the right-hand edge of the dais.

"Where's Tindall?" I said.

"Gone through to the kitchens, with two cops. They checked the dining-room."

I spoke to Buddler, who was conferring with the sergeant again.

"I'd like to use the intercom."

He waved at me impatiently, the professional with a tiresome amateur underfoot.

I studied the keys on the box, found the one for the Stargazer, and depressed it. Ram answered the buzz himself.

"Ram, can you find Dave for me? Soon as he has a moment, I'd like to speak to him."

"Certainly. Have they found Kray, yet?"

"No."

287

As I switched off, I saw that Buddler was watching me.

"So now, Mr Faber, you think we don't know our own job? You bring in your friends in case we slipped up?"

"Tindall's had training with electronic devices."

"I doubt he's had as much as Captain Erasmus. We already searched this whole floor, the roof above, and the floor below as well. There's no bomb."

"Are you saying there's no danger to Mochudi? Knowing what you do?"

"I'm saying Mochudi is safer here, tonight, with maximum police protection, than he'll ever be outside. And I'll say again, you did a good piece of work, telling us about that factory. We'll wipe this gang right off the slate. It's finished. Put your mind at rest."

Almost I thought he was going to give me a kindly pat on the shoulder. And yet I felt once more that warning coldness on my skin.

I went back to the window. Jess murmured, "What is it, Morry?"

I shook my head. My mouth was dry. I felt confused and helpless, an object for ridicule; like the feeling you get when you join a group of people, they're laughing and you join in, but you know that somehow the joke is on you.

A feeling of being conned.

It was six forty-five by my watch. Down in the Moonshot, and out on the pool-deck, I could see the Summit officials moving among the guests. The process of shepherding them in had begun. The delegates responded slowly at first, and then faster, moving into the Stargazer. The uniformed police moved up quietly at the rear, and took up station, two to each doorway, but keeping in the shadows.

The intercom buzzed and I went to it. Tindall's voice said, "Morry?"

"Yes, Dave."

"I found nothing. A cursory search. I did my best."

"Good. Thanks."

"If it's any comfort, I think the fuzz did a good job. The fixtures seem okay. Watch out for anything portable, though."

"We will. Where will you be?"

"I'll stay in the kitchens. That's where most of the stuff will o in from, now."

"Right."

The Moonshot was nearly empty.

Ram Khoosal appeared at the main entry to the Stargazer. The ᵗble reserved for the press was filled, the other tables nearly ᵗ. I spotted Tanda on the pool-deck. A policeman said some‐ ᵗing to him, then moved away.

Five to seven. There was a sudden opening of the bedroom ᵗoor behind us. The president's bodyguards came out, one going ᵗown the spiral stair to the lower hall, the other taking up his ᵗance a little way along the gallery. A moment later, the presi‐ ᵗnt and Amyas appeared.

As they stood together at the head of the stairway, I thought ᵗ what it had cost in grief, in blood, to get these two men ᵗgether; what it might still cost. Yet the price had to be paid, ᵗecause these two—the president with his vast following of ᵗoderate blacks, and Amyas, who could gather up the rebellious ᵗouth of the cities—were the two sides of that last, precious coin ᵗat could buy peace for southern Africa.

Amyas turned and smiled at us. "Stay well, my friends."

"Go well," we said.

He followed the president down the stairs.

Ve couldn't see what happened for the next few moments, since ᵗe exit into the Moonshot was directly under our window. But ᵗe heard voices raised in greeting as the door opened.

Seven o'clock, and the taped music faded. In the total quiet ᵗ the Stargazer, every face turned towards the main doors. I ᵗould hear Jess whispering to herself.

Then the saints went marching in.

The president and the two other leaders went first, walking ᵗbreast. Mochudi followed, alone. Then the rest. They marched ᵗpidly up the centre aisle toward the high table. And the audi‐ ᵗnce, rising in polite applause, saw Mochudi.

A roar went up from them, startled, triumphant. The party ᵗached the dais and found seats, Mochudi taking the place on ᵗe President's right.

The press table emptied as the pressmen hurtled out into the ᵗloonshot, pelting for the telephones over by the bar. Buddler ᵗas speaking without pause into his walkie-talkie. Jess fixed her

K   289

eyes on him. I watched Amyas.

"Mochudi! Mochudi!" The voices crashed into a stead
chant that seemed to rock the slender cupola above. At the high
table the president, still standing, raised both hands. The nois
began to ebb. He leaned over and tapped the table mike. Amya
had turned a little sideways in his chair and was looking up
smiling broadly.

"Brothers and sisters . . ." the president's deep tones cam
clearly over the amplifiers ". . . this is an historic moment. No
only because it marks the start of the Summit conference, fo
which we have all worked so hard and so long . . ."

The sergeant reappeared on the gallery, and Buddler move
to meet him. They seemed to confer urgently. The sergeant ra
down the spiral stairway. Buddler bent over his walkie-talkie
speaking in rapid Afrikaans. What he said was obscured by th
president's words.

". . . the presence among us tonight of an unexpected but mag
nificently welcome delegate—I speak of the man who is a legend
in his own time—Amyas Mochudi. I do not need to tell you . . ."

I called out to Buddler, "Is it Kray? Have they found Kray?"

He nodded, at the same time signalling me to be quiet. Th
intercom next to me buzzed, and I went to it.

"Morry?" Monan Khoosal's voice was close to panic. "Kra
came through here. There was a van at the back, a florist's van
Kray went and met it. He came back with a garland. . . ."

My mind was moving too slowly. Garlands were an India
custom, you hung one round the neck of an honoured guest. Tin
dall said, watch out for anything portable.

"Monan? Where did Kray take it?"

"Towards the lifts. The main bank. But he could change to th
service lift on any floor."

"Yes, okay, I'll take it from there."

I flicked the switch marked "broadcast", grabbed the hand
speaker from the hook at the side and began to intone, "Tindal
Tanda, Ram, come in please. Tindall, Tanda, Ram". The ind
cators for the Stargazer and the pool-deck flashed, showing tha
the signal was being picked up there, but the bulb for th
kitchens stayed dead.

"Ram," I said, "Kray's on his way upstairs. He may be carry
ing a garland. Don't let him take it inside. And tell one of th

waiters to warn Tindall. I can't reach him."

As I started to repeat the message, Buddler's hand closed over my wrist.

"Come now, Mr Faber, you're wasting energy. My men will take care of all that. Nobody's going to throw posies in the restaurant."

I jerked free of him. He shrugged.

"You're making a fool of yourself, man. Look down there."

I went to the window. Buddler must have been calling up reinforcements when he spoke to the sergeant. The uniformed police at the doorways had been joined by a number of heavies in plain clothes.

"I told you," he said, "leave it to us, now. There'll be no trouble."

It was at that point that we heard the ring of the elevator bell. The doors slid back. Strolling towards us with an easy, almost indolent gait, came Lieutenant Kray. He was wearing a sharp dark suit, a striped tie, and his hands were empty. He stopped a couple of yards from us.

"You sent for me, sir?"

Same flat voice as the first time I'd met him, after Calgut's thugs broke up our meeting; same light-blue eyes that gave nothing, took nothing. But tonight he wasn't completely in command of himself. His hands were trembling.

Buddler spoke evenly, "What are you doing here?"

"I'm transferred back again."

"By whom?"

"The boss. The order's on your desk."

"I see. Good then. Very good."

I burst in : "Where's that bloody garland?"

Kray slowly turned his head, as if he'd noticed me for the first time. "I sent it over for testing." He looked back at Buddler. "Coates and Jacobs are checking it out. I don't think they'll find anything. Just flowers. But you can't take chances with this lot."

He moved across to stand next to me, scanning the people in the Stargazer. I saw that Amyas was already on his feet, his voice flowing over the amplifiers, that the moment we'd worked for and dreaded had actually passed without my noticing.

Kray spoke slowly, to no one in particular. "Condor's in Mozambique by now. I had Filey, Lofts staked out for six weeks.

If they'd left me alone, I'd have nailed Condor. He just walked out, this morning. By now, he's out the country."

There was no mistaking it, he was consumed by rage, against himself, against the system that had mucked his chances. And the rage was beginning to focus and search for reasons and demand somebody's blood.

Buddler said placatingly, "Can't blame yourself, jong."

Kray didn't even turn his head. The question, Who, then? seemed to be on his lips, but he suppressed it, tucking in his chin, glancing at the hands stained bright green by the leaves of marigolds.

And as he fell back on silence, so the tumult of doubts and questions began again in my mind.

Condor had walked out this morning. After my first interview with Buddler, before my second, before I'd mentioned the name of his factory in Zululand.

So, had he quit because he smelled the hunt too close, or had he been tipped off? And who could have tipped him, except someone in my own very small circle?

Why was I under such pressure to accept that the Sleepers were finished, when my instincts rejected that, when Hobeni had warned of a much wider organization, still hidden?

If Kray was an honest cop—if he'd killed Calgut merely in self-defence—then who had had him moved out of Durban at such a crucial time?

Who took Buddler off the Ramsay case, and why?

How did Kray get back to this city?

Why was I walking around free, instead of locked up in a maximum-security cell?

Above all, why did I have this deadly sense of being gulled? Who was using me, and for what purpose?

I felt Jess slide her hand into mine.

"Wonderful, isn't he?"

She gestured towards Amyas. She was totally engrossed in what was going on down there, the fears of the past weeks forgotten in the triumphant present.

I thought how it would be spreading now, the news that Mochudi was at the Summit: to the townships, and the executive suites, the editors and newscasters, the consulates and trades missions, here and around the world.

Good news, good news. Mochudi is safe, Mochudi is at the Summit!

The Sleepers are kaput.

That was what was being handed me, and somewhere deep in the heart of this shining red apple, lay the poison.

Which I must seem to swallow.

"Wonderful," I said, smiling at Jess.

LIII

AFTER MIDNIGHT, when we were back at Jess's flat, I 'phoned the leader of my Party and told him the Summit had achieved a spectacular lift-off. I also told him that some of us had had a share in exposing an arms racket, and that I needed to talk to him about that. There could be important repercussions.

He was an old enough hand to read my tone instead of my words. "I'll come tomorrow," he said, "on the first plane. I take it you've consulted the police?"

"There's a police guard on the front and back gates, right now."

"But you are safe? Not under any threat?"

"I think we are perfectly safe for the present."

When I said goodbye to him and hung up, Jess asked me if I meant that about being safe, and I said Yes, I did.

"You mean just till the Summit's over?" she persisted.

"No. Longer than that. You're not to worry." And I put my arms round her and held her close to me so she'd believe it.

EYE-WITNESS

Name :   Unknown
Occupation : Sleeper
Race :   Unknown

LIV

I T I S N O W three weeks since I gave you an abbreviated report
on the shooting of Calgut by Lieutenant Kray of the South
African police.

At that time I had no detailed knowledge of the Ramsay
affair. I arrived in Durban on the morning of 7 March, sum-
moned there urgently because Condor was in trouble.

The situation was worse than I feared. Not only had Hobeni
left Filey, Lofts, not only had he been allowed to learn a good
deal about our operations, but he was known to have visited
the home of Mark Ramsay the night before, probably with the
intention of enlisting Ramsay's help against us.

I must tell you at once that Condor's handling of this whole
sector has been disastrous. You will remember I warned three
years ago that he would prove dangerous. He has no ability to
pick men, because he cannot discern their real character. He saw
Hobeni as an ambitious, surly, black-power protagonist, which
he was. He missed the facts that Hobeni is exceptionally shrewd,
a flaming patriot, and pathologically devoted to his elder brother.

So while Condor deluded himself that he had the hook through
Hobeni's nose, Hobeni was rooting through Condor's territory. He
uncovered certain data relating to the Zululand works. He even
succeeded in buying a Mac 11.

I need not emphasize that with that information, Ramsay
could have destroyed the Natal undertaking. I don't deny, there-
fore, that it was necessary to neutralize Ramsay. He was not a
man who could be bribed or coerced. What I do condemn, most
strongly, is Condor's choice of Calgut to make the hit. What we
needed was a professional, who could do a neat, quiet job and
then fade right out. What Condor chose was a psychopath with
a police record, and a reputation as a bar-room boaster. Had he
lived, Calgut would have been picked up by the police within
hours, and he would have told them a great deal.

When I learned, early that Monday morning, that Calgut had
been hired, I went down to Bayside Buildings. I intended to pick

him up if it should be necessary. I was saved the trouble when he was shot by Lieutenant Kray.

Kray's intervention must not be ascribed to mere ill chance. He is one of those policemen who become obsessed with whatever work is on hand. In June of last year he was allocated to enquiries into the Industria labour troubles. He became interested in Filey, Lofts and sniffed round there for months. Probably he had informers inside. Certainly he knew of the visit Mark Ramsay and his friends paid to the factory on the morning of Wednesday, 23 February.

It appears that after that visit Kray, anxious to find some link between Condor and Ramsay, kept an unofficial watch on Ramsay. On the same Wednesday evening, though supposed to be off duty, he joined one of the blitzpatrol cars, and kept it in the vicinity of the hall where the Ramsay meeting was held.

He was thus on the scene very soon after the riot initiated by Calgut.

Kray also made it his business to attend the Nomination Court on 7 March, but arrived late; heard shots in the building, saw Calgut run out with a Scorpion gun in his hands, and shot him.

In one sense, this was fortunate, since it solved our immediate problem of how to dispose of Calgut. In another, it ensured Kray's involvement in the events that followed the Ramsay shooting. It brought him closer to us than I like. As I have said, he does not give up. Buddler arranged for him to be transferred to the Transvaal, but, somehow, Kray pulled strings, and got back. That indicates he has powerful backing somewhere, and we must proceed against him with great circumspection.

After Ramsay's death, our urgent, our imperative need was to gain time, in which we could safeguard our entire operation throughout southern Africa.

We had, within the shortest possible time, hours at most, to warn our operatives that there had been a breakdown in Natal; to arrange for our stocks to be moved from existing depots to our support depots; and to help certain key people to drop out of sight.

We began at the same time to create in the public and official mind, the belief that Ramsay was killed by a racial fanatic, acting alone. No conspiracy and no organization behind him. We also sought to keep the investigation in Buddler's hands, and away from the Security Police.

Kray himself helped in this. He was so convinced Calgut had a personal vendetta against Ramsay, he underlined it in his reports. This bolstered our efforts. Buddler was able to retain control for several days, during which we made our operation secure over most of our territory.

The exception was Condor's area, namely Filey, Lofts, the Zululand enterprise, and two others. These we wrote off. Hobeni knew of them and might easily have imparted that knowledge to others besides Ramsay. These units were therefore useless to us, and might just as well be thrown as a sop to Cerberus. By convincing the authorities that Condor constituted the whole operation, we could avoid pressure on us in other sectors.

For a short space, things went well. The press, primed by Buddler and Kray, seemed inclined to lay all blame at Calgut's door. A lot was achieved through our agents in the civil service, and it looked for a while as if the Ramsay affair might be settled quickly and to our satisfaction.

Again, it was Condor who marred our success. Dudu Ndhlovu, in his eagerness to get in touch with Hobeni, paid frequent visits to Filey, Lofts; and Condor lost his head and had Ndhlovu shot and dumped in the canal. At that point Kray began to suspect Condor's part in the Ramsay killing, and to search for evidence against him.

Hobeni himself was still at large, and a constant threat to us. There was also Maurice Faber.

Faber, like a number of others, is said to have entertained a deep personal regard for Ramsay. For some days after Ramsay died, he appeared to be inactive, but suddenly he came to light, pressing for full investigation into what he termed a conspiracy; aggressively suspicious, according to Buddler, of the stated views of the police.

(Faber has connections high in the political, business and press worlds. He has succeeded in alerting them. There is now an outcry about the supply of illegal arms to this country, and we must expect the witchhunt to intensify. Since the close of the Summit conference, Faber has been questioned extensively by the Security Police, but is reported to have made a good impression. They are continuing to watch him, naturally, but they do not really suspect him of subversion.)

Buddler and I discussed the question of Faber immediately after Ramsay's death. We decided there could be no quick action against him. A second violent death in the Ramsay camp would have destroyed all hope of laying the blame on Calgut, and would have turned all spotlights onto us.

We decided that Buddler must by some means gain Faber's confidence—not an easy matter, since Faber is one of those liberals who has a built-in dislike of the police. But Buddler did manage to make Faber believe that he was unhappy with the Calgut theory of the killing; that he wished to delve deeper, so to speak; and that he was being prevented from doing so.

Faber seemed to take this bait, and to place some reliance on Buddler. But he did not give up his crusade for a wider investigation.

He began trying to trace Don Hobeni, who had vanished into thin air the day of the Ramsay shooting. We ourselves had no leads to Hobeni. We sent Pitso to try to discover whether Faber had been more successful. All that achieved was the strengthening belief, in Faber's mind, in our existence.

He next turned his attention to those blacks who had associated with Ramsay, notably the men involved in the Black Summit. This indicated to me that he was moving, more by blind instinct than by reason, towards what I may term the Mochudi plan.

He knew we wanted Mochudi and Hobeni.

We knew he wanted them.

It seemed the wisest course for us to let Faber do our work for us. I hoped he would trace the men and lead us to them.

In fact he threw us off. He has the gift, very rare among the untrained, of being able to abandon a set plan without hesitation. On the night he drove Mrs Ramsay and her child to the airport, he exercised this gift. Where most amateurs would have doubled back home to collect clothing, money, make 'phone-calls, Faber simply lit out for the country. Buddler's men lost them at the Brock property.

Thereafter, Faber and his friends established contact with Mochudi and Hobeni somewhere near Brakvlei. Hobeni must have told them what he had learned about us—not only Condor's undertakings, but also our secondary plan to precipitate urban unrest in Natal this year.

Mochudi having made up his mind to attend the Summit, Faber and company undertook to accompany him. They seem to have assumed the rôle of protectors of his person. Their behaviour at this period established that we were dealing with a bunch of amateurs, and not, as I had feared, with trained agents.

They smuggled Hobeni into Zululand and had him plant the Mac 11. Enlisted the aid of the Khoosal clan, who found them a hiding-place somewhere in the Indian quarter. Brought Mochudi to the Summit disguised as a member of the hotel staff. And then revealed a good proportion of their intentions to Buddler.

One could say that this was the pay-off for Buddler's work on Faber. Faber came to him, offering a deal—information in exchange for police protection for Mochudi, that is what it boiled down to. It was easy to discern from this that Mochudi would be at the conference.

We could, then, have assassinated Mochudi more or less at our whim; but, by then, neither the Summit nor Mochudi was of prime concern to us. Mochudi, after all, had never been more than a means of triggering urban riots. It was to that end that we helped to engineer his release from gaol. But with the exposure of Condor, and the collapse of the Natal network, the whole Mochudi plan fell away.

We need urban revolt in order to sell our goods. But the Ramsay affair made it necessary to shift those goods all over the country. Ordinary business matters had of necessity to be suspended. One must know when to abort a plan.

We made the sacrificial moves. We fell in with Faber's demands. Buddler raided the Zululand factory, and "found" the Mac 11. Arrests were made. The raid was heralded in the press as the destruction of an arms ring. Buddler incurred praise from many quarters.

As to the incidents at the Southern Cross Hotel, they are unimportant. The Summit meetings were a success, it seems, but as they are a political matter, they don't interest us in any great degree.

It remains to assess our losses, and make plans for the future.

In the short term, we have suffered extensive damage in Natal. Our presence, as an organization, is known. Buddler and I hold different views about this last.

Buddler believes that Maurice Faber has accepted that our

entire operation died when Condor was exposed. I cannot agree. I believe Faber is far from satisfied, and will continue to agitate against us. He may suspect Buddler's complicity. He is certainly in touch with Kray.

I think these two men present a very dangerous combination. They must be handled carefully. Violence at this time is not to be considered, but we must do all we can to discredit them. Kray can possibly be crushed between the millstones of officialdom. Faber must be made to appear a political crank, one of those who pursue wild theories. One will suggest, perhaps, that he has been thrown off balance by the death of his friend. But we must move very quietly. Quiet is our ally at this time.

Hobeni is another matter. We have taken pains to brand him a revolutionary. The SP are looking for him. If he does not go abroad, he will be found and eliminated, whether by judicial or arbitrary action.

A more difficult decision is that of Buddler's future. He has served us well, particularly over the past few weeks. But he is no longer of use in this sector, or any other in southern Africa. The fact of Kray's return shows that there is mistrust of Buddler in high circles.

Buddler's own wish is to move to another region. He suggests —and I concur—that in a month or two he be allowed to go on vacation. He will take a fishing holiday on one of the offshore islands. From there we will stage some mishap, an overturned boat, some such thing. He will leave the scene, and we will arrange for his transfer along the usual channels to South America. He already has money there. We can use him. He should not be wasted.

You asked me to estimate the long-term damage to us. Sirius has compiled a full report, regarding specific outlets, sales and prospective sales, which will be in your hands this week.

To sum it up, the situation in most sectors of the sub-continent is excellent. By the beginning of June, we will be fully operative again, everywhere except in Natal. There, we will require a little more time to make good our losses. We must secure the new depots, select new agents, and appoint a new regional controller. The man you suggest may do very well. I prefer to offer no opinions until I have seen him at work. We do not wish to repeat the fiasco of Condor.

Materially, we are sound. We have first-class personnel at managerial and executive level, and our key men and women within the Establishment have not been exposed by the recent setbacks.

Political events in the territories to the north favour us. Above all, the policies at present being pursued in this country continue to create a climate which exactly suits our needs.

Our potential market is expanding with each month that passes. We shall have no difficulty, when the time comes, in triggering maximum demand for our merchandise.

I can promise without reserve that in January of next year, when the hot weather starts, we shall be ready to promote our sales campaign.

It will require only a very light touch to awaken the Sleepers.

302